SHAKESPEARE REMAINS

Mark Dooley
Teesside ✓
Nov. '02.

SHAKESPEARE REMAINS

Theater to Film,
Early Modern
to Postmodern

COURTNEY LEHMANN

CORNELL UNIVERSITY PRESS
Ithaca & London

First published 2002 by Cornell University Press
First printing, Cornell Paperbacks, 2001

Printed in the United States of America

Library of Congress Cataloging-in-Publication Data

Lehmann, Courtney, b. 1969
    Shakespeare remains : theater to film, early modern to postmodern/Courtney Lehmann.
        p. cm.
    ISBN 0-8014-3974-4 (alk. paper)—ISBN 0-8014-8767-6 (pbk.: : alk. paper)
    1. Shakespeare, William, 1564–1616—Film and video adaptations.   2. English drama—Film and video adaptations. 3. Film adaptations.   I. Title.
    PR3093 .L45 2002
    791.43′6—dc21

                                                            2001006976

Cornell University Press strives to use environmentally responsible suppliers and materials to the fullest extent possible in the publishing of its books. Such materials include vegetable-based, low-VOC inks and acid-free papers that are recycled, totally chlorine-free, or partly composed of nonwood fibers. Books that bear the logo of the FSC (Forest Stewardship Council) use paper taken from forests that have been inspected and certified as meeting the highest standards for environmental and social responsibility. For further information, visit our website at www.cornellpress.cornell.edu.

Cloth printing   10 9 8 7 6 5 4 3 2 1
Paperback printing   10 9 8 7 6 5 4 3 2 1

For Mom, Dad, and Brooke

Contents

Illustrations

Preface

"*What* was Shakespeare?" asks a recent book cover, instantly replacing the age-old question of *who* Shakespeare "really was." But perhaps we should first ask *why* Shakespeare? Why indeed has Shakespeare been inextricably bound to questions of "who" and "what" constitutes an author? No other literary figure has spawned such an enduring mystery over the nature of authorial practice, past and present. Shakespeare's notorious missing paper trail alone has sent forensic specialists, aspiring detectives, and curious bibliophiles in search of the Bard's textual and bodily remains, hoping to uncover the mystery housed in his Stratford-upon-Avon vault. The fact that nothing has ever been found there, however, seems to point providentially to the status of Shakespeare's remains in literary theory. This book proceeds from the assumption that "Shakespeare"—now housed in obligatory quotation marks—has been disembodied to a fault.

Shakespeare Remains: Theater to Film, Early Modern to Postmodern reexamines the practice of Shakespearean authorship through the lens of film theory. In contrast to literary paradigms of authorship, film theory's concept of "auteur" situates Shakespearean authorial practice within a collaborative, performative, and commercial medium, while simultaneously enabling us to imagine "Shakespeare" as something more than an incidental textual effect. Indeed, I argue that this corpus is most usefully approached as a *montage* effect—a locus of historically illuminating collisions between authors and texts, culture and consciousness, theory and practice—wherein the idea of auteur gives voice to the *singularity* of the agencies vying for articulation.

In assuming the unfinished business of literally coming to terms with Shakespeare, this book differs from recent work in the field in that it does not trace the erosion of Shakespearean textuality and authority in postmodern and early modern culture. Rather, it identifies what *remains* of this contested corpus, focusing on how the plays themselves—and recent film adaptations of them—bespeak an authorial presence under historical conditions of erasure. This intervention is crucial for redefining the place of agency in the aftermath of the "death of the Author" within postmodernity, as well as for understanding the purpose of authorship in the equally anomalous period in which Shakespeare's plays were produced. Situated between the medieval *auctor* and the eighteenth-century Author, the early modern period presents us with an historical habitation—but not a name—for its own authorial practices.

The premise of this book, therefore, is that Shakespeare's plays have always been "screen plays," or, plays that function as screens for our projections—cultural, psychological and, more recently, cinematic—wherein a most profound *something* continues to come from "nothing." And it is this interminable special effect that extends from theater to film, early modern to postmodern, which, I argue, embodies the makings of the auteur. My objective here is not to canonize or to condemn the Bard's real or imagined remains but rather to explore the ways in which this corpus generates ongoing exceptions to our theoretical rules, demanding that we find a way—or at least a will—to make "Shakespeare" matter.

Acknowledgments

I began thinking about the juxtaposition of Shakespeare, cinema, and authorship in early modern and postmodern culture when I was a graduate student at Indiana University, Bloomington. The somewhat peculiar constellation of places, time periods, personages, theories, and practices that drives *Shakespeare Remains* stems from the diverse expertise of the mentors I worked with there. I am indebted to James Naremore, Patrick Brantlinger, Peter Lindenbaum, and especially Linda Charnes, who devoted their energy and enthusiasm to this project from start to finish and beyond. This is my idea of a "dream team," and their voices continue to animate my work. I am also grateful to Susan Gubar, who was my teaching mentor at Indiana, and Stephen Watt, who has helped me through many a professional quandary with instant and enduring wisdom. To Skip Willman, the better half of my best ideas, I am grateful beyond expression.

I have also benefited from the support of several "adopted" mentors. Barbara Hodgdon and Laurie Osborne have read this manuscript at various stages and have challenged me to justify and to hone my arguments at every turn. I thank them not only for their intellectual rigor but also for their patient replies to panicked E-mails and "eleventh-hour" requests. It was Sam Crowl's Shakespeare Association of America seminar "Kenneth Branagh and His Contemporaries" that first introduced me to the emerging community of Shakespeare and film scholars who have left their mark on this project in many ways. For their conversation and encouragement, I am grateful to Doug Lanier, Kathy Howlett, Evelyn Gajowski, Ken Rothwell, H. R. Coursen, Lisa Hopkins, Michael Anderegg, Pete Donaldson, José Ramón Díaz Fernández, Don Hedrick, Bob Willson, Richard Burt, Bryan Reynolds, and Gail Kern Paster, as well as to Lisa S. Starks, whose feedback and friendship I value deeply. Fran Dolan, Darryl Palmer, and Gordon Macmullan have all been generous with their time and timely with their generosity.

While working on this book as an assistant professor at the University of the Pacific, I have received support from my colleagues in the English and Film Studies departments. I am grateful to Diane Borden, Camille Norton, Robert Cox, and Gregg Camfield for their insights and advice, as well as to the students in my Shakespeare classes, who reinvent the Bard for me every year. I owe special thanks to my English department colleagues Cynthia Dobbs and Amy Smith, who lightened my load during the push to complete this book in a semester teeming with teaching and service responsibilities. I thank the University of the Pacific for the Eberhardt Summer Research Fellowship that enabled me to get the book under way and, chiefly, for introducing me to Jim Hetrick, my physicist-husband, who kept me from going out of my mind through the long, late nights by showing me the stars.

I wish to thank Gail Kern Paster and Liz Pohland for granting me permission to reprint Chapter Four, "Strictly Shakespeare? Dead Letters, Ghostly Fathers, and the Cultural Pathology of Authorship in Baz Luhrmann's *William Shakespeare's Romeo + Juliet* "from *Shakespeare Quarterly* (Summer 2001), as well as Julian Yoseloff and Associated University Presses for permitting me to reprint Chapter Seven, "*Shakespeare in Love:* Sex, Capitalism, and the Authorial Body-in-Pleasure" from *Spectacular Shakespeare: Critical Theory and Popular Cinema* (2002) edited by Starks and Lehmann. Passages from *The Riverside Shakespeare* and *The Oxford Shakespeare: Tragedies* are quoted by permission. All illustrations in this book are reproduced courtesy of Photofest, who made the often agonizing labor of obtaining film stills flat-out fun.

I also am grateful to Bernhard Kendler at Cornell University Press for his interest in and support for this book; Teresa Jesionowski for her cheerful willingness to work with me on matters of protocol; and Kristin Herbert for her astute manuscript editing.

Finally, though it goes without saying that none of this would have been possible without my parents, it bears repeating. My mother and father, Carol and Charlie Lehmann, took me to my first Shakespeare play when I was seven years old, and they made me believe that all the world was, in fact, a stage. They are the best teachers I ever had.

Stockton, California   COURTNEY LEHMANN

SHAKESPEARE REMAINS

Introduction

The Author Formerly Known as Shakespeare

Fennyman:	Who is that?
Henslowe:	Nobody. The Author.[1]

Inscribed on a flat stone where Shakespeare's remains are presumed to lie are the following words of warning:

> Good friend, for Jesus' sake, forbeare
> To dig the dust enclosed here.
> Blessed be he that spares these stones,
> And curst be he that moves my bones.

Rumored to have been written by the elusive Bard himself, this prohibition functions more powerfully as an irresistible invitation to search for Shakespeare's remains, a quest that has materialized in the practice of curious gravediggers and, subsequently, in the theory of prying scholars. Remarkably, this necrophiliac desire was nearly satisfied when gravediggers working on the vault adjacent to Shakespeare's revealed a "vacant space...through which one might have reached into his grave" (229), as Washington Irving relates in his account of his visit to Stratford-upon-Avon. But when the Sexton charged with safekeeping the Bard's remains looked into this hole, he found, oddly, "neither coffin nor bones; nothing but dust" (229). Something of a nineteenth-century Geraldo Rivera in search of Al Capone, Washington Irving searched in vain for William Shakespeare, claiming upon his reluctant

---

1. This familiar line is from the movie *Shakespeare in Love,* screenplay by Marc Norman and Tom Stoppard. As a rule, I will be citing dialogue and directions from the published screenplays of the films that I analyze. In the event of discrepancies between screenplay and film, I will cite the film.

departure: "I could not but exult in the malediction which has kept [Shakespeare's] ashes undisturbed in [Stratford's] quiet and hallowed vaults" (238).[2]

To Irving's confident statement we must now add a postscript: undisturbed, perhaps, until 1968, when Shakespeare, along with the entire concept of the Author, experienced a *second* death at the hands of Roland Barthes's famous declaration of "The Death of the Author." Those of us who conduct research in all but the most contemporary historical moments generally find ourselves working with dead authors. Typically, the remains we are bequeathed are comprised not of bodily but of textual matter. I suggest, however, that there is something more to these remains than meets the eye—something that gets under the skin, permeates an affective register, and incites repeated inquiries into and identification with a body of work. The source of this fascination does not reside in the physical materials of the book itself but rather in something that exceeds the familiar confines of ink and parchment, something that John Milton invokes in his 1643 address to Parliament when he claims that "it is of greatest concernment to the Church and the Commonwealth to have a vigilant eye [on] how books demean themselves as well as men.... For books do contain a potency of life in them" (719). Why else, we might ask, are books burned if not to destroy this peculiar potency of life that radiates beyond the text? To adapt a theoretical explanation from Slavoj Žižek, perhaps there is something "in the text more than the text" that activates the inexorable circuit of identificatory desire. According to Žižek, identification is riddled by a primal tension between "meaning" and "enjoyment," giving rise to "a certain signifier which is not enchained in a network but immediately filled, penetrated with enjoyment,... without representing anything or anyone" (76).[3] What is "in the text more than the text," then, is not merely that which eludes interpretation but something that exceeds the narrative frame itself: superfluous *and* vital, it contains the residue of cultural desires, anxieties, and repressions, exerting an affective pull on the reader only to lead to a signifying void. Though Žižek's argument

---

2. I am referring here to the now infamous effort on the part of investigative journalist Geraldo Rivera to expose the mystery of Al Capone's vault. After a great deal of promotional hype, Rivera aired the opening of the vault on live television only to find—along with millions of expectant viewers—that there was nothing there.

3. Žižek has many different names for this elusive but resilient surplus. The phrase "in the text more than the text" is based on Žižek's conception of the symptom-as-*sinthome*,

applies more immediately to human rather than textual bodies, his fundamental logic is that *all* processes of identification—from the psychoanalytic to the critical-textual—produce a certain leftover that cannot be integrated into the totality of the "corpus" concerned. This phenomenon is particularly striking in the theoretical environment of poststructuralism, wherein the desire to destroy even the symbolic remains of already-dead authors suggests that there is, in fact, "something more" emanating from the literary corpus that cannot be reduced to forces exclusively "in the text."[4]

Beginning in the Romantic period and culminating in the high-modernist deification of figures such as Joyce, Eliot, and Pound, this something "in the text more than the text" becomes identified with the mystique of the Author. Based on the notion that the spirit of transcendent genius springs eternal from the text—even after the death of the physical body and the decay of the book—the romantic mythology of the Author defines both the matter and manner of critical rituals undertaken in and around the literary work. Like the ritualistic fascination evoked by the medieval idea of the "king's two bodies," the Author is the site of an enticing surplus, born of a corpus comprised of the "terrestrial body subject to the cycle of generation and corruption" and the "sublime, immaterial, sacred body" invulnerable to the ravages of time (Žižek, *For They Know Not* 254). In 1968, however, Roland Barthes (among others), announced the death of *both* authorial bodies in a polemic directed against the historical romance between literary theory and the sovereign Author. Rallying behind Barthes's battle cry, a wave of poststructuralist theory emerged to liberate critical practice from a mode of interpretation "tyrannically centered" on the author-king and "his hypostases: society, history, the psyche, freedom" (Barthes, "Death" 50, 53). Turning away from the tyranny of authorial intention, post-

---

which Žižek describes as something "in you more than yourself." Emerging from the classic Lacanian opposition between meaning and enjoyment, the *sinthome* is "the life-substance in its most radical dimension of meaningless enjoyment" (*Sublime* 76). The analysand's identification with the *sinthome*—with the impossibility of relinquishing or dissolving the symptom—is the final stage of the psychoanalytic process. In another respect, however, this "something more" is the Lacanian *objet petit a*, the fascinating remainder, the "little piece of the Real" that resists meaning precisely because it is penetrated with enjoyment and, therefore, cannot be integrated into the symbolic order.

   4. In this context, it is significant that Žižek aligns this "something more" with an incarnating effect, that is, with a mysterious presence he identifies as "the life-substance" itself (*Sublime* 76).

structuralism embraced the newly leveled playing field of the text—the locus of contingent traces, supplements, stains, leftovers, and flows that produce multiple meanings and manifest pleasures. But has poststructuralism's interest in these seemingly disembodied textual fragments fallen prey to the trap Barthes unwittingly sets at the end of his essay, which calls for a "revers[al] of the myth" of the Author ("Death" 55)? In other words, does Barthes's manifesto simply mythologize the Text? Suddenly invested with libidinal drives, performativity, and multiple subjectivities, the Text under poststructuralism embodies all the fascinating capabilities that were once attributed to the Author. Perhaps, then, it was *this* peculiar "potency of life" that Washington Irving went in search of as he trod the "intense and thrilling" paths of Stratford-upon-Avon, convinced, as he explains, that "the remains of Shakespeare were mouldering beneath my feet" (229).

But are these remains mouldering or smoldering? Despite the fact that Shakespeare's dramatic corpus precedes the historical birth of the Author in the eighteenth century, Shakespeare has long been identified as *the* Romantic Author—a tradition that continues today in Hollywood, as the extraordinary success of films such as *Shakespeare in Love* (John Madden 1998) attests. Perhaps this is because Shakespeare himself theorized the idea of the symbolic remainder in *Hamlet*—the idea, that is, of "introducing a split between the visible, material, transient body and another, sublime body, a body made of special, immaterial stuff" (Žižek, *For They Know Not* 255). Shakespeare's articulation of this strange surplus that survives the death of the physical body emerges in Hamlet's famous exclamation: "The body is with the king, but the king is not with the body. The king is a thing…Of nothing."[5] As Žižek explains, "The distinction body/thing coincides here with the difference between the material and the sublime body: the 'thing' is what Lacan calls *objet petit a*, a sublime, evasive body which is a 'thing of nothing', a pure semblance without substance" (255). More importantly, Hamlet begs the question: does the "thing" die with the "king"? What is it about the thing that exercises such powers of fascination—so much so that Hamlet, when faced with an opportunity to kill King Claudius, retracts his sword. "What stays Hamlet's arm?" asks Lacan. "It's not fear—he has only contempt for the guy—it's because he knows that he

---

5. See Shakespeare's *Hamlet* 4.2.26–28. All citations of *Hamlet* are from Susanne L. Wofford's edition (1994). Hereafter cited in the text.

must strike at something other than what's there" ("Desire in *Hamlet*" 50–51). Like the warning that presides over Shakespeare's bones urging us not to look for what we can't see, Hamlet's distinction between king and thing forces us to wonder whether or not the thing in "Shakespeare"—the author-king par excellence—died in 1616 or, for that matter, in 1968.

Compared with the critique of the romantic fiction of the Author in other literary periods, the deconstruction of Shakespeare has occurred somewhat belatedly. This is perhaps the case because it took such a long time to install Shakespeare as an "author" in the first place, an arduous process of cultural accretion that Michael Dobson brilliantly documents in *The Making of the National Poet: Shakespeare, Adaptation, and Authorship, 1660–1769*.[6] But what Shakespeare studies may have lost in time, it has made up for in violence. In the last fifteen years, Shakespeare has not only been pronounced dead but also dismembered: un-named by Margreta De Grazia, un-stitched by Michael Warren, un-emended by Randall McLeod, and un-edited by Leah Marcus.[7]

6. Dobson offers the most complete treatment to date of Shakespeare's rising star from the adaptations of the Restoration stage to the apotheosis of Shakespeare as a national hero in David Garrick's staging of *The Stratford Jubilee*. What is remarkable about *The Jubilee* devoted to Shakespeare is that it did not include a single Shakespeare play, nor even a direct quotation of a play because, as Dobson explains, by the 1760s,"Shakespeare is so firmly established as the morally uplifting master of English letters that his reputation no longer seems to depend on his specific achievements as a dramatist: a ubiquitous presence in British culture, his fame is so synonymous with the highest claims of contemporary nationalism that simply to be British is to inherit him, without needing to read or see his actual plays at all" (214). My analysis provides a complement to Dobson's in the sense that it explores Shakespeare's status as an authority and, as we shall see, as an agent of a "national-popular" sensibility in two periods wherein authorship is denied legitimate cultural status but "Shakespeare" nonetheless maintains a semi-ubiquitous, albeit often unacknowledged, presence.

7. See De Grazia's "Shakespeare in Quotation Marks" and *Shakespeare Verbatim*. See also Michael Warren and Gary Taylor's edited collection *The Division of the Kingdom: Shakespeare's Two Version's of King Lear* and Warren's work on "unstitching" and "unbinding" facsimile versions of *King Lear*. Randall McLeod has written many interesting articles on "un-emending" Shakespeare, and his multi-author collection, *Crisis in Editing: Texts of the English Renaissance*, further illuminates the problems associated with early modern textual production, as does Leah Marcus's *Unediting the Renaissance: Shakespeare, Marlowe, Milton*. For further relevant investigations of authorship, drama, and textuality in the early modern period, see G. E. Bentley's *The Profession of Dramatist in Shakespeare's Time, 1590–1642*, Jonathan Goldberg's *Writing Matter: From the Hands of the English Renaissance*, Jeffrey A. Masten's work on collaborative authorship, such as "Beaumont and/or Fletcher: Collaboration and the Interpretation of Renaissance Drama," and Peter W.M.

The crumbling of critical consensus about Shakespeare's authority began in the 1980s, the decade that marked, in Edward Pechter's terms, the "death" of the "one volume anthology"—collections that "did not seem at the time to fracture the containing structure [Shakespeare], or prevent us from understanding modern Shakespeare criticism as a more or less unified discourse" (15). Consequently, since 1985, the year that *Alternative Shakespeares, Political Shakespeare,* and *Shakespeare and the Question of Theory* emerged, respectively, in the spirit of contestation, innovation, and interrogation (Pechter 15), the question of *who* Shakespeare really was—imposter, poetic genius, glover's son—has been replaced with inquiries into *what* constituted "Shakespeare" in material practice.[8] My concern here is not to rehearse these well-known and important critical forays but rather to demonstrate how they have, ultimately, failed to remove Shakespeare completely from the ranks of sublime object, for scholars continue to take particular, even paranoiac, pains to deconstruct the mythology of Shakespeare the Author. For example, Graham Holderness and Brian Loughrey infantilize editorial champions of Shakespeare the Author, describing them as victims of arrested (theoretical) development who desperately "clin[g] to an umbilical cord [by] firmly attaching the texts to an 'author'" (*Shakespearean Originals* 23). As this spirited derision suggests, the very mention of Shakespeare in conjunction with authorship gives rise to an incommensurate anxiety, as if there *really were* something corporeal lurking within this corpus.

The most recent critical approaches to the problem of Shakespearean authorship are similarly preoccupied with extinguishing this tenacious potency of life. Bordering on a nihilistic embrace of the Foucauldian

---

Blayney's exhaustive examination of the process of publishing scripts in "The Publication of Playbooks." For analyses of the challenges posed by dramatic authorship that move from a text-centered to a performance-centered conception of authority, see, respectively, Stephen Orgel's "What is a Text?" and "The Authentic Shakespeare." Robert Weimann's *Author's Pen, Actor's Voice* rounds out this list with an attempt to create a rapprochement between the collaborative and often competing agencies of author, text, and actor. However, Weimann acknowledges that "one difficulty in coming to *terms* with the unfixed, changeful order of relations of 'pen' and 'voice' in the Elizabethan theatre is that the present study has to cope with the lack of a sustainedly helpful *terminology*" (9). The objective of my argument is to supply precisely such a "sustainedly helpful terminology."

8. See *Alternative Shakespeares,* edited by John Drakakis; *Political Shakespeare,* edited by Jonathan Dollimore and Alan Sinfield; and *Shakespeare and the Question of Theory,* edited by Geoffrey Hartman and Patricia Parker.

conclusion, "What matter who's speaking?" (138), the latest trend in Shakespearean authorship studies revolves around the valorization of "non-agential writing." As this phrase implies, non-agential writing posits agency not as a function of the Author but as an effect of the Text, emerging in the random "drift of error, the interruptions of noise" and, ultimately, the system of anonymous "marks on the page" that mandate a critical commitment to not "bothering to look" for "Shakespeare" at all (Pittenger 213)—a far cry from the prurient curiosity of Washington Irving. Subsuming any traces of the authorial voice, "noise," according to this theory, is a catch-all word for the textual interference caused by early modern print technology, whose playful accidents, variants, blots, and blunders become the focus of the scholarly gaze. Accordingly, if random outbursts of noise haunt the Shakespearean corpus, then perhaps, as Marjorie Garber has argued, Shakespeare was himself a "ghost," or at least a "ghostwriter." Offering a theoretical compromise between the heaven of the Romantics and the hellfires of poststructuralism, Shakespeare the "ghostwriter" is a brilliant metaphor for authorship prior to its legal substantiation and historical legitimation. By the same token, however, this "hauntological" variation on the theme of non-agential writing can too often turn a "bad quarto" into a grade B movie, sparking a critical sensationalism around specters, aliens, and cyborgs that carries us euphorically away from the material conditions of Shakespeare's early modern prison-house.[9] Before we rush to usher in the age of the CyBard, then, we might pause to consider the extent to which Shakespeare, as Foucault argues of the figure of the Author more generally, has become a locus for "projections, in terms always more or less psychological, of our way of handling texts" (127). I will approach this idea of projection quite literally, by arguing that there is indeed a ghost in Shakespeare's machine—a cinematic one—which contains the makings of the auteur.

Before exploring this thesis, however, it is necessary to establish why the move from Author-focused criticism to Text-centered theory proves

9. An interesting example of this practice is Janet H. Murray's book *Hamlet on the Holodeck: The Future of Narrative in Cyberspace*, which examines the possibilities of reviving what she calls the "bardic" function of storytelling via websurfing, implicitly ascribing a universalizing, transhistorical role to Shakespeare's *Hamlet* in the evolution of narrative. Subsequently, Murray issues the demand for reconceptualizing authorship along the lines of "storytelling in cyberspace." I borrow the term "hauntological" from Jacques Derrida's *Specters of Marx*.

to be an inadequate representation of all the "things" that constitute the Shakespearean corpus. If there is one prevailing link among poststructuralist critiques of Shakespearean authorship, then it is their persistent projection of human attributes onto the text. Whether construed as the capricious interjections of "noise," the "umbilical cord" of editorial tradition, or the fortuitous hauntings of friendly "ghosts," Shakespeare studies has done away with the fiction of the Author only to endow the Text with a forceful personality of its own. The most thought-provoking illustration of this phenomenon occurs in a compelling derivative of Shakespearean poststructuralism known as the New Textualism. In their influential essay, titled "The Materiality of the Shakespearean Text," Margreta De Grazia and Peter Stallybrass exhort us to forgo the mythology of the Author in order to embrace the idea of "materiality" which, they claim, destabilizes the romanticism that has supported ahistorical readings of Shakespeare's plays for more than two centuries. Emerging in "old typefaces and spellings, irregular line and scene divisions, title pages...other paratextual matter, and textual cruxes" (256), this materiality undermines the traditional interpretive categories of "Work," "word," "character," and "author." The first three sections of this provocative critical practice offer vital demonstrations of how poststructuralism can be used to unrivet the Shakespearean "Work," "word," and "character" from the anachronistic attributes of unity, fixity, and singular identity. In so doing, De Grazia and Stallybrass issue an important countermand to the critical tradition that has falsely rendered Shakespeare as the "onlie begetter" of a dramatic corpus that *cannot* be separated from the collaborative conditions of composition, performance, and reproduction that prevailed in the early modern period. However, when we arrive at De Grazia and Stallybrass's interrogation of the category of "author," we witness an equal and opposite reaction to the very romanticism they set out to critique, precipitating the return of the Author's body in the form of an embodied Text.

De Grazia and Stallybrass begin with a claim that foreshadows this return: "Though now possessing the documents that could dispel it, *we are in danger of remaining hypnotically fascinated by the isolated author*" (279, emphasis added). Oddly attesting to the persistence of the very "thing" they set out to prove as "nothing," De Grazia and Stallybrass deflect attention away from the Author by focusing on "a more helpful way of conceptualizing the text," which "is to be found in the materials of the physical book itself: in paper" (280). But in the process of celebrating the plurality of "paper" over the person of the "isolated author," their critique generates an anthropomorphic treatment of the Text. For example, locating a miraculous karma effect in the metamorphoses of paper, De Grazia and Stallybrass contend that "in the sheets of a book, bedsheets began a new life" (280), implying a not-so-subtle transference of bodily enjoyment between the sheets of a bed to textual enjoyment between the pages—and lines—of a book. But lest this erotic materiality flirt with romanticism, De Grazia and Stallybrass assure us that "[o]ther, less luxurious 'foreign' bodies" such as "rags," "juniper gum, linseed oil, ... lampblack" and even "the residual traces of the urine of the printshop workers" (282) are all contained in the "absorbent surface of the Shakespearean text" (280). And as the secretive "foreign bodies" of the printshop workers lead us to the secret pleasures of readers' bodies, we are drawn into the undulating layers of the Shakespearean text as it panders, or in De Grazia and Stallybrass's words, "coaxes" readers into "assembl[ing] any number and combination of pages" of the author formerly known as Shakespeare (283). Ironically, then, it seems as though any body *but* the authorial body is allowed to participate in this primal scene of textual pleasure.

Though we now place Shakespeare's name in quotation marks to indicate the death of this Author in particular, Shakespeare's epitaph is belied by poststructuralism's tendency to kill the Author without giving up its ghost—that is, without relinquishing its enticing, even "dangerous" aura of fascination. This contradiction is borne out by De Grazia and Stallybrass's closing words, wherein they imagine themselves situated in "a great bibliographic divide," faced with the apparently unfinished task of "tak[ing] our minds off the solitary genius in the text" (283):

This [authorial] genius is, after all, an impoverished, ghostly thing, compared to the complex social practices that shaped, and still shape, the absorbent surface of the Shakespearean text. Perhaps it is these practices that should be the objects not only of our labors but also of our desires.

(283)

As this "ghostly thing" insists, while the authorial body may now be "no thing," it is *something* "in the text more than the text." This is a conclusion that not even De Grazia and Stallybrass can resist, for in their effort to bury the Author once and for all, they succeed in reviving this object of fascination with the specter of their own desire—positing themselves as the aspiring "authors" of a new critical ritual.[10]

As this revolution in Shakespeare studies brings us back around to familiar territory, we are still faced with the question: what do we do with Shakespeare's remains? If, as Herbert Blau contends, contemporary theory has reached a point of crisis, tacitly documenting "the spectacle of a culture whose symbolic is in ruins" (226), then when will it be safe to start constructing again? Is there a way, in other words, to eliminate the oppressive ideology of the Author while retaining a viable, responsible concept of agency that offers a foothold in the midst of this theoretical quicksand? We may begin to answer these questions by considering the historical relevance, or lack thereof, of the term "author" for Shakespeare studies in the first place.

The *Oxford English Dictionary* informs us that the word "author" first appears in the English language circa 1550 as a variant of "auctor," a term from scribal culture designating a literary authority whose status as such is purely derivative, the cumulative product of his affiliation with classical authorities and his posthumous appropriation by his successors.[11] Adapted from the Latin verb *augere*, the High Scholastic definition of the *auctor* as "an increaser of great deeds and thoughts from the past" (Galloway 28) situates this figure not as an individual but as an apparatus, a collaborative nexus of textual production, transmission, and reception enlisted in the creation of *auctoritas*, or established authority. Treading on the heels of the configuration of *auctor*, the "author" springs to typographical life in 1550 but is ontologically premature; this word does not become flesh until the late eighteenth century, when the Author is reborn as the unique creator, proprietor, and benefactor of the fruits of his intellectual labor. The early modern period thus appears to be an inhospitable authorial "no man's land." Of-

10. Although I critique what I perceive to be De Grazia and Stallybrass's idealization of the "materiality" of the Shakespearean text, it is important to underscore the fact that my own work would not be possible without their many contributions to our current understanding of early modern textuality.

11. Throughout this discussion, I will be using the masculine pronoun to speak about the author and authorship. The ideology of authorship, as I will be exploring it in relation to auteur theory and nationalism, is decidedly masculinist. The feminist politics of authorship will be discussed in the final chapter on *Shakespeare in Love*.

fering a particularly useful description of this negative space, Peter Stallybrass highlights the conditions of literary production before and after the historical period in which Shakespeare's plays were written:

> Before, writing as a composite process, involving many hands; after, the individual author's control of every stage of the process. Before[,] patronage; after, the market economy. Before, the shifting orthography in which word bleeds into word; after, the standardized orthography of the individual word. Before, subjecthood, subjection, and the body of the state; after, individuality, republicanism, and the social contract.
>
> ("Shakespeare, the Individual, and the Text," 609)

Representing a pronounced exception to this "before" and "after" paradigm, the early modern period is situated precariously between what we might call the imperatives of the "apparatus"—corresponding to the reiterative ideology of the *auctor*, the feudal economy of patronage, and the contingencies of pre-standardized modes of literary transmission—and the aspirations of the "Author," which are associated with the cultural demand for originality, an autonomous literary marketplace, and the standardization of the literary and legal machinery of authorial production.

Where, then, does Shakespeare fit into this scheme? In order to underscore the extent to which Shakespeare complicates the already precarious space between "before" and "after," it is necessary to traverse some familiar terrain surrounding questions of Shakespearean authorship. As I have demonstrated, over and against the anachronistic tradition of valorizing Shakespeare the Author, contemporary scholarship is devoted to a concept of "Shakespeare" the apparatus, a view that proclaims Shakespeare to be the contingent effect of "the various stages of scripting, acting, printing, selling, [and] patronage" (De Grazia, *Shakespeare Verbatim* 39). This perspective is particularly seductive in light of the fact that roughly two-thirds of the plays in the Shakespeare canon show signs of alteration at these various stages, and sixteen of these plays reveal internal inconsistencies which, in G. E. Bentley's estimation, exceed explanation by printing-house variants.[12] Yet such signs of synchronic and diachronic revision by forces apparently beyond Shakespeare's control are not terribly surprising, for Shakespeare was merely a part of

---

12. For a comprehensive analysis of the textual consistencies in the First Folio, see G. E. Bentley's *The Profession of Dramatist in Shakespeare's Time, 1590–1642.*

a much larger system of patronage, market exigencies, performance technology, and the sociopolitical ideologies of early modern England. Moreover, as an attached dramatist, that is, a dramatist who wrote exclusively for one acting company, Shakespeare was under an ethical obligation to foster the best interests of The Lord Chamberlain's Men which, as of 1603, became The King's Men. This meant that not only were his plays the company's exclusive property to alter and use as they saw fit within the playhouse but also that they were not to be printed for public circulation nor sold to another acting company for profit without express permission. Clearly, then, Shakespeare's relationship to the apparatus of dramatic production alone works against the ideology of possessive individualism typically associated with the figure of the Author. Predictably, there is no evidence to suggest that Shakespeare ever saw a play through the press, leaving Samuel Johnson to complain that "No other author ever gave up his works to fortune and time with so little care" (qtd. in De Grazia, *Shakespeare Verbatim* 61).

In this context, marshaling Shakespeare's missing paper trail as evidence against his authorial ambition is a strategy that ignores the historical conditions of production to which Shakespeare, like other attached dramatists, was bound. Even in the case of independent dramatists, publication was the exception rather than the rule, for as Irvin Leigh Matus notes: "only the most contentious left a revealing paper trail" (41), echoing Foucault's equation of authorship with criminality prior to the installation of copyright.[13] Among Shakespeare's contemporaries, the obvious exception to this rule is Ben Jonson. However, despite Jonson's resemblance to the modern proprietary author who posits both abstract value and personal property in the literary text, Jonson's intervention in the ideological status of early modern textual production is, in Joseph Loewenstein's terms, "neo-conservative" ("Script" 273). For even as he was attempting to create a literary marketplace for the sale of his "Workes," Jonson refused to interact with the mass of consumers, dedicating his Folio plays, poems, and masques to aristocratic patrons as a bid for preferment. Therefore, Jonson's acts of authorship merely adapted a "modern technology of dissemination to

13. In "What Is an Author?" Foucault observes that before copyright "books were assigned to real authors, other than mythical or important religious figures, only when the author became subject to punishment and to the extent that his discourse was considered transgressive" (124).

an archaic patronage economy" modeled, as Loewenstein observes, on the ethos of the *auctor* ("Script" 273). In many respects, then, Jonson was even more "attached"—in his case, to the apparatus of patronage—than Shakespeare was to the dramatic apparatus. In fact, Shakespeare actually possessed one crucial authorial advantage over Jonson. Prior to the creation of copyright laws in the eighteenth century, the only way an "author" could secure property in his work was by also being a member of the Stationer's Company (which maintained a publishing monopoly in England from 1557 to the end of the seventeenth century) or by being a shareholder in the acting company for which his plays were written. It often escapes mention that Shakespeare maintained partial ownership of the products of his intellectual labor because he was a one-tenth shareholder in the acting company.

While it was to Shakespeare's advantage as a shareholder not to see his plays through the press, there is evidence to suggest that he was not altogether lacking a "bibliographic ego."[14] Though extraordinarily little can be confirmed about Shakespeare's life, one of the ways in which he may have acted as an "author" was by implying his sponsorship of the publication of *Venus and Adonis* and *The Rape of Lucrece*. Quite unlike the printed quartos of Shakespeare's plays, which were littered with errors and showed no signs of his authorial sponsorship, these two dramatic poems were submitted as clean copies furnished with elaborate front matter—dedicatory poems, commendatory epistles, addresses to prospective readers, and so on—signaling a self-conscious mode of presentation. In an historical period in which authorship was still predominantly an act of anonymity, authorial sponsorship, as Bentley explains, can generally be detected by the presence of such front matter. And indeed, *Venus and Adonis* and *The Rape of Lucrece* demonstrate the fastidious formality associated with the act of authorial sponsorship, replete with Shakespeare's name printed beneath the dedications.[15] In his analysis of the making of the "bibliographic ego," Joseph Loewenstein explains that, in the pre-Lockean marketplace, authorial consciousness first emerged in the form of the public articulation of a proprietary impulse. Such an impulse would be imperative in the literary marketplace of early modern England, wherein literary works were afforded no

14. I borrow the expression "bibliographic ego" from Joseph Lowenstein. See particularly *"Idem:* Italics and Genetics of Authorship."

15. For a thorough contextualization of the phenomenon of authorial sponsorship in Shakespeare's day, see Richard Dutton's essay on "The Birth of the Author."

legal protection and, consequently, as De Grazia asserts, there was no "preoccupation with who spoke what" ("Shakespeare in Quotation Marks" 57). Significantly, in addition to suggesting his authorial sponsorship of *Venus and Adonis* and *The Rape of Lucrece*, Shakespeare seems to have demonstrated a very keen sense of "who spoke what" when he believed his reputation as an "author" to be at stake, allegedly objecting to having verses that were written by Thomas Heywood attributed to him in *The Passionate Pilgrim* (De Grazia, *Shakespeare Verbatim* 172n). This protest is predicated on the self-conscious assertion of both authorial propriety *and* property. It is particularly ironic, then, that aside from the six surviving legal signatures ascribed to Shakespeare, the only material trace of Shakespeare the "author" actually testifies to the existence of "Shakespeare" the apparatus, namely, the *Sir Thomas More* manuscript, wherein Shakespeare's hand has been detected alongside five other dramatists working on the play, among them, Thomas Heywood.

The riddle posed by Shakespearean authorship clearly confounds what Foucault refers to as the "singularity of the name of the author" (122). The early modern period compounds this riddle in its failure to present us with a consolidated notion of authorship. However, a closer examination of the early modern rhetoric of production suggests a burgeoning theory of agency that may help us to resist the false choice between Shakespeare and "Shakespeare." Rather than tipping the balance of production in favor of either the "author" or the apparatus, early modern discourse tends to eliminate the distinction between producer and product. This elision is reflected, for example, in Montaigne's 1580 preface to his essays, which presupposes a transubstantial relation between his body and his text: "I have no more made my book than my book has made me" (23). Bodies and texts are also intertwined in the early modern printing rhetoric of "typeface" and "bodytype," in handwriting manuals that delineate letters by endowing them with "heads" and "tails," and in pedagogical definitions of the writing surface as the "author-text," as if the separation of these terms was unthinkable. This productive constellation of bodies and texts is particularly relevant to the dramatic medium which, Linda Charnes reminds us, has an "intrinsically 'double' nature" as both written text and embodied script, the convergence of which "produces something that cannot be deconstructed" (*Notorious Identity* 99).

Indeed, it could be argued that theatrical performance is the ideal locus for propelling Shakespearean authorship beyond theoretical dead ends posed by the singular Author and an anonymous textual apparatus, for on stage, the body is textualized and the text is embodied. But as W.B. Worthen argues in *Shakespeare and the Authority of Performance*, theatrical performance subscribes to a binary logic of its own by situating "authoritative" texts against "transgressive" performances of them. More problematic, according to Worthen, is the fact that even within the text vs. performance paradigm, the Author enters the scene not as a legitimate third term but as a sign of reversion toward "a point of privileged meaning to which both frames of interpretation finally appeal" (36). Worthen's fascinating investigation of the ways in which authority of a distinctly "Shakespearean" variety is performed in the rhetoric of directors, on the surfaces of actors' bodies, and between the lines of performance scholarship both continues and complicates the crucial work initiated by the first wave of alternative Shakespeare criticism that sought to disrupt the "stabilizing, hegemonic function of the Author" (Worthen 2) in Shakespeare studies more generally. However, despite its move to posit a third term in the idea of dramatic "labor," a concept which is embodied in stage performances and reading practices that generate "a new production of the work" (21), Worthen's analysis of performance relies on and, in the process, ultimately resurrects the straw categories of the "absent author" and its "Trojan horse...the text" (2).

I propose both interrogating and *changing* the terms of the Shakespearean authorship equation. However, moving beyond the seemingly ineradicable oppositions of Author vs. Text, text vs. performance, and performance vs. Author demands a change of venue, a site less susceptible to distinctly "Shakespearean" ideas of authority and, therefore, capable of defamiliarizing our associations with such critically entrenched terminology. If we begin the search for this site by returning to the phrasing of Shakespeare's authorial legacy as it was articulated by the compilers of the First Folio, John Heminge and Henry Condell, we find that they, too, went in search of third terms when they bequeathed to posterity neither Shakespeare's body nor "Shakespeare's" book but, rather, his "remaines."[16] What is alluded to here, as in the tenuous sites

---

16. In their 1623 dedicatory epistle to the Earls of Pembroke and Montgomery, Heminge and Condell explain that they "most humbly consecrate...these remaines of your servant Shakespeare" (94). I cite this excerpt from a facsimile of Heminge and Condell's "To The Most Noble and Incomparable Paire of Brethren" in *The Riverside Shakespeare*.

of early modern textual "theory" explored above, is a kind of montage of bodies *and* texts that matter, a locus of a resilient remainders that undermines totalizing interpretations and, more importantly, resists total deconstruction. Might the idea of montage suggest a means of obeying the warning that presides over Shakespeare's "corpus"—a way of keeping his bodily and textual remains intact—rather than slicing "Shakespeare" into either an Author or a Text? The concept of montage, from the French verb "monter" meaning "to assemble," implies a site for this act of *splicing* to occur: film theory.

The figure in film theory most associated with ideas of montage is Sergei Eisenstein, who located the rudiments of this cinematic concept in the protocinematic experimentation conducted in Kabuki Theater, as well as in other cultural forms that simulate contrapuntal collisions of visual and aural stimuli. However, while theater was a useful site of incubation for what Eisenstein called "montage thinking" (27), he ultimately found the dramatic medium lacking. Bound by the principles of real space and time, theater proved incapable of representing *"collateral vibrations"* (67) across historical and political landscapes that the cinematic concept of dialectical montage fully realized. Indeed, according to Eisenstein, third terms can only be generated from simultaneity—from collisions that replace "an 'aristocracy' of individualistic dominants" in the visual-aural field with a "'democratic' equality of rights for all provocations, or stimuli" (66).[17] Thus, following a series of failed experiments with theatrical forms, Eisenstein explains that "we found ourselves in the cinema" (16). So, too, I will argue that the "remaines" of the author formerly known as Shakespeare may be found in the cinema and, more specifically, in film theory. In contrast to literary paradigms, film theory's approach to authorship, embodied in the concept of "auteur," is based on constitutive tensions between bodies and texts, authors and apparatuses—similar to the early modern praxis described above. Perhaps this is why Eisenstein, in another intriguing moment of synthesis, referred to montage as *"the dramaturgy of the film-story"* (55).

Citations of Shakespeare works other than *Romeo and Juliet* and *Hamlet* are quoted with permission from the second edition of *The Riverside Shakespeare*.

17. Montage, as Eisenstein conceives it, is based on the dialectical "view that from the collision of two given factors *arises* a concept" (37).

Even after Andrew Sarris dubbed it a formal theory, the short story of auteur theory took shape more as a "structure of feeling" that reflected changing expectations about agential relationships within film produc-tion.[18] Spanning more than three decades, auteur theory focused specifically on the relationship between a film's "author," or director, and the filmic "apparatus," or the mechanical and ideological struc-tures involved in a film's creation, distribution, and reception. In the late 1940s through the 1950s, auteur theory evolved as a revival of the Romantic theory of the author applied to the film director. The auteur was considered to be an uncompromising artist who transcended the constraints of the Hollywood studio system to inscribe an inimitable signature across a series of films. Consequently, in the 1960s, the irre-sponsible excesses of this phase of auteur theory were balanced by auteur-structuralism, which refocused attention from the film-author to considerations of the function of the filmic apparatus. In this context, the apparatus is identified more closely with the camera and also with the ideological apparatuses that structure perception. With the help of Freud and Lévi-Strauss, the author of a film becomes reconstituted as a "deep structure," inflected with a nexus of collaborative agents whose contingent interactions lead to the film product. But the pivotal phase of auteur theory with which this project is concerned begins, oddly enough, with the death of the Author.

Having arrived by 1968 at a predictable impasse between Romanti-cism and poststructuralism, auteur theory distinguished itself from its brethren in literary theory by refusing, as film theorist Edward Buscombe describes it, to "throw out the baby with the bathwater" (qtd. in Heath 218). Resisting the temptation to eliminate the idea of agency along with the figure of the Author, *Cahiers du Cinema* editors Jean-Louis Comolli and Jean Narboni demanded a new direction for film theory and practice in their 1969 manifesto, "Cinema/Ideol-ogy/Criticism." In the wake of the political and pedagogical upheavals in France in 1968, Comolli and Narboni repositioned the concept of agency according to the principles of dialectical montage as formulated by Sergei Eisenstein. Generating a theory of authorship based on con-stitutive conflict, critics such as Peter Wollen, Serge Daney, Jean-Pierre Oudart, and Robin Wood followed suit by arguing that the collision of

18. Sarris's coining of the phrase "auteur theory" occurs in his "Notes on the Auteur Theory in 1962." Raymond Williams defines a structure of feeling as an emergent forma-tion which "is indeed social and material, but...in an embryonic phase" (131).

an "author" and an "apparatus" produces a concept of auteur-as-*remainder*. Consequently, these critics went in search of symptoms of this surplus, which they described, provocatively, as "patterns of energy cathexis"—the remainders, gaps, and seams in the filmic text and texture that betray a struggle for agency occurring beneath the cinematic surface.[19] Offering an example of this search in terms uncannily similar to the critical rhetoric I have been exploring, Peter Wollen employed the principles of auteur analysis to explore the irreducible surplus generated by the collision between "Fuller or Hawks or Hitchcock, the directors," and " 'Fuller' or 'Hawks' or 'Hitchcock,' the structures named after them" (168). Thus, as authorship itself is reconceived of as a montage effect, the idea of auteur comes to offer a local habitation and a name for that which is "in the film-text, more than the film-text."

> Cudgel your brain, tear away every covering in your breast
> and expose the viscera of feeling, demolish every defense
> that separates you from the person you are reading about,
> and then read Shakespeare—and you will be appalled at the
> collisions.
>
> —Søren Kierkegaard, *The Sickness Unto Death*

Robin Wood once launched a defense of Alfred Hitchcock based on a comparison of Hitchcock to Shakespeare.[20] But perhaps we should rethink Shakespeare in relation to Hitchcock. De Grazia and Stallybrass remind us that "we need . . . to rethink Shakespeare [the Author] in relation to our new knowledge of collaborative writing, collaborative printing, and the historical contingencies of textual production" (279). The only barrier to the articulation of this important knowledge lies in the fact that "Shakespeare's work," as James Kavanagh argues, exists at "the threshold of a new practice which lacks the word that will give it a

19. The phrase "patterns of energy cathexis" is from Wollen's *Signs and Meaning in the Cinema*.

20. See Wood's 1965 introduction to *Hitchcock's Films Revisited*, in which Wood answers the question "Why should we take Hitchcock seriously?" by insisting upon the cultural value that Hitchcock and Shakespeare share.

discursive ideological presence" (147). Might the concept of auteur answer both of these critical calls? To refocus the Shakespearean corpus through the lens of auteur theory is to recognize "Shakespeare" as a montage of historically charged collisions between bodies and texts that cannot be reduced to the work of either a solitary "author" or an ever-metamorphosing dramatic and textual "apparatus." At the same time, however, the concept of auteur renders visible what *remains* after all is said and undone, by drawing attention to how the plays themselves—and recent film adaptations of them—generate intriguing traces that testify to an authorial presence despite historical conditions of erasure. In projecting film theory from the postmodern to the early modern and back again, my objective is not to relegate history to "costume drama" which, in Catherine Belsey's words, is to reconstruct "the past as the present in fancy dress" (2). Rather, my intent is to expose— through deliberate collisions of two historical periods in which "authors" fear to tread—the provocative ways in which Shakespeare keeps coming back, as it were, from the future, to illuminate the shared pathologies and possibilities of a practice that defines a habitation but defies a name. As Jacques Derrida argues, such specters or, in cinematic terms, "projections"—from the historical to the cinematic—are always the bearers of a message, imploring us, like the Ghost in *Hamlet*, to do a doubletake, for "what seems to be out in front, the future, comes back in advance from the past, from the back" (*Specters of Marx* 10). So, too, I shall argue that the idea of auteur only appears to be "out in front," coming back in advance—ahead of its time—from the past, indeed, from Shakespeare.

Beginning with the early modern period, the first three chapters trace the evolution of Shakespearean authorial practice in three plays which, I argue, encode allegories of authorship in the dramatic collisions they stage between aspiring authors and repressive cultural apparatuses, culminating in the representation of the early modern auteur in *Hamlet*. Chapter One, "Shakespeare Unauthorized: Tragedy 'by the book' in *Romeo and Juliet*," analyzes Romeo's struggle for agency within the historical void separating the medieval *auctor* from the eighteenth-century Author. *Romeo and Juliet* stands out in the Shakespeare canon as a play that relies almost exclusively on a single source or *auctor:* Arthur Brooke's *The Tragicall Historye of Romeus and Juliet*. Through its unusual preoccupation with phrases such as "by the book," "by rote," and other expressions of textual compulsion, Shakespeare's play reveals an irrepressible anxiety about its exceptionally close relationship to its source.

Romeo, too, acts as if he were aware of his own "tragicall historye" in Brooke's poem and attempts to alter this fatal trajectory by becoming "author" of his own destiny. But Romeo's rebellion precedes the historical separation of authorship from established authority and, therefore, he cannot ultimately extricate himself from "what's in his name": literally, the letters prescribing his destined arrival in "sour misfortune's book."[21] Thus, Romeo's version of his story emerges only in the form of a dead letter—the irreducible remainder of his untimely attempt at authorship.

If the early modern nondramatic author occupies the volatile space between *auctor* and Author, then the predicament of the early modern dramatist is even more problematic, for this figure must also struggle against the tensions internal to the theater itself. Chapter Two, "Authors, Players, and the Shakespearean Auteur-Function in *A Midsummer Night's Dream*," explores the relationship of Shakespearean drama to the growing rift in the public theater between an "authors' theater" and a "players' theater," a conflict that precipitated the fin de siècle War of the Theaters (1599–1601). Given the fact that the War etched an enduring fault line between elite and popular playgoing tastes in England, theater historians have long puzzled over why Shakespeare's company didn't claim a position in this debate about repertoires, audiences, venues, and actors. I argue, however, that Shakespeare's company both entered into and derived a solution for this theatrical crisis before the War even began by experimenting with social, aesthetic, and political montage effects in *A Midsummer Night's Dream*. Staging a proleptic war between Oberon's "authors' theater" and Bottom's "players' theater," *Dream* generates a third term from this collision—an auteur's theater—materializing, appropriately, in a playhouse named for its encompassing stature and appeal: the Globe.

Chapter Three, "The Machine in the Ghost: *Hamlet*'s Cinematographic Kingdom" investigates the limits of theatrical authorship itself, based on Hamlet's admission that he has "that within which *passes* show" (1.2.85, emphasis added). Building on the Derridean logic that ghosts return from the future, this chapter explores *Hamlet* as a locus of early cinematic thinking, arguing that Hamlet's notorious failure to act may be explained by his failure to think in "live" or theatrical terms. Be-

---

21. See Shakespeare's *Romeo and Juliet* 5.2.82. All citations of this play are quoted with permission from Stanley Wells and Gary Taylor's edition, *The Oxford Shakespeare: Tragedies*. Hereafter cited in the text.

cause the Ghost's commandments require Hamlet to occupy two conflicting temporalities, future ("revenge") and past ("remember"), Hamlet is forced to envision a mode of fulfilling these demands that defies the narrative logic of space, time, and even causality. This modality will crystallize three hundred years later in cinema's ghostly ability to subvert theater's reliance on live action and spatio-temporal constraints. Thus, despite Hamlet's inability to project and, therefore, to exorcise the ghost in his machine, Shakespeare's play, I shall argue, remains thoroughly "cinematic."

As a play that begins with a struggle over remains and ends with the remains of a struggle, *Hamlet* dramatizes a crisis of legacies and literacies. Focusing on Shakespeare's authorial legacy in postmodern culture, Chapters Four through Seven explore the crisis of legitimacy that forms the historical continuum between early modern and postmodern authorship. Just as the early modern "author" exists before the historical birth of the Author, the postmodern "author" arrives on the scene only after the theoretical "death" of this figure. Chapter Four, "Strictly Shakespeare? Dead Letters, Ghostly Fathers, and the Cultural Pathology of Authorship in Baz Luhrmann's *William Shakespeare's Romeo + Juliet*," offers an introduction to the precarious status of authorship in postmodern culture. Indeed, the title of Luhrmann's 1996 film alone announces its apparent concession to the disabling logic of the postmodern aesthetic, representing what Fredric Jameson describes as "the failure of the new, the imprisonment in the past" ("Postmodernism and Consumer Society" 190). In a world in which "stylistic innovation is no longer possible," Jameson concludes, postmodern authorship can aspire to little more than "speech in a dead language," or, a "blank parody" of the past (190). In its quest to create a distinctly cinematographic language for articulating Shakespeare's authorial legacy, *William Shakespeare's Romeo + Juliet* poses the central challenge of authorship in the age of blank parody: generating an alternative to "speech in a dead language."

Against the prevailing logic of the postmodern, film historian Leo Braudy argues that the adaptation process does not stem from a compulsion to repeat the dead language and styles of the past but, more profoundly, from unfinished *cultural* business.[22] In postmodern culture, the practice of authorship cannot be separated from struggles of race, class, gender, and sexuality. Though rarely characterized as such, the

22. This idea of adaptation as unfinished cultural business is a theme of Leo Braudy's essay on "Rethinking Remakes."

Shakespearean adaptations of Kenneth Branagh emerge from an ongoing crisis of "unfinished cultural business," for his films generate a singular confrontation between the postmodern and the postcolonial. Branagh's work is deeply inflected with what he describes as a uniquely Anglo-Irish sense of alienation, born of his precarious status as a Belfast native and honorary Englishman. Chapter Five, "Dead *Again*? Or, the Cultural Logic of Late Auteurism," uses Branagh's films as a springboard for exploring the emergence of the postmodern auteur as a figure who undertakes the modernist search for a legitimating identity within and against the leveling operations of mass culture. Locating this practice in historical precedents such as the Irish renaissance, this chapter defines the work of the postmodern auteur as the attempt to reinvent the high-modernist notion of artistic production within a low-postmodern mode of mass cultural reception.

This complex negotiation between high and low culture assumes the coordinates of what Antonio Gramsci defines as "the national" and "the popular," as Branagh attempts to create a "united kingdom" of moviegoers through his Shakespeare films for the masses.[23] By appealing to an economically and ethnically diverse constituency of "the people," Branagh's films do indeed promote a certain degree of aesthetic populism at the level of *reception;* but at the level of *production*, the content of his films hinges on an internal dynamic of social exclusion which, ironically, keeps a certain faction of "the people" in their place. Chapter Six, "There Ain't No 'Mac' in the Union Jack: Adaptation and (O)mission in *Henry V*," explores what gets *left out* of Branagh's vision of a national-popular cinema. Branagh promotes his debut film of *Henry V* (1989) as both "quintessentially English" project and a "truly popular" film.[24] However, these "national" and "popular" interests fork in the face of the Irish Captain Macmorris, who emerges not only as a theatrical stereotype of the "wild Irish" but also as a staple of the minstrel tradition—wearing blackface—underscoring the historical slander of the Irish as "white niggers." Calling the bluff of Branagh's postmodern pledge of making Shakespeare for the masses, Macmorris represents what Paul Gilroy describes in *There Ain't No Black in the Union Jack* as the "enemy within," a symbol of social antagonisms internal to the

23. The term "national-popular" appears throughout Antonio Gramsci's *Selections from Cultural Writings*.

24. This national-popular rhetoric is a recurrent theme in Branagh's description of the making of *Henry V* in his autobiography, *Beginning*.

United Kingdom. Ultimately, then, *Henry V* reserves its modernist pay-off exclusively for Branagh, who creates a vision of a working United Kingdom in which "no Irish need apply" only by positing himself as an exception to the rule.

Chapter Seven, "*Shakespeare in Love:* Sex, Capitalism, and the Authorial Body-in-Pleasure," explores the gender and labor exploitation that underlies Hollywood's romance with the figure of Shakespeare the Author. What makes John Madden's 1998 film such a provocative endpoint for this analysis is its focus on the authorial body itself as the privileged site of the adaptation process. Reinventing the "death of the Author" as a "little death," this bedroom farce playfully links poetic labor to sexual expenditure. In so doing, however, *Shakespeare in Love* poses a theory of authorial production that is grounded in the conspicuous consumption of the *female* flesh, producing, through Will's unacknowledged collaboration with Viola, a vision of the once vulnerable Shakespearean corpus as a smooth, seamless, sexually viable hardbody. Thus, what *Shakespeare in Love* teaches us is that the play is *not* the thing, for only the capital-driven logic of the cinema can create such a pleasing mystification of labor in the name of love—and this is a love which, as the film repeatedly suggests, "creates riot in the heart" and *re*creates Shakespeare—as Hollywood's Ur-Auteur.

Writing in France in the volatile context of 1969, American filmmaker and expatriate Noel Burch observed that "many of the most important break-throughs in film in the last fifteen years" have been, to a great degree, "a matter of vocabulary" (*Theory Of Film Practice* 3).[25] The Shakespearean authorship question is very much a matter of vocabulary and, peculiar as it may sound, auteur theory provides us with a means of articulating conclusions which, contrary to the literary theories at our dis-

25. Burch refers here specifically to the French concept of *decoupage:*

Decoupage in its third French meaning refers to what results when the spatial fragments, or, more accurately, the succession of spatial fragments excerpted in the shooting process, converge with the temporal fragments whose duration may be roughly determined during the shooting, but whose final duration is established only on the editing table. The dialectical notion inherent in the term *decoupage* enables us to determine, and therefore to analyze, the specific form of a film, its essential unfolding in time and space. *Decoupage* as a structural concept involving a synthesis is strictly a French notion ... *It may never occur to English-speaking film-makers or English-speaking critics that these two oper-*

posal, stand the chance of making *Shakespeare* matter. Cinema has always argued the ontological priority of bodies over texts, claiming,
from its earliest moments, that the movies "give us back our bodies,
and particularly our faces, which have been rendered illegible, soulless,
unexpressive by the centuries-old ascendancy of print" (Sontag, "Film
and Theater" 373).[26] Taking its cues from cinema, *Shakespeare Remains*
gives the Shakespearean corpus back its body—but it does so with a
difference—by initiating a long-overdue process of *theoretical* adaptation that replaces the burning of historical bridges between the early
modern and the postmodern, Romanticism and poststructuralism, theater and cinema with the timely creation of montage effects. With the
help of this truly "deep focus," then, we may discern within these ongoing sites of Shakespearean energy cathexis an undetected pattern: the
making of the auteur.

ations stem from a single underlying concept, simply because they have at their disposal no single
word for this concept. (4, emphasis added).

26. Susan Sontag is paraphrasing early filmmaker Bela Belazs's exuberant promises
about the new cinematic medium.

I

Shakespeare Unauthorized

Tragedy "by the book" in *Romeo and Juliet*

One should not, in principle, be able to say where the book
stops and identity begins.

—Stephen Greenblatt, *Renaissance Self-Fashioning*

Emerging for the first time in the literature of the early modern
period is a peculiar, seemingly symbiotic relationship between bodies
and texts. However, this illusion of reciprocity actually conceals a collision of two conflicting modes of authorial production, both vying for
dominance prior to the historical onset of capitalism. In vastly over-
simplified terms, this clash is generated on the one hand by the residual ideology of *auctoritas,* which is rooted in the feudal system of hierarchy, deference, and propriety that designates fixed roles for the
individual within society—and, on the other hand, by an emergent
ideology of self-authorship, which begins to drive a wedge between
the individual and the community by privileging social mobility through
acquisitive appropriation.[1] It is important to note from the outset of
this discussion that these perspectives on authorship and the individual do not simply undergo a tectonic shift of emphasis in the late
fifteenth century when the Renaissance throws off the shackles of the
"Dark Ages" to herald the birth of modernity. Rather, these ideologies
are unstable in and of themselves; for just as the more modern term
"author" can invoke the deified, vatic status associated with the High

---

1. For an extensive exploration of the point at which the literary ethos of "imitation"
takes on an "acquisitive aspect" to reflect changes in early modern culture at large,
see Robert Weimann's "'Appropriation' and Modern History in Renaissance Prose
Narrative."

Scholastic notion of *auctor*, so, too, the concept of *auctoritas* can indicate—particularly during the late Middle Ages—a more modern understanding of authority as derived from distinctly human agency. As we have begun to see, the upshot of these historical tensions is a hybrid sense of agency in which neither bodies nor texts resonate independently of each other as unique "things" but rather function collectively and performatively as "actions."[2] This provocative friction between the producing body and the yet-unauthorized text is consistently ignored in analyses of the Shakespearean corpus, based on the assertion that Shakespeare's elusive authorial body cannot be materially linked to his texts. What this perspective crucially obscures is that Shakespeare's body was, in fact, deeply inscribed in his texts—as an actor of them. In the absence of surviving authorial manuscripts, then, we must look for evidence of concerns about authorship within the plays themselves.

Romeo and Juliet is a play that dramatizes the problematic relations between bodies and texts in early modern culture, generating, in the process, an emergent discourse on authorship. Though this play about the excesses of young love seems an unlikely source of commentary on authorship, *Romeo and Juliet* hinges on another kind of excess: an excess of preexisting literary influence. Accordingly, I shall argue that Shakespeare explores the effects of source on subjectivization through Romeo who, unlike his legendary precursors, attempts to become the "author" of his own destiny by *separating* his body from his tragic text. Ultimately, however, Romeo becomes little more than a vanishing mediator of this historically premature process, foiled by the bizarre early modern interspace wherein two conflicting modes of authorship collide and leave only a "kind of nothing" in their wake.[3] A powerful historicization of the Lacanian theory that language is anterior to subjectivity, the tragedy of

2. As Mark Rose argues in "The Author in Court: *POPE v. CURLL* (1741)," it is not until the eighteenth century, when texts become commodified as "things" and "action" becomes the creative prerogative of the Author, that bodies and texts become truly separable.

3. In *Enjoy Your Symptom!* Slavoj Žižek describes the "vanishing mediator" in the context of the competing world views of the classical detective and the hard-boiled or *noir* detective. The former exists in an ordered universe, while the latter operates in a conspiratorial, radically indeterminate universe. The "vanishing mediator" is therefore the figure who "emerges for a brief moment in the interspace" of these two worlds, existing paradoxically as "a subject prior to his subjectivization" (161). The phrase "a kind of nothing" occurs in Shakespeare's *Coriolanus* at the point where Coriolanus forbid[s] all names" and becomes "a kind of nothing" (5.1.13).

Romeo and Juliet culminates when flesh becomes word.[4] In so doing, Shakespeare's play renders visible the ideological limits and material consequences of both poststructuralist theory and early modern practice, wherein bodies are destined to become mere functions of texts.[5]

In early modern English pedagogy, as Jonathan Goldberg explains, "the individual produced by writing is not an individualized subject but one conforming to the characters inscribed—the letters and, ultimately, the words of copy-texts.... [which are in turn] inscribed within social practice" (*Writing Matter* 317). It is a well-known fact that Shakespeare's "copy-text" for *Romeo and Juliet* is Arthur Brooke's verse-tale *The Tragicall Historye of Romeus and Juliet* (1562). What has not been adequately theorized, however, is the fact that *Romeo and Juliet* is the only play in the Shakespeare canon that relies almost exclusively on a single source, suggesting a relation between this early tragedy and the kind of compulsory inscription Goldberg describes. In his eight-volume analysis of Shakespeare's sources, Geoffrey Bullough makes a case for the consistently loose-plotting of the early plays, which tend to draw on a smatter-

---

4. In his seminar on "The Purloined Letter," Lacan utters the famous conclusion that "the letter always arrives at its destination," which typifies his view that the subject is inexorably inhabited by and bound to language. In other words, language is anterior to the subject, who, according to Lacan, receives his "decisive orientation" from the "itinerary of a signifier" (qtd. in Muller and Richardson 62).

5. In her fascinating analysis titled "The Sonnet's Body and the Body Sonnetized in *Romeo and Juliet*," Gayle Whittier explores the ways in which "the displaced Petrarchan poetic word...turn[s] into Shakespearean dramatic flesh" (33). Likening the influence of the Petrarchan sonnet form to the all-powerful Word of God in Genesis, Whittier examines the fatality that inheres in "the inherited Petrarchan word" as it "declin[es] from lyric freedom to tragic fact through a transaction that sonnetizes the body, diminishes the body of the sonnet, and scatters the terms of the *blason du corps*" (27). For example, Whittier astutely notes that Shakespeare's Juliet is nearly fourteen years old (whereas she is sixteen in Brooke's poem), subtly suggesting her similarity to "the sonnet's fourteen-lined body" (40, n26). Romeo's authorial moves, according to Whittier, are situated within an anxiety of inheritance stemming from his dependency on Petrarchan sonneteering. She claims that "Romeo seeks to become author of the [Petrarchan] persona he imitates.... That is, he would create his own pre-creation, and so preempt inheritance" (30). My argument is similar to Whittier's in that it explores the dynamics of flesh and (preexisting) word, but I read Romeo's dependency on Petrarch as a mere symptom of a much larger historical crisis of authorship and authority in the Renaissance, locating Romeo's intervention well beyond his negotiations with the sonnet form.

ing of sources as well as indulge in significant deviations from them. *Romeo and Juliet* remains the exception to this rule, following *The Tragicall Historye* "with extraordinary exactness" (Moore 117), as if Shakespeare were "[w]riting with Brooke at his elbow" (Pearlman 23). And if we trust traditional dating schemes, then *Romeo and Juliet* is situated between two plays lacking identifiable principle sources, *Love's Labors Lost* and *A Midsummer Night's Dream*, making the early tragedy still more conspicuous. It also seems significant that around the time Shakespeare was composing *Romeo and Juliet*, Robert Greene accused him of being an "upstart crow," a player-turned-plagiarist seeking to beautify himself with the poetic plumage of other playwrights (*Complete Works* 12: 144). Though *Romeo and Juliet* is a product of a period wherein judicious "borrowing" was encouraged according to the ethos of imitation, Shakespeare's play persistently encodes an uneasy self-consciousness about operating "by the book."[6] And though I don't wish to imply that Shakespeare suffers explicitly from the "anxiety of influence," I'm convinced that the play's citational preoccupation with books suggests more than a casual interest in their intertextual power. I will argue, therefore, that *Romeo* becomes the site of Shakespeare's own displaced struggle between the proper imitation of his source-text and his burgeoning "bibliographic ego," a struggle that is writ large in Romeo's attempts to be "his own 'original'" rather than suffer the tragic destiny prescribed for him in Brooke's poem.[7]

More than any other Shakespearean play, *Romeo and Juliet* is obsessed with the metaphor of "the book."[8] Phrases such as "by the book,"

6. Many studies have been devoted to ferreting out the verbal echoes of Brooke's poem in Shakespeare's play; this is not my purpose here. Rather, I wish to suggest that potentially displaced authorial anxieties about following Brooke in such an unprecedented manner are legible in certain characterological effects, particularly in Romeo's proleptic paranoia and radical insistence on becoming "author of himself." In this context, it is significant that, atypical of legends as a genre, the legend of Romeo and Juliet reflects a trajectory of transmission that is almost entirely literary (as opposed to oral) in character.

7. I borrow the provocative phrase "his own 'original'" from Linda Charnes's influential book, *Notorious Identity: Materializing the Subject in Shakespeare*. Charnes explores the problem of "notorious identity" as a characterological effect in Shakespeare's legend plays: *Richard III*, *Troilus and Cressida*, and *Antony and Cleopatra*. I will transpose some of the problems which Charnes ascribes to the pre-scripted nature of the legendary into the realm of literary production by exploring the dynamics of early modern "authorship" within the historical regime of compulsory reiteration.

8. In his chapter on *Romeo and Juliet* in *Shakespearean Metadrama*, James Calderwood was perhaps the first critic to point out that this play contains an unusual number of references to books.

"without book," "from [the] book," "by rote," and so on, are continually interjected without precedent from Brooke's *Tragicall Historye*.
Significantly, all of the play's references to books either refer to or occur
in the presence of Romeo's character, with one exception: Lady Capulet's
bibliographic inventory of Paris's qualities. Lady Capulet's description
of Paris establishes the ideological script against which Romeo will attempt to define himself, for while Paris and Romeo represent rival suit-
ors for Juliet's hand, they also represent rival approaches to authorship.
Attempting to persuade her daughter to marry Paris, Lady Capulet ex-
tols Paris's features as though he were a book glossed with conventional wisdom:

> Read o'er the volume of young Paris' face,
> And find delight writ there with beauty's pen.
> Examine every married lineament;
> And see how one another lends content;
> And what obscured in this fair volume lies
> Find written in the margin of his eye.
> This precious book of love, this unbound lover,
> To beautify him only lacks a cover....
> That book in many's eyes doth share the glory
> That in gold clasps locks in the golden story.

> (1.3.81–88, 91–92)

The specific kind of book that Lady Capulet describes is a commonplace book, which is representative of an approach to authorship derived from a long-standing and distinctly medieval tradition of locating
authority in a collection of voices. Consonant with Lady Capulet's
clichéd description of Paris, the commonplace book is a host for aphorisms articulated by *auctores*, or textualized authorities, which are transcribed from "marginal" glosses in other texts into the "lineaments" of
one's own personal "volume." In likening Paris both to a "precious book
of love" shared by "many's eyes" and a "fair volume" that Juliet can
personalize with her own gloss, Lady Capulet literalizes the idea of the
commonplace book as a "'common-place' between a 'public memory'
and [a] personal situation" (Carruthers 181). But there are considerable
limits to the concept of the "personal" that this collective and reiterative
mode of authorship extends to individual subjects. As Mary Carruthers
argues, the "fundamental symbiosis of memorized reading and ethics"
represented in the commonplace book exists to perform the socially

regulative function of "stamping the body-soul," of producing "*charak-ter*" (180).[9] This concept of producing "character" through textual authority is exemplified in Gregory the Great's adage: "what we see in a text is not rules for what we ought to be, but images of what we are" (qtd. in Carruthers 182). These images are in turn committed to memory through their transcription in commonplace books, which produce the subject not as a unique " 'self' or even 'individual,' " but rather, as "a subject who remembers" (Carruthers 182).

Although this regime of molding character is still in place in the early modern period, as indicated by the enduring popularity of commonplace books in Renaissance pedagogy, the confining interdependency between memory, ethics, and operating "by the book" is beginning to be called into question. In fact, this process begins as early as the fourteenth century, wherein, as Andrew Galloway explains, "new intellectual structures of authority...were fundamentally challenging the shop-worn claims of clerical and aristocratic dominance (in the old Gelasian formulation, clerical *auctoritas* and royal *potestas*) and the traditional interlocking structure of society presumed on these bases" (28).[10] Consequently, words like "commonplace" begin to acquire more modern, pejorative meanings like "base" or "doltish," even "promiscuous," and the injunction to imitate is gradually replaced by an acquisitive, as opposed to reiterative, mode of literary and intellectual production. This emerging dynamic between "authoritarian austerity and rebellion" is most visible in the literary negotiations of Shakespeare's late medieval predecessors like Chaucer, who challenged the earlier medieval reliance on ancient and patristic *auctores* by initiating the crucial cultural work of "de-authorizing old patterns of authority [by] implying positive, not yet nameable new structures of authority" (Galloway 33). Chaucer, as Galloway contends, "invariably emphasizes the historical agent behind a text (his usual meaning, in fact, for *auctoritee*) rather than accepting any transcendently authoritative 'sentence'. Indeed, his sensitivity to human origins of knowledge is so great *that encounters with 'olde bokes' usually involve some degree of crisis regarding*

9. Here we see the convergence of the multiple meanings of "character" which, in its verb form means "to inscribe" and in its noun forms means both "persona" and "letter."

10. For further analysis of the circulation of authority from the late Middle Ages through the eighteenth century, see also Larry Scanlon's *Narrative, Authority, and Power: The Medieval Exemplum and the Chaucerian Tradition,* Roger Chartier's *The Order of Books,* and Ronald J. Deibert's chapter on "Print and the Medieval to Modern World Order Transformation" in his book *Parchment, Printing, and Hypermedia.*

their claims to authority" (29, emphasis added). Shakespeare's play picks up this struggle against the strictures of medieval scholasticism where Chaucer leaves off. Resisting the older convention of operating "by the book" embodied in pre-scripted figures like Paris, *Romeo and Juliet* conveys the perils of challenging *auctoritas* through Romeo, who attempts to compose himself, both literally and literarily, "*without* the book."

Like Shakespeare and Chaucer, however, Romeo embraces new but "not yet nameable" structures of authority and, therefore, his defiant acts of self-composition take place within the available modes of composition dictated by medieval and Renaissance pedagogy. Modeled on classical oration, the practice of composition at this historical juncture was, essentially, an exercise in memorization. Carruthers describes this process as follows: "The memory bits culled from works read and digested are ruminated into a composition—that is, basically what an 'author' does with 'authorities'" (189). Students aspiring to "authorize" or, more appropriately, "re-author" a composition (Carruthers 168), would begin this process with *inventio,* a pre-writing phase involving meditation (*meditatio*) upon and collection (*collectio*) of sources (*auctores*).[11] The next phase, cogitation (*cogitatio*), forms a bridge between pre-writing and writing and often produces emotional episodes that enable the transposition of one's thoughts from psyche to tablet, leading to the rough draft (*res*) of the composition. *Compositio,* or writing-proper, is then enlisted in the service of forming the more complete draft (*dictamen*). This phase also involves revision and "the more precarious fortunes of improvisation" (*ex tempore dicendi*), including attempts at excision (*excisio*) and dilation (*dilatio*)(Carruthers 205). Following revision, the *dictamen* is transcribed from wax to parchment and, subsequently referred to as the *exemplar,* is subjected to the communal process of "authorization," the public glossing and approval of the composition.

Romeo's efforts to engage in *self*-composition correspond to this process with increasingly subversive variations, leading to a model of the early modern author *not* as a "subject who remembers," but as a subject who *dis*members. Though Romeo's end is scripted by the Chorus before he can even begin to write his destiny anew, he nonetheless attempts to redirect his "star-cross'd" trajectory (Pro. line 6) by engaging in what Alan Sinfield calls "scripting from below." Reading Shakespearean plays as a "contest of stories," Sinfield defines "scripting" as

---

11. I have extracted the fundamental stages of composition from Carruthers's more detailed chapter on "Memory and Authority" in *The Book of Memory.*

the drive to create the "conditions of plausibility" for belief in a particular story. A story is typically enlisted in the (re)production of dominant ideology, which "makes plausible...concepts and systems to explain who we are, who the others are, how the world works" (*Faultlines* 32)—precisely the role that Gregory the Great ascribes to the text or *auctor*. "Scripting from below," however, is generated from a position of relative disempowerment and, as such, it "immediately appears subversive" because it creates "faultlines" in existing power structures (Sinfield 33). The two major "stories" in tension in *Romeo and Juliet* involve characters who operate "by the book"—those who live by the still dominant script embedded in textual *auctoritas*—and those who operate "without the book" and reject the overdetermination of pre-authorization. But Romeo can only "script from below" the triumval arches of memory, authority, and the sovereign book for so long; like Paris, he is destined to become a commonplace, a source of commonly experienced wisdom, at the expense of personal identity. After all, by his own admission, he, too, must ultimately resign his authority to "sour misfortune's book" (5.2.82).

When we are first introduced to Romeo, we encounter him steadfastly operating "by the book," specifically, the aforementioned "book of love" represented by Paris. As Gayle Whittier points out, as an apprentice lover-poet and Petrarchan devotee, Romeo does not "choose [his] language, the words, in a sense, choose [him]" (18). Accordingly, in the beginning of the play, Romeo appears to be engulfed in the early stages of composition. For example, although Romeo's father laments the fact that his son is "to himself so secret and so close" (1.1.146), Romeo's antisocial behavior is particularly conducive to "invention," which requires that "wherever we are, in a crowd, on a journey, at a party, we must practice fashioning a secret inner sanctuary ('*secretum*')" (Carruthers 214). Romeo is particularly adept at creating such a sanctuary, so much so that his father fears "Black and portentous must [h]is humour prove" (1.1.138). But at this point Old Montague has nothing to fear, for Romeo has merely been engaging in "meditation," as his father's lamentation unknowingly implies:

> Away from light steals home my heavy son,
> And private in his chamber pens himself,
> Shuts up his windows, locks fair daylight out,
> And makes himself an artificial night.
>
> (1.1.134–37)

Before we learn that Romeo's reclusiveness is the result of his unrequited love for Rosaline, this description could easily characterize a
lover or a student, and Romeo is clearly both, for he is studying courtier-
ship, hoping to compose himself as worthy of Rosaline's attention.

Romeo continues to operate "by the book" in his first speaking part,
emerging from his sanctuary performing the task of "collection," as his
contrived and derived description of Rosaline suggests:

> ...She'll not be hit
> With Cupid's arrow; she hath Dian's wit,
> And, in strong proof of chastity well armed,
> From love's weak childish bow she lives unharmed.
> She will not stay the siege of loving terms,
> Nor bide th'encounter of assailing eyes,
> Nor ope her lap to saint-seducing gold.
> O, she is rich in beauty, only poor
> That when she dies, with beauty dies her store.
>
> (1.2.205–13)

If composition originates with the act of formally processing memorized reading, then Romeo's collection of clichés from love poetry,
along with his frequent outbursts of exclamatory "O's," oxymorons,
and hyperbole (1.1.168–79; 182–92), demonstrates the rote style of this
apprentice lover-poet par excellence. Indeed, Romeo "runs through the
repertory...[of] variations upon a hundred sonnets in the official
mode" (Colie 138). But the fact that the above rhyme falters *in medias res*
("terms / eyes / gold" do not a couplet make) suggests that Romeo is
not yet prepared to enter the more sophisticated stages of composition,
for he is unable to improvise his own rhymes where memory fails to
supply him with commonplaces. More importantly, at this stage in
what will become Romeo's tragic education, he is also unprepared to
recognize the implications of his slavish dependency on "the official
mode" of the book in which his legendary fate is written.

"Fate," according to Lacan, is constituted by "misrecognition"
(*meconaissance*). In other words, through a tendency to mistake external
compulsion for personal agency, subjects unwittingly set into motion a
chain of events that they assume to be under their control. Reversing
this relationship, Lacan argues that subjects do not possess the agency
they presume; quite to the contrary, the "signifying chain...*traverses
them*" ("Purloined" 43, emphasis added). Similarly, in the beginning of

Romeo and Juliet, Romeo misrecognizes the fact that his tendency to operate "by the book" is not volitional. Rather, his clichéd words and actions
are scripted by the sundry literary accounts that precede Shakespeare's
version of this star-crossed lover. Shakespeare's unique twist on this
tragic legend, however, is to refigure Romeo's crossed stars as a constellation of crossed literary trajectories embodied in divergent modes of
authorship, which redefine Romeo's legendary struggle within the troubling and, at times, tragic provenance of literary production in early
modern England. By the end of Romeo's first scene in Shakespeare's
play, the distinctly literary course of his fate is summarized, albeit mis-
recognized, in a single couplet. In one breath, Romeo begs Benvolio to
"teach" him how "to forget" his unrequited love for Rosaline (1.1.222)
and, in the next breath, he preempts further assistance:

> ROMEO: Farewell, thou can'st not teach me how to forget.
> BENVOLIO: I'll pay the doctrine, or else die in debt. (1.1.234–235)

This couplet is of singular importance in that it establishes the coordinates of Romeo's process of scripting from below. Emerging in opposition to the union forged by memory and *auctoritas*, "forget" and "debt"
mark the beginning and end, respectively, of Romeo's attempts at authorship, for his unsuccessful efforts to "forget" the book in which his
fate is inscribed will result in his outstanding "debt" to the "doctrine,"
or *auctoritas*, that he will, in fact, "pay" with his death.

This drama of remembering and forgetting is encoded in the play's
references to books, which demarcate Romeo's progress through the
various stages of composition en route to self-authorship. Romeo's first
rhetorical encounter with "the book," however, only offers further evidence of his misrecognition of his tragic fate, as Peter the servant asks
for help reading the guest list for the Capulet ball:

> PETER: God gi' good e'en. I pray, sir, can you read?
> ROMEO: Ay, my own fortune in my misery.
> PETER: Perhaps you have learned it without book.
>   But I pray, can you read anything you see? (1.2.58–60)

As Peter suggests, Romeo has not corroborated this blithe reading of
his fortune with the *auctoritas* of the book, which would have revealed
to Romeo just how miserable his fortune really is. What is more striking

about this scene, however, is the fact that it permits Shakespeare to suggest that Romeo's fate is actually constituted by misrecognition. Unlike in Brooke's poem, where Romeus simply shows up to the Capulet Ball without provocation, here, Shakespeare's Romeo peruses the Capulet guest list in Peter's possession and, seeing Rosaline's name but (predictably) not his own, proceeds to write himself into his own tragedy by determining to go to the ball where he will meet Juliet.[12] In one sense, then, Romeo's first act of independent authorship is also his last, for at this moment the signifying chain traverses him and, hereafter, his fate is sealed. In another sense, however, Romeo's naïve exuberance temporarily shields him from the force of textual compulsion that haunts this play, establishing at least the conditions of possibility for his later attempts to authorize his own fate "without book."

The next occurrence of the phrase "without book" signals a turning point for Romeo, who begins to experience a disturbing feeling of distinctly textualized déjà vous. Against the sense of decorum and pre-authorization embodied in Paris's "precious book of love," Romeo, Mercutio, and Benvolio determine to enter the Capulet ball as uninvited guests, or as Benvolio puts it, "without book," claiming that he has no use for the pretensions of a

> ...without-book Prologue faintly spoke
> After the prompter for our entrance.
> But let them measure us by what they will.

$$(1.4.7-9)$$

Despite Benvolio's confident use of the acting metaphor, which suggests that they can improvise the evening as they go along, Romeo suddenly experiences stage fright. Announcing that he will not dance at the ball, Romeo complains that he feels listless from the burden of being "proverbed with a grandsire phrase" (1.4.37). This exceptionally unusual conversion of the noun "proverb" into a verb not only suggests the performative power of language that will eventually convert Romeo to a commonplace but also indicates the genealogical underpinnings of this process: Romeo's "grandsire" literally *is* a "proverb"—a common-

---

12. " 'Fate,' " as Slavoj Žižek affirms, "always asserts itself through such contingent encounters, giving rise to the question: 'What if I had missed that remark? What if I had taken another route and avoided that scene?' " (*Enjoy* 11).

place about star-crossed love. At this disturbing juncture, then, Romeo is less concerned about his lack of a prologue than he is about the certainty of his epilogue, as he suggests upon entering the Capulet mansion:

> ...my mind misgives
> Some consequence yet hanging in the stars
> Shall bitterly begin his fearful date
> With this night's revels, and expire the term
> Of despised life, closed in my breast,
> By some vile forfeit of untimely death.
> But he that hath the steerage of my course
> Direct my sail! On, lusty gentlemen.

(1.4.106–13)

In Brooke's poem, no such anxiety exists for Romeus; in fact, the opposite is true, as Brooke's Juliet exclaims: "Oh Romeus (of your lyfe) to[o] lavous sure you are."[13] Only Shakespeare's Romeo finds himself in the throes of "cogitation."

Cogitation, a process of formalizing ideas occurring between invention and composition-proper, ushers in a loss of linguistic innocence for Romeo. Cogitation literally means "knowing," and in *Romeo and Juliet*, as Linda Charnes argues of *Troilus and Cressida*, the characters are "afflict[ed]...with a historical 'knowledge' that contaminates most, if not all, of their verbal intercourse" (*Notorious Identity* 76). This "knowledge," as the perfect sonnet formed by Romeo and Juliet's first verbal exchange reveals, is generated "by the book," that is, by the force of textual compulsion that prescribes Romeo and Juliet's actions in Shakespeare's play.[14]

---

13. All excerpts from Brooke's *Tragicall Historye* are quoted from J. J. Munro's 1908 edition, hereafter cited in the text.

14. The sonnet is as follows:

> ROMEO: (to Juliet, touching her hand) If I profane with my unworthiest hand
> This holy shrine, the gentler sin is this:
> My lips, two blushing pilgrims, ready stand
> To smooth that rough touch with a tender kiss.

> JULIET: Good pilgrim, you do wrong your hand too much,
> Which mannerly devotion shows in this.
> For saints have hands that pilgrims' hands do touch,
> And palm to palm is holy palmers' kiss.

But Romeo and Juliet's pedantic exchange is to be expected from Romeo's engagement in the preliminary stage of cogitation, which involves the mulling over and reworking of information gathered during invention. In this spirit, then, the formal poem both initiated and completed by Romeo upon meeting Juliet suggests his reworking of material gathered during the Rosaline affair. However, Juliet's peculiar response to Romeo—"You kiss by th' book" (1.5.109)—indicates that she is not impressed with his tendency to kiss (and tell) "by the book" and, more importantly, implies that Romeo's fear of being "proverbed" has contaminated her through his kiss. Shifting from infatuation to panic, Romeo reveals his knowledge of this double loss of innocence when he exclaims:

> Is she a Capulet?
> O dear account! My life is my foe's debt.
>
> (1.5.117–18)

At this moment, the pieces of prior misgivings come together for Romeo, as the earlier couplet formed by "forget" and "debt" triangulates to include "Capulet." But Juliet is also the figure who becomes the catalyst of Romeo's attempt to forget his debt to the book—by teaching him to become a "subject who remembers"—remembers, that is, what's in his name.

If the first stage of cogitation demands the passive retrieval of information gathered during the earlier phases of invention, meditation, and collection, then the later stages of cogitation involve intense agitation, mobilizing various "transports of fear and desire" as a mechanism

---

ROMEO: Have not saints lips, and holy palmers, too?

JULIET: Ay, pilgrim, lips that they must use in prayer.

ROMEO: Oh then, dear saint, let lips do what hands do:
They pray; grant thou, lest faith turn to despair.

JULIET: Saints do not move, though grant for prayers' sake.

ROMEO: Then move not while my prayer's effect I take.
[He kisses her]

(1.5.92–105)

for sifting out and identifying those materials fit for composition-proper (Carruthers 202). Such agitation becomes an opportunity for Romeo, who, at Juliet's prompting, begins to explore and, ultimately, eliminate the tragic text(s) of his name. During the balcony scene, Juliet propels Romeo's cogitation out of the comfort zone and into chaos, urging him to "Deny thy father and refuse thy name.... 'Tis but thy name that is my enemy" (2.1.76, 80). At this point, Romeo experiences a strange loosening of the correspondence between his first name, "Romeo," and his father's name, "Montague," which in turn creates a growing distinction between his "subjectivity" and his "identity," respectively. Subjectivity, according to Charnes, is "the unstable heterogeneity that simultaneously constitutes and unfixes even the most 'fixed' of names," while identity is "that which fixes meaning (both personal and political)" (*Notorious Identity* 74). Juliet draws this distinction between Romeo's subjectivity and his identity, as well as between his body and "text(s)," when she muses:

> Thou art thyself, though not a Montague.
> What's Montague? It is nor hand, nor foot,
> Nor arm, nor face, nor any other part
> Belonging to a man. O, be some other name!
> What's in a name? That which we call a rose
> By any other word would smell as sweet,
> So Romeo would, were he not Romeo called,
> Retain that dear perfection which he owes
> Without that title. Romeo, doff thy name,
> And for thy name—which is no part of thee—
> Take all myself.
>
> (2.1.81–91)

Here again, however, the logic of "owing"—of debt and accounting—contaminates the more Utopian trajectory of Juliet's speech. For the "dear perfection" that Romeo retains by abandoning "Montague" will eventually lead to the dire debt that Tybalt will take upon himself to collect. But the more immediate consequence of Juliet's speech is the double-bind that it creates for Romeo: first she tells him that the nominal rub lies in "Montague" and then she claims that "Romeo" is equally odious to her. Thus, when she commands Romeo to "doff thy name," we, along with Romeo, must wonder *which* name?

Unlike Shakespeare's other legendary figures, who are known simply as "Antony" or "Cleopatra," or "Troilus" or "Cressida," Romeo is forced to negotiate the symbolic inheritance of two names. However, Romeo's two names are perfectly in keeping with the confusing province of the early modern "author," for in the gap between "Montague" and "Romeo," Shakespeare encodes the diachronic clash of two conflicting modes of authorship in the synchronic space of Romeo's body. On the one hand, "Montague" refers to the historical house and political faction of the Montecchi, invoking the *auctoritas* of the powerful family name, the landed estates of a feudal economy, and the source of the tragic legend that will crystallize in the "notorious identities" of Romeo and Juliet. In other words, "Montague" corresponds quite literally to the pedagogical, political, and literary name of the Father. On the other hand, "Romeo," which Shakespeare changes from Brooke's protagonist "Romeus," suggests Romeo's (if not Shakespeare's) desire to roam from genetic and generic overdetermination. In the spirit of self-determination introduced by Juliet's "what's in a name" speech, "Romeo" looks ahead to the emergent mode of self-authorship associated with the new market economy, the mobility of social station, and the literary subversion of representational mimesis or imitation.[15] Shakespearean shorthand for the agitating function of "Romeo" would perhaps be "upstart crow," a nickname specifically inflected with the notion of "scripting from below." The difference between "Montague" and "Romeo" thus involves more than the space that separates surname and proper name, for it invokes a metonymic chain of associations pulling in opposite historical directions, leaving Romeo, like the early modern "author," with "two bodies" but "no thing" to show for them.

It is no wonder, therefore, that Romeo anxiously awaits his "new baptism," pledging to Juliet:

> I take thee at thy word.
> Call me but love and I'll be new baptized.
> Henceforth I never will be Romeo.
>
> (2.1.90–92)

---

15. Robert Weimann theorizes these important changes in authorial attitudes in "'Appropriation' and Modern History in Renaissance Prose Narrative."

But Romeo's names are easier unsaid than undone, for in demanding to be "new baptiz'd," he is denying his "primal baptism," the preordained plan that names were believed to contain and confer in the early modern period. Indeed, Romeo's desire to separate his body from his "text" suggests a debate of great consequence in Shakespeare's day: the debate over the relationship between words and things. The two central camps in this debate are the "nature" and "convention" constituencies. The nature argument, which was the favored argument in the Renaissance, maintained that there was a likeness and perhaps even a destiny inferable in the relationship between words and things. This view, clearly based on the logic of *auctoritas*, conceived of words as conferring knowledge "not immediately obvious" but, rather, as "a legacy of the wisdom of the past" (Donawerth 31). This claim was particularly compelling when it came to names, as the educator Richard Mulcaster argued: "God himself... doth planelie declare...what a cunning thing it is to giue right names, and how necessary it is, to know their forces, which be allredie giuen" (qtd. in Donawerth 29). Romeo and Juliet, on the other hand, represent a burgeoning school of skeptical thought embodied in the "convention" argument. Troubled by a proleptic knowledge of the "forces allredie giuen" in his name(s), Romeo, like Juliet, maintains that the connection between words and things is purely arbitrary and retained only through social practice, an idea articulated by figures like Montaigne, who contended that "the name, is neither part of the thing nor of substance: it is a stranger-piece joyned to the thing, and from it" (qtd. in Donawerth 27). This approach to the "name" as "stranger" is illustrated in Romeo's echoing of Juliet's description of his name as an "enemy":

> By a name
> I know not how to tell thee who I am.
> My name, dear saint, is hateful to myself
> Because it is an enemy to thee.
> Had I it written, I would tear the word.
>
> (2.1.95–99)

As a figure torn between two names, two sets of historical imperatives, and two modes of production, Romeo completes his agonizing cogitation with a statement that looks ahead to the Lacanian reformulation of Descartes' *cogito* as "I am only insofar as I doubt," as he suddenly becomes a stranger to himself.

With Juliet's help, then, Romeo realizes the lethal implications of "what's in [his] name" and, subsequently, seeks to dis-member the tragic associations between his body and his "text." As we have seen, Romeo begins this process by writing his name and tearing it—an image that evokes the cliché of the author at work, crumpling his rejected drafts (*res*) into paper balls. But "tearing" has a particularly violent ring to it, and necessarily so, for this action suggests the violent processes of "expropriation," "deformation," and "displacement" required to remove the burden of imitation (Weimann, "Appropriation" 483–91). In other words, because *imitatio vitae* implies not only "a given set of literary schemata, but [also] literary modes of social propriety and age-old forms of cultural and economic property" (Weimann 481), writing as we know it cannot begin without a significant "tearing" away from this deeply sedimented literary and world view. In *Romeo and Juliet*, the next reference to books confirms the fact that Romeo is engaging in this process of dis-membering and beginning to operate on his own authority, that is, "without book," as he assures Juliet: "Love goes toward love as schoolboys from their books" (2.1.201). Here, Romeo emphasizes his break with *auctoritas* and his readiness to embrace a more progressive, experiential school of thought. Consequently, when Juliet reappears on her balcony to wish Romeo good night, her language is contaminated with Romeo's earlier image of the violence of this subversive process:

> Bondage is hoarse, and may not speak aloud,
> Else would I tear the cave where Echo lies,
> And make her airy tongue more hoarse than mine
> With repetition of my Romeo's name. Romeo!
>
> (2.1.205–8)

Juliet wishes in graphic form to "tear the cave" or mouth of "Echo"—a representative, in this case, not only of tragic love but also of a pedagogy based on mnemonics and repetition, which Romeo has just attempted to dis-member in likening himself to a deviant schoolboy who goes from his books. Following this cue, Juliet aspires to recreate "Romeo" without the echo of "Montague," repeating his first name until his dreaded surname is forgotten. Appropriately, then, the closing balcony interchange between Romeo and Juliet includes four references to "forgetting" in six lines, concluding with Romeo's complete abandonment of the House of Montague: "And I'll still stay, to have thee still forget, / Forgetting any other home but this" (2.1.219–20).

∿

In many respects, Juliet is the more compelling of the two authorial candidates in Shakespeare's play, for from the very beginning, she is far less text-bound than Romeo. Indeed, Juliet resists the *auctoritas* of her mother's bookish entreaties, her father's patriarchal authority, and the feuding tradition of Romeo's family name. The reason that this analysis focuses on Romeo, then, is because it is his body that becomes the stage wherein the historical tensions between *auctoritas* and self-authorship are, quite literally, incorpsed. Incorpsing is the term that Margaret Ferguson derives from *Hamlet* to describe the uncanny power of words which, in Shakespeare's tragedies, "almost always resul[t] in a literal death" (292). In *Romeo and Juliet*, references to the preexisting authority of books incite this incorpsing power. Following cogitation, however, Romeo is able to forestall this threatening power by aligning himself with the burgeoning ideology of the Author, emerging from his liminal state with the desire to engage in *self*-composition. Immediately impressed with Romeo's "revisions," Friar Laurence barely recognizes his pupil who, just yesterday, boasted of a "love [that] did read by rote, that could not spell" (2.2.88–89).[16] Despite the fact that Friar Laurence testifies to the success of Romeo's emphatic rejection of the schoolboy mode of rote or bookish memorization, the friar's use of the phrase "by rote" simultaneously suggests the futility of this enterprise, for "rota" is Latin for "wheel," implying that Romeo will come around—both literally and literarily—to his former ways. Tybalt emerges as a catalyst of this process, confronting Romeo as a "subject who remembers" his debt to the house of Montague by issuing him a new challenge—not by rote, but by writ.

The letter that Tybalt sends to Romeo's home throws into relief the collective consequences of Romeo's historically premature attempts at authorship, a process that corresponds in illuminating ways to the Lacanian theory of the "letter in sufferance." The concept of the "letter in sufferance" reflects Lacan's attempt to theorize the intersubjective consequences of a letter, or signifier, temporarily diverted from its path. Subjects, Lacan reminds us, follow the itinerary of the signifying chain. However, when a letter is "in sufferance," its symbolic circuit gets disrupted, and signifiers proceed with blind automatism to cross and corrupt the paths of subjects at random. Although "the letter always arrives at its destination," for every near miss along the way, the letter

16. Carruthers notes that the phrase "by rote" began to acquire the pejorative meaning of "mere" memorization in the Renaissance (252).

leaves a symbolic debt in its wake that must be paid, as Lacan explains: "if *it* be in sufferance *they* shall endure the pain" ("Purloined" 44). Consequently, as Romeo becomes a kind of letter in sufferance, imagining himself to be an unchained signifier, others suffer in his stead; and the string of tragic events is halted only when Romeo arrives at his "destination"—as a *dead* letter—in "sour misfortune's book."

Tybalt starts the letter on its symbolic circuit by issuing Romeo a written challenge, the purpose of which is to hasten Romeo's recognition of himself as a Montague. This process unfolds through Benvolio and Mercutio's casual conversation about Romeo following his mysterious disappearance from the Capulet ball:

> BENVOLIO: Tybalt, the kinsman to old Capulet,
> Hath sent a letter to his father's house.
> MERCUTIO: A challenge, on my life.
> BENVOLIO: Romeo will answer it.
>
> (2.3.6–9)

In addressing the letter to Romeo's *father's* house, Tybalt challenges Romeo to answer to the patronym and to obey the injunction to imitate his feuding forefathers. The fatal result of Romeo's evasion of "Montague," however, is suggested by the apparent non-sequitur uttered by Mercutio upon hearing of Tybalt's challenge: "Alas, poor Romeo," Mercutio sighs, "he is already dead" (2.3.12). Slavoj Žižek explains that because the letter is a kind of "memory trace," what "propels a letter on its symbolic circuit is always some outstanding debt" (*Enjoy* 16), an observation that is particularly evocative of Romeo and Juliet's debt-ridden discourse. This debt, Žižek continues, oddly reveals itself in a "tiny detail of no significance" (15). Accordingly, Mercutio's odd remark dovetails with another detail of apparent insignificance to reveal Romeo's outstanding debt to a different "letter"—one addressed not to Montague but to Romeo's proper name. Helping Romeo with his wedding plans, the Nurse asks:

> NURSE: Doth not rosemary and Romeo begin
> Both with a letter?
> ROMEO: Ay, Nurse, what of that? Both with an "R."
> NURSE: Ah, mocker—that's the dog's name. "R" is for the—
> no, I know it begins with some other letter, and she
> hath the prettiest sententious of it, of you and rosemary,
> that it would do you good to hear it.
>
> (2.3.197–204)

This exchange condenses several elements of Romeo's fate. First, we learn that through the letter "R," Romeo is linked with rosemary. In this context, Mercutio's chilling comment that Romeo is "already dead" becomes particularly ominous, for traditionally, rosemary is sprinkled on the bodies of the dead and is synonymous with *remembrance*. Secondly, we learn that the letter "R" is performative; "R" is the dog's letter because it growls as it is spoken, suggesting the ways in which words hunger for flesh in this play. Indeed, as Žižek suggests of the Lacanian letter compelling one's fate, the problem "consists in the overlooking of its *performative* dimension" (*Enjoy* 12, emphasis added). Finally, the Nurse reveals that Juliet has been inscribing Romeo *in her commonplace book* as the "prettiest sententious." In this botched attempt to sound the Latin word "sententiae," the Nurse makes it painfully clear that Juliet has been translating "Romeo" into "rosemary," converting him into a memory trace rooted in *auctoritas*. Ironically devoted to removing Romeo from the realm of referentiality, Juliet knows not what she does. Rather, the fact that she reproduces Romeo as a commonplace reveals the degree of textual compulsion at work in the play, materializing "the [already] dead letter" emanating from Brooke's *Tragicall Historye*.

In more ways than one, then, this capitalized "R" emerges as the placeholder of Romeo's proper name, that is, the culturally "proper" place to which he must return when he recognizes that he is the inevitable addressee of both Tybalt's and Juliet's "letters." While these letters comprising Romeo's name remain "in sufferance," however, Romeo enjoys a false sense of security, as he presents the new, improved, un-Montagued version (*dictamen*) of himself for public perusal and emendation by Tybalt, another of the play's representatives of "the book." As Joan Ozark Holmer argues, Tybalt's meticulous attention to fencing etiquette and jargon reveals his preoccupation with operating "by the book": specifically, Vincentio Saviolo's widely read Renaissance fencing manual.[17] Offering sharp criticism of the new Romeo, Tybalt challenges him to a fencing duel according to the dictates of decorum detailed in Saviolo's book. Tybalt's plan is foiled, however, when Romeo not only fails to receive his letter but also refuses to respond "by the book" to his verbal challenge: "thou art a villain" (3.1.60). Proper etiquette requires Romeo to retort: "Thou liest," but he insists, provocatively, on "standing mute."

17. See *Vincentio Saviolo His Practise* (1595).

According to the early modern system of English jurisprudence, the most severe form of torture was reserved for those who refused to enter a plea of guilty or innocent, commonly known as "standing mute." Because the act of standing mute constituted a threat to the coercive power of established authority, the extortion of the accused's voice was undertaken by "pressing" the prisoner, if necessary, to death. As Margreta De Grazia explains, "this procedure attempted the...seizure of the prisoner's voice...the voice it needed to conduct its procedure, in this case pressuring the body to release the consent of the accused" ("Sanctioning Voice" 295). Resisting his body's impressment by the text of his name, Romeo refuses to enter a plea that would identify him, villain or no villain, as a Montague. Instead, he responds to Tybalt's challenge by offering the unscripted version of himself:

> I see thou knowest me not....
> So, good Capulet—which name I tender
> As dearly as mine own—be satisfied.

> (3.1.64, 70–71)

The central stake involved in "standing mute" is the attempt to "avoi[d] conviction," thereby maintaining one's property, good name, and, most importantly, "a will or testament of [one']s own" (De Grazia, "Sanctioning Voice" 295). In refusing to permit his body to resonate as a text in this public forum, Romeo asserts personal, not collective, property in his own person. What is inscribed in this battle of wills between Tybalt and Romeo, then, is an investigation of the early modern conflict "between absolutist authority and its coercive forms, and a contrary fantasy...represented explicitly during this time, of the possibility of a 'self-authored' subjectivity" (Charnes, *Notorious Identity* 74).

Although Romeo disarms Tybalt verbally and momentarily dodges the force of his "letter," its symbolic debt remains, and Romeo's fantasy of a "self-authored subjectivity" becomes accountable to the letter's penchant for "materializ[ing] the agency of death" (Lacan, "Purloined" 38). Mercutio becomes the letter's first victim when he takes Romeo's place in the duel. In the clash with Tybalt that follows, Mercutio dies by Tybalt's sword and Romeo's word, struck by Tybalt in the midst of Romeo's attempt to pacify the quarrel. But Mercutio's last words suggest a more fatal force at work, revealing his assumption of the letter's symbolic debt as he proceeds to die "by the book," that is, with his discourse overwhelmed by commonplaces:

No, 'tis not so deep as a well, nor so wide as a church door, but 'tis enough. 'Twill serve. Ask for me tomorrow, and you shall find me a grave man. I am peppered, I warrant, for this world. A plague o' both your houses! Zounds, a dog, a rat, a mouse, a cat, to scratch a man to death! A braggart, a rogue, a villain, that fights by the book of arithmetic! Why the devil came you between us? I was hurt under your arm. (3.1.96–103)

Even the play's most brilliant mincer of words is no match for a fight with "the book." What Mercutio's dying words suggest to Romeo is that the agency of death comes from something within Romeo's very person, something "in him more than himself," as his reflections on Mercutio's death imply:

> This gentleman, the Prince's near ally,
> My very friend, hath got this mortal hurt
> In my behalf, my reputation stained
> With Tybalt's slander....
> This day's black fate on more days doth depend.
> This but begins the woe others must end.

> (3.1.109–12, 119–20)

Implicating himself in future as well as present tragedies, Romeo begins to realize that there is more than an incidental connection between his acts of self-composition and others' decomposition. As Romeo's use of the word "stain" implies, "the letter i[s] ultimately such a stain...an object resisting symbolization, a surplus, a material leftover circulating among subjects and staining its momentary possessor" (Žižek , *Enjoy* 8). Indeed, before arriving at its destination, the letter proceeds with a will of its own to claim surrogate bodies for its rite of remembrance—another stunning illustration of which occurs when Romeo, in a sudden fit of "fire-eyed fury" (3.1.124), slays Tybalt only to repent immediately, crying: "O, I am fortune's fool!" (136). From here forward, then, Romeo is left with no recourse but to engage his authorial energies in "the more precarious fortunes of improvisation" (Carruthers 205).

What distinguishes this perilous phase from Romeo's earlier attempts to sever the relationship between his body and his text is that now the rhetorical gesture of tearing his name is revisited in violent assaults that tear into his body. This approach is a distinctly "neurotic" mode of authorship which, "by its nature, helps reinforce and hold in place the original structures of oppression against which it reacts. This is, finally, what makes it neurosis—it is a politics of rebellion turned back upon the self" (Charnes, *Notorious Identity* 72). Romeo's authorial neurosis culminates in his suicidal attempt to excise (*excisio*) his name from his body. When the Nurse delivers news of Juliet's grief, which stems from Tybalt's death and Romeo's banishment, Romeo, confessing once again that he has "stained" their married joy (3.3.94), attests to the deadly power of his own name:

> As if that name
> Shot from the deadly level of a gun
> Did murder her as that name's cursed hand
> Murdered her kinsman. O tell me, friar, tell me,
> In what vile part of this anatomy
> Doth my name lodge? Tell me, that I may sack
> The hateful mansion.
> [*He offers to stab himself, and the Nurse snatches the dagger away*]
>
> (3.3.102–7)

But Romeo's name is what is in him more than himself—a point that Juliet underscores when she exclaims, upon learning of Romeo's murder of Tybalt, "Was ever book containing such vile matter / So fairly bound?" (3.2.83–84). Here, Juliet draws a striking distinction between Romeo's "fair" binding or body and the "vile" matter of his text—the vile family name that dictates both the violent social relations within the play and Romeo's "tragicall historye" beyond the play. As his masochistic gesture implies, however, Romeo has read further along in this text than Juliet, for he now understands that his body *cannot* be separated from it. Indeed, "the real letter is not the message we are supposed to carry but our being itself" (Žižek, *Enjoy* 7).

In the process of railing against the bodily inscription of his name, Romeo undergoes a temporary change in authorial status, suddenly troping himself as "female." From the perspective of early modern pedagogy, the female body is often likened to something to be written upon; it is a pliant and absorbent surface, akin to wax or parchment, intended for receiving marks.[18] Echoing this sentiment, the friar admonishes Romeo for his "womanish behavior," explaining to him that "Thy noble

---

18. For both primary and secondary texts exploring female stereotypes in the Renaissance, see, for example, *Half Humankind*, edited by Katherine Usher Henderson and Barbara F. McManus; Pamela Joseph Benson's *The Invention of the Renaissance Woman*; Linda Woodbridge's *Women and the English Renaissance*; and *Daughters, Wives, and Widows*, edited by Joan Larsen Klein.

shape is but a form of wax, / Digressing from the valour of a man"
(3.3.109, 125–26). But "digression" is precisely the answer to Romeo's
self-destructive mode of improvisation, for it suggests a means of keeping the letter "in sufferance" without making Romeo suffer. Consequently, in *Romeo and Juliet*, as Patricia Parker argues of *Hamlet*, "Dilation in its sense of amplification as well as delay becomes in this play a
multiplication of occasions and images for the postponement or put-
ting off of [an] end or 'fine'" (219). Friar Laurence promises Romeo
such amplification of his happiness if he can first abide its delay in
Mantua, where, pending the Prince's removal of Romeo's banishment,
the friar claims,

> thou shalt live till we can find a time
> To…call thee back
> With twenty hundred thousand times more joy.
>
> (3.3.149–52)

In Romeo's absence, however, the letter continues on its symbolic circuit, and Juliet becomes the next object of its inscription. Acting as a
surrogate text for Romeo, Juliet suddenly finds herself at the mercy of
auctores figured in her father and his chosen son-in-law Paris, both of
whom seek to claim her as textual and sexual property. Like her rebel-
lious Shakespearean "sister" Hermia, who is also forced to endure
phallocratic tyranny, Juliet is to her father-*auctor*

> …but a form in wax,
> By him imprinted, and within his power,
> To leave the figure, or disfigure it.
>
> (*Dream* 1.1.49–51)

When Juliet defies her father's script by protesting that she will not wed,
her father replies by saying "My fingers itch" (3.5.164), as if he were indeed on the verge of "pressing" her into consent. So, too, Paris attempts
to force the issue when he encounters Juliet at Friar Laurence's cell:

> PARIS: Happily met, my lady and my wife.
> JULIET: That may be, sir, when I may be wife.
> PARIS: That "may be" must be, love, on Thursday next.
> JULIET: What must be shall be.
> FRIAR: That's a certain text. (4.1.18–22)

Encoded in this exchange is a battle between the authorized and the improvised, and the fact that the conversation ends with a commonplace
adds to Juliet's sense of fighting a losing cause. Consequently, upon Paris's
departure, Juliet turns suicidal in her refusal to be forsworn to Romeo:

> Tell me not, Friar, that thou hear'st of this,
> Unless thou tell me how I may prevent it....
> Do thou but call my resolution wise,
> [*She draws a knife*]
> And with this knife I'll help it presently.
>
> (4.1.51, 53–54)

With uncanny accuracy, Juliet replays Romeo's last scene with Friar Laurence "to the letter," and, in the spirit of textual repetition-compulsion,
the Friar offers Juliet a solution identical to Romeo's: dilation. Likewise
warning Juliet not to be "womanish" in the execution of his plan
(4.1.119), Friar Laurence concocts a scheme for Juliet to feign death, buying time for Romeo to retrieve her and return to Mantua, where they will
live together in anonymity. Friar Laurence assures Juliet that "In the
meantime,...Shall Romeo by my letters know our drift" (4.1.114). But
the sense of déjà vu that pervades this scene suggests the presence of
what Lacan calls the "repetition automatism" of the letter—the sense
that even the most original of schemes are in some way bound to the
"itinerary of a signifier" ("Purloined" 28–29). There is, in other words,
no place for anonymity among legendary, always-already known
figures like Romeo and Juliet, and the Friar's plan to "drift" away from
or dilate upon their "certain text" is destined to fail by way of the letter
that "does not forget [the]m" (Lacan, qtd. in Muller and Richardson 63).

A letter always arrives at its destination.... [when] the
sender, we tell you, receives...his own message in reverse
form.

—Lacan, "Seminar on 'The Purloined Letter'"

FRIAR LAURENCE: Who bare my letter then to Romeo?
FRIAR JOHN: I could not send it—here it is again—

The dizzying reversals and returns that occur in the final scenes of *Romeo and Juliet* reveal the twisted agency of the letter en route to its destination. Juliet is the first to "receive her message in reverse form" when, as a prelude to her actual death, she is sprinkled with rosemary (4.4.106), just as she had imagined Romeo and rosemary together in her commonplace book. Subsequently, Romeo has a dream that replicates Juliet's earlier vision of him as "one dead in the bottom of a tomb" (3.5.56). Imagining that "my lady came and found me dead" (5.1.6), Romeo believes his dream to "presage some joyful news at hand" (1.1.2); but when he is informed of Juliet's "death" he cries: "Then I defy you, stars" (1.1.24). Here again, Romeo misrecognizes his fate, for he is not defying so much as he is complying with the stars that warned him earlier of his "vile forfeit of untimely death" (1.4.111). Indeed, the Chorus's opening invocation of the "star-crossed" nature of Romeo and Juliet's love alone suggests these twisted trajectories of the letter in sufferance. The most striking of these twists occurs when Romeo is prompted by news of Juliet's death to call for "ink and paper" (5.1.25) in order to write the letter that will serve as his suicide note; meanwhile, the letter that was supposed to prevent this rashness fails to arrive via Friar John and is returned to its sender, Friar Laurence. Žižek explains that the letter typically arrives at its destination not in its literal form but in its characterological effects, that is, "when the subject is forced to assume the true consequences of his activity" (*Enjoy* 13). Recognizing that his attempts at authorship have sentenced a host of others to death, Romeo at last proceeds to the Capulet monument to assume his long-awaited place in his own "tragicall historye." It is particularly significant that Paris, the play's representative of the conventional and pre-authorized, emerges to prevent Romeo's passage at this threshold moment. But Romeo must take Paris's place, and upon slaying him, Romeo recognizes that his letter has arrived at its destination:

> noble County Paris! ...
> O, give me thy hand,
> One writ with me in sour misfortune's book.

> (5.3.75, 81–82)

Borrowing Paris's hand as a prosthetic, authorized writing instrument, Romeo inscribes himself in "sour misfortune's book"—necessarily the last of the play's references to books.

This line returns us to Brooke's *Tragicall Historye*, which is not merely a book about "unfortunate lovers" but also a cautionary tale about those who "neglec[t]...authoritie." The reader, Brooke concludes, will learn by this "exaumple, [which] ministreth good lessons, to the well disposed mynde" (qtd. in Bullough, 1:284). Romeo must therefore submit himself as an example, or in compositional terms, an *exemplar*, to serve the pedagogical origins of the book in which he is inscribed. Having used Paris's hand to write himself "in sour misfortune's book," Romeo's own aspirations to authorship must cease, as he assures the dead Tybalt:

> O, what more favour can I do to thee
> Than with that hand that cut thy youth in twain
> To sunder his that was thine enemy?
>
> (5.3.98–100)

Pledging to sunder the authoring activity of his hand from his body once and for all, Romeo pours over the dead-seeming body of Juliet and, improvising just a moment longer, makes a Petrarchan blazon of himself:

> O, here...
> Will I set up my everlasting rest,
> And shake the yoke of inauspicious stars
> From this world-wearied flesh. Eyes, look your last.
> Arms, take your last embrace, and lips, O you
> The doors of breath, seal with a righteous kiss
> A dateless bargain to engrossing death.
>
> (5.3.109, 111–15)

At this moment, we recognize the force of Robert Weimann's observation that "The burden of 'historie' upon the hero is such that his defeat is most hurtful and in its implications most tragic where he has become the interpreter of the text of his own enterprise" ("Appropriation" 492). Interpreting the text of his own *Tragicall Historye*, Romeo engages in a remarkable final moment of composition, as he restores his body's bargain with his name part by part, annulling the earlier contract that severed "Romeo" from "Montague." Thus, Romeo Montague begins his "dateless bargain" with the book, christening his reluctant agreement with poison.

Upon seeing the ruinous consequences of his plan, Friar Laurence can offer no consolation to the revived and bewildered Juliet, confessing that "A greater power than we can contradict / Hath thwarted our intents" (5.3.153–54). This greater power that claims Romeo's life and then compels Juliet to draw her own conclusion with Romeo's dagger is, of course, the *auctoritas* of the book—and specifically, Arthur Brooke's book, made widely available by the rise of the printing press in early modern England. Old Montague's lament over Romeo's body punningly testifies to the contaminating, even preposterous influence of the printed word on the "impressionable": "O thou untaught! What manners is in this, / To press before thy father to a grave?" (5.3.213–14). Indeed, Romeo has been "to press" both before and after his father, whose claim to paternity is a matter of little consequence in the rude, virtually unregulated literary marketplace of Shakespeare's day. But Romeo requites his father by returning to his sender, arriving at his destination in the form of the "dead letter" he always already was, as Balthasar reproduces Romeo's suicide note addressed to Old Montague (5.3.274). Romeo's letter also satisfies his literary father, or "grandsire," as proof of Brooke's cautionary tale about the consequences of neglecting "authoritie." Subsequently, this transcript of Romeo's affair but merely the trace of his authorship is submitted as the *exemplar*—the complete, revised text intended for authorization by the subjects of Verona. As Carruthers explains, this last stage of medieval authorship requires the relinquishment of self-aggrandizing motives in the interests of "the communal process of…public comment and readerly response" (212). This process of authorization is completed by the Prince's closing commentary, wherein "Romeo" becomes a trope for "woe": "For never was a story of more woe / Than this of Juliet and her Romeo" (5.3.308–9). As Romeo takes his place as a commonplace, plans for an illustrated edition of this "story" are consolidated by the two families, who vow to memorialize Romeo and Juliet in the form of a "statue in pure gold" (5.3.308, 298). Meanwhile, Romeo's untimely attempt at authorship is consigned to a sculpted silence, waiting for history to catch up with his "story." The letter always arrives at its destination.…

Romeo's authorial efforts, while defeated in the play, receive a kind of belated acknowledgment by the fact that a certain resistance to *auc-*

toritas haunts the publication history of *Romeo and Juliet*, which boasts of no one authorized version. Indeed, Romeo's attempts within the dramatic narrative to authorize different versions of himself are uncannily revisited in the play's multiple quarto versions; and a peculiar irony resides in the fact that the first or "bad" quarto is the product of memorial reconstruction. But in a perverse sense, this "unauthorized" version must have proved a certain point embedded in the play. After all, doesn't *Romeo and Juliet* ratify this piracy, by dramatizing the neurotic positioning of the early modern "author" who, as "a kind of nothing," remains in social, legal, and material "sufferance" until the eighteenth century? Similarly, doesn't the play suggest that there is a certain madness endemic to the text itself under conditions of early modern authorship, wherein a lack of standardized orthography and typography, as well as non-existent copyright laws, cause letters to bleed and proceed via a kind of blind automatism? For that matter, isn't the Shakespearean corpus always in sufferance—in one sense because we lack the paper trail to authorize it, but in another sense, because it is always being pressed into consent with editorial agendas that alternately banish the body or the text? In this respect, *Romeo and Juliet* proleptically encodes the ongoing debate over the connection, or the lack thereof, between Shakespeare's body and his texts. But this play also insists, through Romeo's unauthorized struggle for voice amidst the noise of *auctores* seeking to claim him for their own authority, that there *is* something in the Shakespearean text, more than the text. And this something is the insistent, actorly "body beneath," whose silence speaks volumes about what it means to be a "singular kind of nothing."[19]

19. I refer here to Peter Stallybrass's analysis of the provocative, insistent "body beneath" the Shakespearean actor's clothing in "Transvestism and the 'Body Beneath': Speculating on the Boy Actor." The attempt to cover-over this potentially subversively sexed/gendered body via layers of clothing bears a suggestive likeness to the recent efforts of Shakespearean poststructuralism to paper-over the author's body with textual clothing.

2

Authors, Players, and the Shakespearean Auteur-Function in A Midsummer Night's Dream

In the 1590s, the English public theater became the site of contestation between two distinct modes and views of authorship. As Richard Helgerson explains in *Forms of Nationhood*, the theater's traditional reliance upon players who doubled as "authors," a practice which began on the English public stage in the 1580s with Richard Tarlton, Robert Wilson, and the Queen's Men, began to be challenged in the 1590s by "new nonplayer writers," men "who had no other theatrical function than to write" (199).[1] But there was more at stake than determining the proper division of labor in this conflict between what Helgerson describes as a "players' theater" and an "authors' theater." Class-consciousness was the driving force behind the emergence of the "authors' theater," wherein the so-called "university wits" set out to distinguish the intellectual labor

1. In his chapter on "Staging Exclusion" from *Forms of Nationhood*, Helgerson explores the thesis that beginning with the history plays, Shakespeare followed the trajectory of the "authors' theater" in banishing the low in favor of the high. According to Helgerson, Hal's "totalizing fantasy of power," which "subordinates subplot to main plot, commoners to aristocrats, comedy to history," is also Shakespeare's fantasy of authority (227). Helgerson locates evidence for Shakespeare's politics of exclusion "in the attempt Shakespeare and his company made to secure a private playhouse closer to the center of fashion and government, in their actual move from Shoreditch to the Globe, in the disappearance of Will Kemp from the company and the jig from its repertory, [and] in the transformation of Shakespeare himself from player to author" (227). No longer interested in "a popular theater that mingled kings and clowns," Shakespeare, according to Helgerson, "awoke and despised that dream" (227). Quite the contrary, I argue that Shakespeare imagines montage effects in *A Midsummer Night's Dream* that enable him to resist false choices between an "authors' theater" and a "players' theater."

of poetry from the stigmatized physical labor of playing, arguing that "they had won the right to gentility along with a university degree" (200). Fetishizing the university degree was crucial to the nonplayer-authors' claim to gentlemen's status, for they hailed from backgrounds no different from the artisanal player-authors whom they spurned; the fathers of Chettle, Greene, Kyd, Marlowe, Munday, and Peele were a dyer, a saddler, a scrivener, a shoemaker, a draper, and a clerk, respectively. A social drama contained in a stage drama, these emergent cultural tensions between high and low, "authors" and players proved tenacious, culminating at the turn of the century in what would become known as the War of the Theaters (1599–1601). Forming the backdrop to this fin de siècle conflict, the 1590s was, according to Helgerson, "the crucial decade, the decade of maximum tension," inaugurating "a marked shift from inclusion to exclusion, from public to private, from 'hodge-podge' to 'art'" (203). On which side of the divide was Shakespeare to be found? According to Robert Greene, Shakespeare was a mere pilfering player, an "upstart crow" who tried to poach on the gentility of poetry by aspiring to authorship from the base rabble wherein he meddled. But Shakespeare's position was far more complicated than Greene and his university wit companions suggest:

> As the player-poet who presented the most direct competition to the scholar-poets at their own specialty of producing artful and learned theatrical texts,... [who] could "bombast out a blank verse" with the best of them, Shakespeare became an indigestible lump in the craw of the new authors' theater. He had either to be swallowed or spat up, assimilated as an author or rejected as a player. (Helgerson 203)

Irreducible to either category, Shakespeare requires a third term.

Since the pathbreaking work of the New Bibliography in the first half of the twentieth century, theories about Shakespearean authorship have moved away from romantic myths of authorial embodiment toward what I call "negative space" theories. In the absence of a Shakespearean paper trail, such theories construct a stronghold out of absence itself, and Shakespeare becomes synonymous with a peculiar *negative* surplus. For example, it is common practice to relegate "Shakespeare" to the negative space of quotation marks. This typographical flourish alienates the concept of the proper name in favor of invoking a vast apparatus of theatrical, mechanical, and editorial production to which credit for the plays is (over)due, as Margreta De Grazia contends: "a bibliographic rubric rather than a proper name, 'Shakespeare' functions synecdochally, the authorial part standing in for the collective whole of production" ("Shakespeare in Quotation Marks" 39). So, too, Michel Foucault uses Shakespeare as an example of how the "name of the author" functions (122), but he subsequently fails to include the early modern period in his genealogy of authorship. Rather, the very idea of the early modern "author" is again consigned to negative space, becoming the mere signpost of an untheorized epistemological break between the Classical *auctor* and the singular Author of eighteenth- and nineteenth-century Europe (131). It is not surprising, then, that Peter Stallybrass and Allon White describe authorship in sixteenth-century England as a "series of negations" (67) or "leave-takings—from other writers, from theatrical audiences, from actors, even from patrons" (78).[2] Taking this position to its logical extreme, Marjorie Garber describes a mode of production wherein " 'Shakespeare' is present as an absence—which is to say, as a ghost. Shakespeare as an author is the person who, were he more completely known, would not be the Shakespeare we know" (11). While all of these theoretical commitments share a useful and "poststructurally correct" interest in signifying absences, plurality, and subjective fragmentation, there is something profoundly dissatisfying about their reliance upon a *negative* theory of *production*. I propose a spin on these "negative space" theories of Shakespearean authorship: for the "author" who occupies a non-position, I recommend a "non-theory"—one that maintains Shakespeare and "Shakespeare" in the historical and theatrical craw between *auctor* and Author, player-author and nonplayer-author—as an auteur.

Significantly, the word "auteur" is actually an etymological precursor of the word "author," appearing in Old French well before the English variant "author" emerged in the sixteenth century. More importantly, however, this unremarked precursor has an afterlife in film theory that suggests a form of cultural mediation uncannily similar to that of Shakespearean drama. Auteur theory, as James Naremore points

2. In all fairness to Stallybrass and White, in their chapter titled "The Fair, the Pig, Authorship," they are exploring Ben Jonson's attitude toward dramatic authorship. Nonetheless I would argue that they misdiagnose Jonson as too representative of the sixteenth century "author" when he was, in fact, quite exceptional.

out, "was never really a formal theory; it took on different political meanings at different conjunctures" (21). It was indeed better characterized as a "structure of feeling" which, in Raymond Williams's classic definition, is a "kind of thinking and feeling which is indeed social and material, but...in an embryonic phase" because it exists "at the very edges of semantic availability" (131, 134). For our purposes, the most useful articulation of this "non theory" occurred when it became virtually non-existent—when, following Roland Barthes's sounding of the authorial death knell and the upheavals of May 1968, auteur theory went the way of the Author. In the period from 1969 to 1972, traditional auteurism was completely eclipsed and film theorists turned to the idea of " 'filmic writing' considered in its social relations" (Browne 1). Generated in the wake of political insurgence and social uprisings, this new direction for film theory and practice took shape as an ultimatum formulated by the editors of the pioneering French film journal *Cahiers du Cinema*, who demanded "a critical theory of the cinema...in direct reference to the method of dialectical materialism" articulated by Sergei Eisenstein (Comolli and Narboni 64). In response to this call to action, film theory embraced the idea of "filmic writing" as productive of a *material trace*, based on Eisenstein's definition of dialectical montage as a dramatic principle which derives its force from conflict, a "view that from the collision of two given factors arises a [new] concept" (Eisenstein, *Film Form* 37). This new theoretical investment in filmic writing led to a more comprehensive concept of the authorial subject "as an effect of the signifier and as an agency of historical forces" (Browne 13).

Consequently, the few remaining practitioners of auteur theory reconsidered ideas of film authorship from Eisenstein's sociopolitical perspective. For Peter Wollen, this meant adding to *Signs and Meaning in the Cinema* (1969) a post script (1972), which theorizes the "patterns of energy cathexis" that an auteur film reveals beneath its final, "worked over," "smoothed out" surface (167). Beneath the film façade, a volatile, contestatory production process "remains latent in the film unconscious" which, Wollen argues, "an auteur analysis disengages from the film" (167). Akin to Wollen's view of the auteur film as both a product and a producer of constitutive conflict, Serge Daney and Jean-Pierre Oudart also argued in 1972 that "the nom-de-l'Auteur" emerges as a third term or symptom of the collision between a subversive directorial desire and the ideological prohibitions of a film's historical moment of production, becoming the site of convergence between "a camera and a consciousness" (312). Still others such as Robin Wood maintained that despite the 1968 paradigm shift, it was inappropriate "to throw out ideas of personal authorship altogether," for the idea of the individual artist could be productively refigured as "medium" of ideological, aesthetic, and sociological tensions ("Ideology" 475, 479). Accordingly, auteur theory's "last words" might be articulated as follows: from the collision of the "author" and the "apparatus," arises a concept of auteur-as-"material trace"—the inextinguishable afterlife of this collision. The concept of auteur is hereby refigured as a kind of montage effect in its own right, for montage, as Nick Browne explains, "rearranges significant relations, transforms pre-texts (the culturally and normally invested fields of fixed sense), interrupts and renegotiates notions of liaison and continuity. *Its deconstructive form of productivity is the result of both action and negation*" (1, emphasis added). Flirting with negative space but not reduced to it, the auteur—like Shakespeare—becomes an "indigestible lump" born of the collision between an insistent authorial presence and the contingent machinations of a collaborative mode of production.

The double-negative constituted by this non-theory of auteur, in combination with Shakespeare's non-position as an "author," suggests a positive hermeneutic for exploring Shakespeare's dramatic corpus. As I argued in the preceding chapter, authorship in Shakespeare's day was treated as "a kind of nothing." Moreover, in the specific context of the theater, Shakespeare poses a "not yet nameable" challenge to the emerging dichotomy between player-authors and nonplayer-authors—as both a player *and* an "author" who could "bombast out a blank verse" with the best of his university wit rivals. The only term that approximates Shakespeare's unique position in the Renaissance theater as dramatist, actor, and shareholder in his own company is the Spanish word "autor," the term for the leading actor of late sixteenth century Peninsular troupes who also "served as manager, financier, and employer of the other members of the repertory group" (Cohen 176). Despite its likeness to the word author, *autor* does not refer to the act of composition and, therefore, strikes at only part of the Shakespearean equation. The term auteur, however, which led to significant variations such as *auctor*, actor, and eventually author, suggests not only a historically appropriate habitation but also a name for Shakespearean dramatic authorship. In addition to reconciling contemporary debates between Romantic and poststructuralist theories of Shakespearean authorship, which respectively privilege either the author or the apparatus, the idea of auteur implicitly invokes a practice whose principal destination is not print but rather a fundamentally *performative* medium. Might we then move Shakespeare from the negative space of quotation marks and ghostwriting into the constitutive haunts of the auteur? To do so is to reconceive of Shakespeare himself as a montage effect—born of the conflicting historical trajectories embodied in *auctor* and Author, of the competing agencies generated by an "author" and an apparatus, and, as we shall see, of the opposing representations staged by the "players' theater" and the "authors' theater." These productive collisions ultimately betray the presence of what I wish to call the Shakespearean auteur-function, which first emerges in the 1590s under the pretext of *A Midsummer Night's Dream*.

The Athenian setting of *A Midsummer Night's Dream*, the site of the play's so-called main plot, provides the decoy for the Shakespearean negotiations that take place in the metadramatic space of the green world subplot. As if picking up where *Romeo and Juliet* leaves off, *A Midsummer Night's Dream* begins with an assertion of *auctoritas* and a haunting image of being "pressed to death," as Egeus "beg[s] the ancient privilege of Athens" to punish his daughter's refusal to accept his chosen suitor, Demetrius.[3] For a defiant Hermia's benefit, Theseus, ruler of Athens, explains this ancient privilege:

> To you your father should be as a god;
> One that compos'd your beauties; yea, and one
> To whom you are but as a form in wax,
> By him imprinted, and within his power,
> To leave the figure, or disfigure it.
>
> (1.1.47–51)

Theseus's explanation and Egeus's prompting together reflect the male parthenogenic fantasy sustained by the concept of *auctoritas*, whereby the ancient privileges of the text, in this case, Athenian law, are rendered perpetual and absolute by their phallocratic impersonators, who are capable of enforcing not only mental but also bodily impressions.

---

3. See Shakespeare's *A Midsummer Night's Dream* (1.1.41), quoted with permission from the second edition of *The Riverside Shakespeare*. Hereafter cited in the text.

Wishing to prevent the latter consequence, Theseus assumes a pedagogical tone, appropriating another metaphor of inscription and prescription in order to urge Hermia to revise her desire for Lysander and conform to her father's script:

> For you, fair Hermia, look you arm yourself
> To fit your fancies to your father's will
> Or else the law of Athens yields you up
> (Which by no means we may extenuate)
> To death or to a vow of single life.
>
> (1.1.117–21)

Unimpressed by such displays of rhetorical muscle, Hermia and Lysander decide to foil the ancient privilege of Athens by fleeing beyond the city limits where, they conclude, "the sharp Athenian law / Cannot pursue us" (1.1.162–63). Parting ways at this point with *Romeo and Juliet,* wherein paternal law cannot ultimately be countered, the opening sequence of *A Midsummer Night's Dream* represents *auctoritas* as "the failure of a particular generic structure...to reproduce itself" (Jameson, *Political Unconscious* 146). According to Fredric Jameson, this failure "not only encourages a search for those substitute textual formations that appear in its wake, but more particularly alerts us to the historical ground, now no longer existent, in which the original structure was meaningful" (146). Within the magical world of romantic comedy and the changing real world of the literary and theatrical marketplace, the structures of meaning supported by *auctoritas* are being replaced by "structures of feeling," as the play turns toward an alternative setting, the forest, in order to initiate its search for "substitute textual formations."

These textual formations destined to supercede *auctoritas* acquire specifically dramatic contours if we interpret Hermia and Lysander's quest for liberty beyond the city limits as an allusion to the London liberties, the site of the public theaters in Shakespeare's day. As Steven Mullaney has notably argued: "London's liberties, extending up to a mile from the city proper, were a part of the city yet set apart from it; they were free or 'at liberty' from manorial rule or obligation to the crown, but they were also outside the jurisdiction of the Lord Mayor. They formed a transitional zone between the city and the country, various powers and their limits, this life and the next" (21). In Shakespeare's play, the forest or green world represents both a transitional and a theatrical zone. And, though one might expect the green world sequences of a play about midsummer madness to facilitate a holiday from the friction generated by the social realignments of the late sixteenth century, the forest scenes relentlessly dramatize the tensions between "a rising bourgeoisie, urban—as opposed to rural—residence, a centralizing monarchy, and an emancipated peasantry" (Cohen 190). With all of these constituencies loosely or directly represented in Shakespeare's forest—in Hermia and Lysander's self-serving flight from feudal strictures, Titania and Oberon's fairy kingdom, and the rude mechanicals' farcical pursuit of class mobility—it is no wonder that, as Jean-Christoph Agnew argues, the theater itself became "a 'physiognomic metaphor' for the mobile and polymorphous features of the market" during England's uneven transition from feudalism into capitalism (11). Marking Shakespeare's singular intervention in the rampant social realignments of the 1590s, *A Midsummer Night's Dream* makes the theater accountable to its own representational logic, as the metadramatic forest sequences translate class conflicts into a clash of competing modes of theatrical production in ways that uncannily anticipate the War of the Theaters.

In the spirit of fin de siècle restlessness, the War of the Theaters began in 1599, several years after Shakespeare composed and performed *A Midsummer Night's Dream*. The War was, according to Andrew Gurr, "a curious little fracas" that turned an emergent vogue for satirical "railing" against the playwrights themselves (159). The logical result of tensions between player-authors and nonplayer-authors during the 1590s, this metatheatrical railing staked out two principal positions. In one camp were the antitheatrical playwrights, or proponents of the "authors' theater" who, scornful of the public theater and its rude, citizen-taste repertory, produced more learned theatrical texts replete with Latinisms and obscure scholarly allusions, which served as veiled insults to the less-educated sectors of the playgoing public. Consequently, the social antagonisms fueled by the university wits in the early 1590s led to a change of venue, audience, and repertory with Jonson, Marston, and eventually Webster, when the semi-private and financially exclusive boys' companies of Blackfriars and St. Paul's re-emerged in 1599. Throughout the brief life span of the boys' companies (1599–1608), the "authors' theater" poets "went to great lengths to emphasise what a different clientele they enjoyed compared with the crowds at the Shoreditch or Bankside playhouses" (Gurr 23)—as in Marston's notorious distinction between the "choice selected influence" of the Hall-goers and the "stinkards" among the amphitheater-attendees.[4] Predictably, satire and a penchant for the outrageous defined the modus operandi of these aspiring "authors."

On the other side of this dispute were the Henslowe company dramatists such as Munday, Chettle, Heywood, and, to a lesser extent, Dekker, who maintained their association with the more traditional "players' theater" and its predominantly citizen and artisan tastes. They did not, however, remain unprovoked by railing. For instance, Dekker's response to Jonson's attack on adult players in *Poetaster* (1601) was *Satiromastix* (1601), a play retaliating against Jonson and the Black-friars boys with a tone of violent condemnation. Indeed, for a mere "fracas," the theatrical exchanges got quite heated, and Heywood, too, joined the fray in an explicitly moralizing manner, arguing that the "bitterness" featured in the "authors' theater," coupled with its "liberal invectives against all estates," should not be committed to "the mouthes of Children" (qtd. in Gurr 155).

Shakespeare, meanwhile, occupied a rather curious position in this theatrical contest. On the one hand, his company virtually initiated the fashion for railing by staging Jonson's *Every Man in His Humour* (1598), following the success of which the boys' companies ran with the new fashion. On the other hand, when Jonson abandoned the Lord Chamberlain's Men to join the boys' companies, Shakespeare's company responded by staging Dekker's attack on Jonson, *Satiromastix*. In Shakespeare's own oeuvre, *Hamlet* is the only play that is explicitly linked with the War of the Theaters. Explaining the return of the boys' companies to an incredulous Hamlet, Rosencrantz informs him of an "aery of children," whose "little eyases . . . cry out on the top of the question, and are most tyrannically clapp'd for't. These are now the fashion, and so [berattle] the common stages—so they call them—that many wearing rapiers are afraid of goose-quills and dare scarce come hither" (2.2.330–35). Elaborating on his preposterous suggestion that weapon-wearing adults are

4. For the purposes of this discussion, I am somewhat oversimplifying the relations between the playwrights involved in the War of the Theaters. Marston, for example, entered the War by attacking Jonson, whom he saw as his chief rival among aspiring "non-player authors." Another complicated example is Dekker, the commercial hack who was associated with the "player-authors" but who teamed-up with Marston to write *Histriomastix* and eventually wrote for the Children of St. Paul's. For a thorough account of the War of the Theaters, see James Bednarz's essay "Marston's Subversion of Shakespeare and Jonson: *Histriomastix* and the War of the Theaters."

afraid of boys and goose-quills, Rosencrantz explains the new theatri-cal vogue as a battle between "the poet and the player," who "[go] to cuffs in the question" (2.2.346). When Hamlet asks, "Do the boys carry it away?" Rosencrantz replies, alluding to the boys' "theft" of playgo-ers from the Globe, "Ay, that they do, my lord—Hercules and his load too" (2.2.350–2). Though the play's reference to the "aery of children" is typically glossed as a reference to the hawking metaphor of fledg-lings in the nest, it also contains within it the suggestion of insubstan-tiality—precisely the patronizing "aery nothing" status which, as we shall see, Shakespeare systematically debunks on behalf of *his own* the-atrical enterprise in *Dream*.

But did Shakespeare tacitly desire the elite clientele that the boys' companies and their "authors," for a short time, enjoyed exclusively? Taking up this question, the milieu studies and metadramatic criticism of the 1970s contend that this desire is encoded in Shakespeare's inter-nally staged productions which, as Alvin B. Kernan and others have ar-gued, are *all* private entertainments performed for aristocratic patrons.[5] Many critics have concluded, therefore, that these internal perfor-mances were intended to court Shakespeare's "ideal" audience: the no-bility and, of course, the monarch. And yet, when Shakespeare officially became a royal servant as a member of The King's Men, he still catered to a distinctly popular audience, writing plays which, even after the Blackfriars acquisition of 1608, were also intended for performance in the public venue of the Globe. According to Andrew Gurr, then, Shakespeare's company remained decidedly neutral in the War of the Theaters, escaping contention by avoiding "the 'public' or popular tag which clung to Henslowe's companies as well as the risks which the boys ran to get their 'private' or 'select' playgoers into their seats" (157). But neutrality is not exactly what we might expect from Shakespeare, so how exactly did he write himself both into and out of the War under the guise of remaining neutral?

Some time around 1600, hedged in on both sides by the War, Shake-speare's company risked positioning itself as something more than a theatrical haven for either complacent citizens or acerbic aristocrats by

5. See, for example, Alvin B. Kernan's *The Playwright as Magician* and "Shakespearian Comedy and Its Courtly Audience"; Theodore B. Leinwald's "'I believe we must leave the killing out': Deference and Accommodation in *A Midsummer Night's Dream*"; Calder-wood's *Shakespearean Metadrama;* and Laurie E. Osborne's "Staging the Female Playgoer: Gender in Shakespeare's Onstage Audiences."

creating the Globe theater in the spirit of social, aesthetic, and political montage effects. This decision, I shall argue, was made possible by the dramatic experimentation conducted in *A Midsummer Night's Dream*. Ideally suited for such experimentation, the pretext of a "dream"—with its traditional function of divination and its emergent, early modern association with madness—enables Shakespeare both to imagine the fin de siècle spectacle of theatrical war and to resolve its madness according to the bizarre logic of dreamwork, or, in the play's language, "the fierce vexation of a dream" (4.1.69). In the late sixteenth century, dreaming and the theater were implicitly connected, as theories about the theater of the mind were also undergoing shifting alignments. As Carol Schreier Rupprecht observes, at this transitional point in dream theory

when a person had a dream, no single criterion could be comfortably or systematically invoked to assess its origin. . . . Some [dream theorists] evaded the question of prophecy by associating dreams and astrology with a new external celestial force—stars and planets—or with an extremity of intrapsychic existence such as madness, or with a nonnatural, external, suprahuman force like magic. (125)

Anyone familiar with the forest scenes of Shakespeare's play will recognize all of these excuses for the "dream"—the rebellion of the natural world, Bottom's madness, Puck's magic—but none of these theories are singularly endorsed. Rather, they are condensed into Theseus's assessment of the imagination at the play's conclusion: "The lunatic, the lover, and the poet / Are of imagination all compact" (5.1.7–8). Indeed, the connection between the poet, passion, and pathology cannot be understated when speculating about the maddening aspirations of the early modern "author," and, particularly, the early modern dramatic "author." For if the former signifies a "kind of nothing," the latter signifies *less* than nothing, indeed, an "aery nothing," as Theseus condescendingly describes the work of the stage poet in Shakespeare's play (5.1.16). This status is all but confirmed by Dekker's description of the dramatist as one who "barters away that light commodity of words for a lighter ware than words—plaudits and the breath of that great beast which like the threatenings of two cowards, vanish all into air" (qtd. in Kastan 160). Building on these nightmarish aspersions that so berattle the public stage, Shakespeare's play likewise represents the pathology of early modern dramatic authorship in the threatenings of two cowards, embodied in the petite war between Bottom's "players' theater" and Oberon's "authors' theater." But Shakespeare stages this war with a difference; for as the player and the poet go to cuffs in the question and collide under the cover of the play's rarified green world/dream world, they leave in their wake a montage effect that enables Shakespeare to end the War—before it even begins.

Examples of how other Renaissance visions draw on narrative and conceptual modes akin to dreamwork help to further contextualize the ways in which Shakespeare's play achieves these desired effects. In her analysis of "Renaissance Dreams," Rana Goffen examines the capacity of Renaissance cultural forms that depict or suggest dreams—particularly the secular works of Quattrocento painters—to function as "real" dreams, that is, as mediums for exploring wishes and exorcising anxieties. Combining historical and Freudian perspectives on dreamwork, Goffen observes that a common tableau created and commissioned by male Renaissance artists and patrons is the representation of fantasies and fears about distinctly female power. Similarly, in his famous approach to *A Midsummer Night's Dream*, Louis A. Montrose uses Simon Forman's actual dream of Elizabeth I as a window onto the larger, "cultural contours of [the] Elizabethan psyche" (63) represented in Shakespeare's *Dream*. Like the Quattrocento imagination, the Elizabethan psyche is beset by male anxieties associated with female rule and, more specifically, a ruler whose image was dispersed across the seemingly incommensurate cultural categories of maiden, mother, and monarch. My objective in briefly rehearsing these New Historical perspectives on the early modern sex/gender system is to add something new to this equation, by pointing out that Elizabeth—in her self-consciously theatrical, "triune" cult image of maiden, mother, and monarch (Montrose 85)—offers a working model of the kind of metadramatic collision that Shakespeare produces under the auspices of *A Midsummer Night's Dream*. For if, as Montrose argues of Forman's dream, "in the context of cross-cutting relations between subject and prince, men and women, the dream insinuates into a gesture of homage, a will to power" (65), then Shakespeare's *Dream* goes one step further, making good on the cinematic analogy that Montrose casually invokes. Indeed, in "cross-cutting" between representations of a "players' theater" and an "authors' theater," Shakespeare's generates not an homage but a montage—the effects of which imply a most potent Will to power in the form of an auteur's theater.

While dreams may vanish into thin air, they do not merely emerge from it, for they are produced by what Freud calls "day residue," or the leftovers of waking life. In this spirit, we might consider Robert Greene's 1592 attack on Shakespeare to be the textual residue informing the first half of the authorial nightmare represented in *Dream*. Part of the first generation of aspiring nonplayer-authors, Greene warned his fellow university wits of a usurper in the ranks, bastardizing a conceit from Shakespeare's highly successful *Henry VI* plays in order to inform Marlowe, Nashe, and Peele of "'an upstart crow, beautified with our feathers, that with his tiger's heart wrapped in a player's hide supposes he is as well able to bombast out a blank verse with the best of you'" (*Complete Works* 12, 144). Adding insult to injury, Greene also refers to Shakespeare as a "rude groom," completing his coda to Nashe's earlier indictment of "those 'mechanical mate[s]'" who "'think to outbrave better pens with the swelling bombast of a bragging blank verse'" (qtd. in Parker 305). The forest/dream sequence of *A Midsummer Night's Dream* thus begins by revealing Shakespeare's deflection and condensation of these derogatory epithets into the "rude mechanicals," who share bombastic fantasies of playing, authorship, and social climbing. Because censorship plays a critical function in a dream's self-defensive distortion of the day residue, dreams will not permit the direct representation of certain persons, localities, and events; rather, through the mechanisms of condensation and displacement, the dream-work creates "relation[s] of similarity, consonance, or approximation" (Freud 343, 354). Accordingly, the rag-tag crew that emerges in scene two of Shakespeare's play, representing a constellation of the "mechanical arts"—carpentry, joinery, weaving, bellows-mending, tinkering, and tailoring—provides a rough analogue to the collaborative apparatus of dramatic art. And, as Patricia Parker points out, players *were* "culled from the ranks of joiners, weavers, and other artisans" and, therefore, "ranged 'i' the statute' with vagrants and vagabonds" (87). Though traditional commentary on the rude mechanicals suggests that Shakespeare creates them in order to distinguish his own professional company from the ranks of such amateurs, my analysis is more concerned with the idea that the rude mechanicals serve as a worst-case scenario for *all* players (including Shakespeare) deemed illegitimate by "the statute" and continually reminded of this status by the reluctant "jury of their peers," the nonplayer-authors. Doubly inflected with derogatory stereotypes of handicraft and stagecraft, the rude mechanicals represent the nightmarish status of players and player-authors both in the early modern and Shakespearean imagination.

In *A Midsummer Night's Dream* it is Bottom who, by virtue of his name alone, represents the lower-limit of the individual and collective nightmares voiced in the play, for he emerges not only as the doltish spokesman for the player-authors but also as the poster-boy for existing anxieties about social miscegenation. Though Peter Quince is the character typically identified as the stand-in for the "author"/Shakespeare among the rude mechanicals (and as writer, actor, and business manager of the troupe he does present a provocative parallel), Bottom appears to command more attention in the eyes of the crudely assembled acting "company" (1.2.1), since he is the figure who is continually improvising new scripts, stage-directing, and attempting to play all the parts as if he had written them. This somewhat uneven distribution of power in the troupe is revealed to us through the sequence of commands that Bottom issues to Peter Quince, the decoy director-figure of the amateur entourage. Following Quince's call to attention, Bottom runs the show, scripting even the procedure for the mechanicals' pending rehearsal of *Pyramus and Thisbe*—a play culled, appropriately, from the ranks of "citizen tastes": "First, good Peter Quince, say what the play treats on; then read the names of the actors; and so grow to a point" (1.2.8–10). As an aspiring *player*-author, however, Bottom's desire to devise scripts quickly merges with his wish to perform them, as he stage-directs himself upon receipt of the part of Pyramus: "That will ask some tears in the true performing of it. If I do it, let the audience look to their eyes. I will move storms; I will condole in some measure" (1.2.25–28). Unable to resist this opportunity to make good on his poetic and playerly bravado, Bottom suddenly extemporizes:

> The raging rocks
> And shivering shocks
> Shall break the locks
> Of prison gates;
> And Phibbus' car
> Shall shine from far,
> And make and mar
> The foolish Fates.

> (1.2.29–38)

Adding an exclamation point to his attempt to "bombast out a blank verse with the best of them," Bottom cries, "This was lofty!" (1.2.39).

But as his low execution of his lofty subject matter reveals, Bottom is repeatedly hindered not only by basic mispronunciations, as in his rendering of Phoebus as "Phibbus," but also by nagging malapropisms
such as "call them generally, man by man" (1.2.2–3) and "we may rehearse most obscenely and courageously" (107–8). While such impedi-
ments to cogent speech could be attributed to dream language, which
generates slips-of-the-tongue and neologisms (Freud 330), Bottom's
botched authorial efforts suggest a more compelling origin in the invective of the university wits who, fearful of the "semiotic contagion"
of the low (Helgerson 201), stake their claim to superiority on stereotypes of the uneducated and plodding player-author. The prophetic
quality of Shakespeare's vision of Bottom and the rude mechanicals is
uncanny; for Marston will resurrect this troupe of amateur players in
Histriomastix as "Sir Oliver Owlet's Men" who, forced by Marston to act
out their own incompetence, strike the first blow against the "players'
theater" in the War of the Theaters.

As a living metaphor for the apparatus of dramatic production, the
rude mechanicals also introduce us to the ideological apparatuses associated with theatrical patronage and censorship. In the process of the
rehearsing the popular play *Pyramus and Thisbe* in preparation for Duke
Theseus's wedding, Bottom's amateur troupe testifies to the pressures
posed by these ideological apparatuses when they fall to bickering over
who should play the Lion. It is significant that the part de résistance in
the mechanicals' pending production is that of the Lion, since it suggests the dream-work's altered version of Greene's indictment of
Shakespeare as the *tiger*-hearted player who, much to Greene's chagrin,
receives the lion's share of applause. In *Dream*, Quince gives the part to
Snug, but Bottom immediately insists on playing the Lion as a reflection of his upstart ambitions:

> BOTTOM: Let me play the lion too. I will roar, that I will do any
>   man's heart good to hear me. I will roar, that I will make
>   the Duke say, "Let him roar again; let him roar again."
> QUINCE: And you should do it too terribly, you would fright the
>   Duchess and the ladies, that they would shrike; and that
>   were enough to hang us all.
> ALL: That would hang us, every mother's son. (1.2.70–78)

This brief and comical exchange between the members of the troupe
delineates the dual nature of the apparatus, or the "Janus-face of Re-

naissance theatrical authority" (Wilson 9), with which all theatrical projects in Shakespearean England were held in precarious tension. First, Bottom's desire to play the Lion and thereby to please the Duke reveals the strict system of patronage that both maintained and threatened the livelihood of players under Elizabeth I. In 1572, Elizabeth banned all companies that lacked patronage or peerage, a crack-down on amateur and professional troupes which, in the 1590s, resulted in the radical reduction of acting companies to a mere happy few. By 1598, after *Dream*'s debut, the Vagrancy Act went further to ordain punishments of whipping and even death for unlicensed playing. In the context of this historical moment, then, Bottom's repeated desire for the Duke's endorsement of his skillful roaring suggests the pressing need to be numbered among and legitimized by the few remaining patronized acting companies. At the same time, however, the implicit risks involved in playing before patrons—particularly royalty—are articulated by Peter Quince's fear of frightening the ladies with the lion's roar, which could be "enough," as the other players confirm, "to hang us all, every mother's son." Indeed, Elizabethan censorship was characterized by a "nervy inconsistency," and "[t]hough no Elizabethan actors were hanged or mutilated for libel,... they were right to be apprehensive about such a system, which might one day tolerate them and the next haul them before the judges" (Wilson 8). It is no wonder that at the close of the mechanicals' first meeting, Quince, fearful of being "dogg'd" within city limits (1.2.104), instructs the players to hold their next meeting in the marginalized space of "the palace wood, a mile without the town, by moonlight" (1.2.101–2). Here, the aspiring players confront both social and artistic marginalization; rehearsing in the city liberties—the haunts of asylums and leprosariums—their mechanical and theatrical labor must compete with the performances of lunatics and lepers.

This confrontation between the mechanical players and the ideological apparatuses of patronage and censorship also illustrates why the "authors' theater" worked so vehemently to distinguish itself from the collaborative ethos of the "players' theater." Simply put, the "authors' theater" sought to valorize self-determination over and against collaboration. The broader social implications of this distinction are rendered succinctly by Hobbes, who declared that " 'Natural persons' were those individuals who could be said to represent themselves; 'artificial persons,' on the other hand, were those whose words and deeds were 'owned' by those whom they represented. The former were *authors;* the latter were *actors* but actors in the sense of mere hirelings" (Agnew 99).

Shakespeare dramatizes this distinction between "authors" and "actors" most conspicuously by making his representatives of the "players' theater" truly mere hirelings, emphasizing their irreducibly collaborative and exclusively mechanical work of plotting, playing, and prop-making and, in so doing, drawing attention to their status as mechanical or "artificial" persons. Moreover, the fact that the rude mechanicals conclude their meeting by agreeing to hold their next rehearsal at the "Duke's Oak" reminds us that their theatrical enterprise is virtually sprung from the Duke's loins and dependent upon his "purse."[6] Whether or not the rude mechanicals will hang from this tree remains to be seen. Either way, the play suggests that these yet-unweaned "mothers' sons" will not snap out of their state of arrested development. Unable to authorize anything other than the most mechanical pursuits, they are destined to remain rock bottom.

In *The Place of the Stage*, Mullaney describes the unique ability of Shakespearean drama to create an aura of "two-eyedness," to "produce, in dramatic form, an anamorphic scene that always seems to call for yet one more perspective, for what are oftentimes mutually exclusive points-of-view, if it is to be adequately comprehended" (54). More specifically, in his discussion of narrative as a "socially symbolic act," Jameson reminds us that hidden under the auspices of romance and even romantic comedy is "a transitional moment in which two distinct modes of production, or moments of socioeconomic development, co-exist" (*Political Unconscious* 148). In *A Midsummer Night's Dream*, a play in which "every thing seems double" (4.1.190), Shakespeare provides us with an anamorphic nightmare of the "authors' theater" as well. Indeed, it is not long before the world of fairy productions reveals that these aspiring "natural persons" are not only profoundly unnatural but also as rude as their playerly counterparts.

Immediately following the exit of the rude mechanicals, the fairy kingdom unfolds through Puck, a mediating character between the play's two representations of authorship. Puck introduces us to Oberon, who, in addition to being a Hobbesian "natural person," is also

6. In early modern discourse, the word "purse" encodes a double-entendre, operating both as a site of economic expenditure in its evocation of "purse-strings" and as a site of sexual expenditure as slang for testicles.

the supernatural King of the Fairies. Oberon is the play's other internal dramatist and, like Bottom, he, too, is planning something special to commemorate Theseus's wedding—although his performance will involve a series of masque-like revels befitting an elite audience. Oberon's "theater" is thus more aptly described as a theater of influence—of "choice selected influence" (Marston)—that enables Oberon to further his own spectacle of power. In this respect, then, we might consider Oberon to be the play's central representative of the claims of the "authors' theater," as he emerges, in characteristic "railing" style,

> ...passing fell and wrath,
> Because she [Titania] as her attendant hath
> A lovely boy stolen from an Indian king;
> She never had so sweet a changeling.
> And jealous Oberon would have the child
> Knight of his train, to trace the forests wild...
>
> (2.1.20–25)

Already Oberon appears to be demonstrating both the pettiness and extravagance associated with the boys' companies' productions at Blackfriars and St. Paul's. And, if we substitute "troupe" for "train," we might indeed interpret Oberon's desire for the changeling boy in the specifically theatrical context of *Dream*'s pending war of the theaters, particularly since Oberon plans to use the child as the main attraction of the revels he will be staging for Theseus's wedding. Since the mid-sixteenth century, fairies were frequently associated with royal masques, and their parts were most often performed by boy choristers; in making Oberon King of the Fairies, then, the play suggests his connection both to the aristocratic tastes of the "authors' theater" and its partnership with the boys' companies. But in *Dream*, Oberon's hopes of satisfying the exotic tastes of a select theatergoing audience are foiled by the Indian child's overbearing mother-figure, Titania, who prevents Oberon's savvy move and unwittingly provides him with the seeds of his revenge plot. "Well, go thy way," Oberon exclaims to Titania, "Thou shalt not from this grove / Till I torment thee for this injury" (2.1.146–47).

Though *A Midsummer Night's Dream* is staged well before the return of the boys' companies in 1599, Oberon's "theater" reveals further, striking affinities with the emerging "authors' theater." This affiliation is suggested by the division of labor Oberon's title implies. Alternately hailed as King of the Fairies or Shadows (shadows, significantly, being

slang for actors), Oberon is immediately invested with a sense of superiority over, rather than collaboration with, players. And, not surprisingly, Oberon's theater does not involve the "author" in the dirty work
of production, as his first stage-directions to Puck insist: "Fetch me this
herb, and be thou here again / Ere the leviathan can swim a league"
(2.1.173–74). Similarly, Oberon's implicit description of his positioning
vis-à-vis the production—figured spatially as an elevated or invisible
vantage—intimates an authorial posture of superiority unimaginable
in the "players' theater":

> Having once this juice,
> I'll watch Titania when she is asleep,
> And drop the liquor of it in her eyes;
> The next thing then she waking looks upon
> (Be it on lion, bear, or wolf, or bull,
> On meddling monkey, or on busy ape),
> She shall pursue it with the soul of love.
> And ere I take this charm from off her sight
> (As I can take it with another herb),
> I'll make her render up her page to me.
> But who comes here? I am invisible,
> And I will overhear their conference.

(2.1.176–87)

Unlike the laboring player Puck who is firmly entrenched in the downstage activities, Oberon's position in this scene is sheer authorial fantasy, conveying the desire to be an autonomous force independent of
the drama below but all the while pulling the strings.[7] We might consider Oberon's simultaneous desire for recognition and anonymity to
represent a conflation of two changes in the social architecture of the
theater that develop during the rise of the "authors' theater": the practice of stool-sitting and the retreat of the playwright from stage to page.

Stool-sitting, which never occurred in the public amphitheaters, was
a short-lived practice that conformed to the brief life-spans of the boys'
companies in the late 1570s and 80s and early 1600s. Essentially an

---

7. As in film versions that position Oberon atop trees and other perches, the Renaissance stage would place him in the "locus" or upstage setting, in the illusionistic space
above the "platea," the downstage site of anti-illusionistic representation. For further
analysis of *locus* and *platea* conventions, see Robert Weimann's *Shakespeare and the Popular
Tradition in the Theater*, as well as *Author's Pen and Actor's Voice*.

early modern mode of conspicuous consumption, stool-sitting was reserved for the VIPS in attendance, who would actually sit on stage and
display themselves in a manner that suggested direct competition with
the performance of the actors themselves. Often, stool-sitters would
add a crowning touch to their sartorial splendor by sporting tall feathers in their hats, hoping to claim the "highest" position on stage. As a
kind of stool-sitter looking down on the action, Oberon embodies the
non-player authors' own ambitions of rising to superior social standing
through a different kind of feather-in-their-caps: the university degree.
However, Oberon's simultaneous investment in invisibility reflects
these same dramatists' desire to emerge as VIPs not on stage but in
print—a medium that enabled the "authors' theater" to obscure the
base theatrical body beneath their scripts as well as to remove the taint
of collaboration with rude mechanicals and an unsophisticated playgoing public. This mandatory air of resignation that true "authors"
adopted toward the dramatic medium would become standard practice after the War, as demonstrated by Webster's surly preface "To the
Reader" in the printed version of *The White Devil* (1612):

...should a man present to such an auditory, the most sententious tragedy that
ever was written, observing all the critical laws as height of style, and gravity of
person, enrich it with the sententious *Chorus*, and, as it were Life and Death,
in the passionate and weighty *Nuntius:* yet after all this divine rapture, *O dura
messorum ilia*, the breath that comes from the incapable multitude is able to
poison it; and, ere it be acted, let the author resolve to fix to every scene this
of Horace:

—*Hæc hodie porcis comedenda relinques.* (3)[8]

Thus, in this ongoing battle between the bibliographic ego and the base
theatrical body, a seemingly false set of antagonisms emerges, pitting
"printed texts against staged plays, gentlemen poets against common
players" (Helgerson 200).

Many critics suggest that Shakespeare was not incapable of professing similar revulsion for his medium, deriving evidence for their case
from Sonnet 111. Lyric affinities among the Sonnets and plays such as
Romeo and Juliet and *A Midsummer Night's Dream* have led critics to date

---

8. "*O dura messum ilia*" is from Horace's *Epodes*, translating as "O strong stomach of
harvesters"; similarly, "*Hæc hodie porcis comedenda relinques*" is from Horace's *Epistles*,
translating as "what you leave will today become food for pigs."

them in close proximity to one another, and if we grant this dating conjecture, Sonnet 111 does provide an interesting gloss on Shakespeare's metatheatrical *Dream*. In this sonnet, the speaker engages in an extended lament presumably about his position in the public theater:

> O, for my sake do you [with] Fortune chide,
> The guilty goddess of my harmful deeds,
> That did not better for my life provide
> Than public means which public manners breeds.
> Thence comes it that my name receives a brand,
> And almost thence my nature is subdu'd
> To what it works in, like the dyer's hand.
> Pity me then, and wish I were renew'd,
> Whilst like a willing patient I will drink
> Potions of eisel 'gainst my strong infection,
> No bitterness that I will bitter think,
> Nor double penance, to correct correction.
> Pity me then, dear friend, and I assure ye,
> Even that your pity is enough to cure me.

Assuming that Shakespeare and the poetic "I" here are the same, it would seem at first glance as though he is joining the ranks of the "authors' theater" in descrying the depravity associated with and generated by the public theater, its players, and its playgoers. However, if, as I have suggested, the shaping day residue of the Sonnets is similar to that of *Dream*, namely, Greene's (among others') attacks upon Shakespeare, another reading emerges in which the "I" laments not his medium but rather the "brand" his name wrongfully receives from *other playwrights*. This reading becomes more compelling when we realize that, also around the time Shakespeare was writing *Dream*, he was engaged in an attempt to procure a coat-of-arms for his family name. This kind of endeavor was the subject of violent denunciation by those with "natural pedigrees" who argued against the unnatural phenomenon of "gentlemen made...cheap in England" (Sir Thomas Smith, qtd. in Parker 23), as well as the source of satire for aspiring "authors" such as Ben Jonson, whose famous postscript to a rustic's rise to gentility in *Every Man in His Humour* (1598)—"not without mustard"—is believed to be a sardonic reply to the granting of arms to Shakespeare in 1596.[9]

---

9. *Non sans droit* is the motto on the Shakespeare coat of arms.

Viewed in this light, it is surprising that the playwright-figure in Sonnet 111 vows to absorb the poison of his detractors without rebuttal: "No bitterness that I will bitter think, / Nor double penance, to correct correction." But according to Russ MacDonald, this reticence is in keeping with the historical perception of Shakespeare as someone who "remain[ed] aloof from public controversy," allowing "future generations to imagine him as a private, diligent artist, untainted by the personal and literary squabbles of the times" (3). However, MacDonald adds that while "this image may be accurate...it is almost surely an oversimplification promoted by scant evidence" (3). *A Midsummer Night's Dream* might thus be conceived of as "evidence" of Shakespeare's overdue reply, or "correction," to charges left unanswered by the Sonnets. In this context, then, the vitriolic Oberon, who strives to be a Hobbesian "author" by making all the world his "actors," emerges as the dreamwork's nightmarish representative of Shakespearean sabotage from on high, just as the rude mechanicals project this fear of sabotage from below.

While Marston borrowed from the "bottom" half of *Dream*'s two-eyed vision for his portrait of Sir Oliver Owlet's Men in *Histriomastix*, Ben Jonson testifies to the divinatory nature of the other half of Shakespeare's vision by naming his 1611 masque and main protagonist "Oberon." As Joseph Loewenstein has argued, Jonson's masques hinge on an authorial fantasy likening the figure of the "author" to the King, and Shakespeare's "King of the Shadows," I would suggest, provides the prototype for this presumptuous analogy.[10] To Shakespeare's Oberon, Jonson's masque adds a specific nod to King James I:

> Before his presence, you must fall, or flie,
> He is the matter of vertue, and plac'd high.
> His meditations, to his height, are even:
> And all their issue is a kin to heaven.
>
> (*Works* 7:353)

As Jonson's description implies, the divine right of author-kings is "to identify oneself with the high and to spurn the low" (Helgerson 201). The masque, with its two-eyed form, is ideally suited to fulfilling this

10. See particularly Loewenstein's "Printing and 'The Multitudinous Presse': The Contentious Texts of Jonson's Masques," and, to a lesser extent, "The Script in the Marketplace."

authorial ambition, for it was comprised of the antimasque, a "low" vision of chaos performed by professional actors, and the masque proper, a "high" vision of order-restored performed by aristocrats and occasionally nobility. The more closely we look at the forest sequence of *A Midsummer Night's Dream*, the more it resembles this antimasque/masque structure, a likeness perhaps inspired by *Dream*'s conjectured origin as a piece commissioned for a noble wedding, the most common masque occasion.[11] Whereas Bottom and his cohorts clearly represent the disorder associated with the antimasque, the more esoteric fairy sequence stages the attempts of would-be "authors" to establish an altogether new vision of order restored, reflected, for example, in the lovers' defiance of Athenian law and Titania's assertion of the matriarchal prerogative. But to "discreet observers," as Kirby Farrell notes, this convenient ceremonial structure moving from disorder to order "may well have seemed blasphemous or cynical political trumpery" and, consequently, it was necessary that the "illusionistic and manipulative aspects of the masque…remain hidden. Were the magical process itself exposed, comprehended as a predictable *technique*, its efficacy would cease" (45). Such are the seeds of Shakespeare's own plot to deconstruct the lofty illusions of the "authors' theater" in *A Midsummer Night's Dream*, that is, with the technical assistance of a few mechanicals.

While the structure of the masque crystallizes two competing modes of authorship vying for hegemony in Renaissance England, the boundaries it erects between high and low, "authors" and players, order and improvisation were continually being contested within the realm of actual theatrical performance, where, as Helgerson reminds us, "the terms would not stay fixed" (201). Accordingly, in *Dream*, it becomes increasingly difficult to determine where the border lies between antimasque and masque, as the disorder of Bottom's artisanal stage subtly infiltrates Oberon's absolutist state. If we return, for example, to the initial juxtaposition of "antimasque" and "masque"—the exit of Bottom's company with the entrance of the Fairies—hints of Oberon's slackening

11. The suggestion that the play is influenced by the masque genre is borne out by the conditions surrounding its original performance, for it is likely that *Dream* was not only an occasional piece for a noble wedding but also may have been performed in Whitehall, the most popular locale of the Jamesian masques. It should be noted that the antimasque/masque structure is a Jonsonian trope used in his Jamesian masques, so this form is itself an unconsolidated "structure of feeling" when Shakespeare is composing *A Midsummer Night's Dream*.

grip on the world around him are already visible, as Titania's opening tirade unfolds a state of nature in rebellion. Lamenting the proliferation of "contagious fogs" (2.2.90), incontinent "rivers" (91), "rotted" and "drowned field[s]" (95, 96), and "alter[ed] seasons" (107), Titania makes it clear that Oberon's petty "brawls" (87) are to blame for this ubiquitous devolution of order—a spectacle we hardly expect from a budding "author"-king. The assertion of infallible authority is the defining feature of the masque-proper, which revolves around "the ability to overcome gravity, control the natural world, reveal the operation of the heavenly spheres" as "the supreme expression of Renaissance kingship" (Schmidgall 58). Our initial glimpse of the fairy kingdom, however, suggests that Oberon's illusion of power is, in fact, illusory.[12]

With the ensuing entrance of Puck, we begin to see the efficacy of both Oberon's and Bottom's performances diminished by what is known in film theory as "noise." "Noise" is a catch-all phrase used to account for the tension between the aspirations of the author and the contingencies associated with the apparatus of production. Puck, Oberon's understudy, is the first to hamper Oberon's production with noise, mistaking his cue to charm the eyes of a young Athenian. Puck is told by the aloof Oberon to "anoint [the] eyes" of a disdainful lover decked in "Athenian garments" when "the next thing he espies / May be the lady" (2.1.261–64). Seeing Hermia and Lysander lying apart from one another on the ground, Puck takes them for the alienated couple (Helena and Demetrius) whom Oberon intends to unite. Essentially, in the absence of certainty as to how to carry out Oberon's stage-directions, Puck improvises—a decision that is completely fitting with the dramatic lineage of his character, situated somewhere between the medieval Vice figure and the more contemporary Clown.[13] However, whereas improvisation was the trademark of the "players' theater," it was anathema in the "authors' theater." But Puck has not intentionally switched loyalties; rather, without necessarily meaning to, he has demystified the claim of the "authors' theater" to absolute control over their productions by exposing the consequences of Oberon's refusal to interact with the dramatic apparatus. In other words, Puck serves as a

12. I refer here to Stephen Orgel's influential book on Inigo Jones and the masque form, *The Illusion of Power*.

13. For a detailed account of the genesis of this figure, see Robert Weimann's chapter on "Popular Myth and Dramatic Poetry: Robin and Puck" in *Shakespeare and the Popular Tradition in the Theater*.

reminder that Oberon is an "author"/King of the Shadows only to the extent that he is present as a kind of *actor* himself to insure that his troupe will obey his script. Intent on denying the collaborative realities of dramatic production, Oberon, despite his occasionally impressive use of magic, is plainly dreaming.

The distinction between masque and antimasque all but disappears when the miscarriage of Oberon's authorial plot is juxtaposed with the reappearance of Bottom's mechanical players, who proceed to deconstruct their illusion-making potential all on their own. Because the mechanicals lack a sophisticated dramatic apparatus, they must make do with the props that nature provides them, a concession evinced by their efforts to create a playing space: "This green plot shall be our stage, this hawthorn brake our tiring-house, and we will do it in action as we will do it before the Duke" (3.1.3–6). As Patricia Parker argues, the mechanicals' unwitting "insistence on laying bare the mechanics of theatrical illusion (on exposing the means of its construction rather than producing the seamless or naturalized) calls attention both within and beyond the play to the production of other illusions and spectacles, including the theatrics of power itself" (106). But even as the mechanicals' rough-hewn wooden theater deconstructs the illusionistic space of the stage, the actions they perform therein testify to their enduring belief in the magic of theatrical representation, for the mechanicals are again fearful that their performance of *Pyramus and Thisbe* will "fright the ladies." Bottom, still playing the aspiring player-author, cries: "Not a whit! I have a device to make all well" (3.1.16) and insists that a prologue be written which "say[s] we will do no harm with our swords, and that Pyramus is not kill'd indeed; and for the more better assurance tell them that I Pyramus am not Pyramus, but Bottom the weaver. This will put them out of fear" (18–22). In one breath, Bottom systematically debunks the theory that Hamlet will refer to as "the purpose of playing," namely, to "hold a mirror up to nature" by maintaining, rather than maiming, theatrical illusion (*Hamlet* 3.2.20, 22). The imperative toward disillusionment demonstrated within Bottom's "players' theater" is not to be dismissed as purely accidental, however, for Bottom's ensuing attempt to compose a prologue reveals a desire not merely to elude censorship or punishment for the mechanicals' pending production but, more importantly, to promote a certain kind of *self*-presentation: "speak [the lines]...saying thus, or to the same defect: 'Ladies,' or 'Fair ladies'...If you think I come hither as a lion, it were pity of my life. *No!*

I am no such thing; I am a man as other men are' " (3.1.38–44, emphasis added). Buried in this bumbled moment of improvisation is a kind of "apology for actors" such as Heywood would publish in 1612 and, above all, an entreaty to be disburdened of the illusion that players are "artificial" or "mechanical" persons, despite the disparaging assertions of the "authors' theater."

At this point in the dream-work, Shakespeare's discrete visions of a sub-par "players' theater" and an overbearing "authors' theater" merge into a single nightmare through the creation of a composite figure. According to Freud, the composite figure emerges in a dream when it is clear that what connects its constitutive parts are shared hostilities toward the dreamer (356). Because these hostile elements combine to create an unrecognizable mix, the composite figure is easily "admissible to the dream-content without censorship" (357), prompting the dream-work to attempt to resolve the nagging hostilities it represents. In Shakespeare's play this composite figure is generated by the ever-metamorphosing, noise-inducing figure of Puck when he stumbles upon the mechanicals' rehearsal and announces that he will intervene as "an auditor / An actor too perhaps, if I see cause" (3.1.79–80). Almost immediately, Puck sees cause to transform Bottom's top into an ass's head, frightening the rude mechanicals out of their wits and, consequently, out of the woods. "O Bottom, thou art chang'd!" Snout cries in the act of fleeing, "What do I see on thee?" (3.1.114–15). Unaware of his change, Bottom replies: "What do you see? You see an ass head of your own, do you?" (116–17). Indeed, before the mechanicals can prove themselves men and defend themselves from the indictments of the "authors' theater," their fears are realized in Bottom's conversion to an ass. To make matters even worse for the self-legitimating cause of the "players' theater," Bottom degenerates into the stereotype of the player-author most despised by the nonplayer-authors, as he begins "piperly extemporising and Tarltonising" (Harvey, qtd. in Gurr 121).

Popularly known as clowning, Tarltonizing alludes to the stage-figure invented by Richard Tarlton, the original player-author. Tarlton was the country-bumpkin impersonator of lower-class grievances who made jigging and jesting all the rage in Elizabethan England, leading the "authors' theater" to declare its independence from such ribaldry in what Ben Jonson contemptuously called "these jig-given times" (qtd. in Gurr 225). Portraying a classic fall guy and gullible victim, Tarlton would typically sing and dance his way out of harm's reach. Bottom draws on this comic tradition when, suddenly conscious of the fact that someone is trying "to make an ass of me, to fright me" (3.1.120–21), he decides to

> ...walk up and down here, and...sing, [so]
> that they shall hear I am not afraid.
> The woosel cock so black of hue,
> With orange-tawny bill,
> The throstle with his note so trye,
> The wren with little quill —
>
> (3.1.122–28)

The piping voices of the wren, throstle, and woosel cock require only the addition of a tabor to recall verbatim the image of Tarlton consciously making an ass out of himself. In the latter part of the 1590s, however, Tarltonising met with increasing elitist denunciation and became generally passé.[14] Accordingly, Bottom's mulish reversion to Tarltonizing in a moment of crisis suggests in no subtle fashion the halted intellectual development of both the "players' theater" and it players, who face their theatrical future, as the play's punning logic insists, "ass backwards."

Despite Tarlton's popular reputation as a clown or fool, he also became known as an off-stage figure who enjoyed the favor of Queen Elizabeth herself. And it is in this spirit of Tarltonizing that Bottom suddenly finds himself in favor with Oberon's Queen Titania. Framed by Oberon's magic to fall in love with the first creature she spies, Titania wakes to find herself enamored of her unlikely ass-headed suitor. At this point in the dream-work, then, playerly anxieties about being counted among the asses collide with authorly anxieties about social miscegenation. One of the great complaints of the "authors' theater" was that players, especially during the unprecedented commercial success of the adult companies in the 1590s, waxed wealthier than the "authors" who devised scripts for them. Perhaps the most famous and symptomatic example of such a complaint was the attack launched by a group of anonymous university wits on the profession of playing in the *Parnassus* plays (1598–1601). These plays bemoan the fact that despite the consistently high nature of their accomplishment, "authors"

---

14. In 1599, William Kemp, Tarlton's living legacy, retired from the Lord Chamberlain's Men to effectively silence the tradition.

fall progressively lower in social and economic status when compared with players, who defy all established codes of rank and sumptuary legislation by "jet[ting] under gentlemen's noses in suits of silk," as Stephen Gosson bitterly complained (qtd. in Helgerson 201). In *Dream*, this very real fear of contagion from below is embodied in the social translation of Bottom (whose name alone implies that the only way is up) when he becomes the new favorite at the court of Oberon's fairy queen. Despite its farcical nature, Bottom's temporary promotion to royalty has dramatic social implications, for simply dismissing the ass-head as a symbol of stupidity is inappropriate in the context of Renaissance iconography, which interprets the ass as an image of vanity and, more significantly, licentiousness (Wyrick 438). After all, the ass was known as a beast of superior phallic endowment. Thus it is not surprising to find that Titania's language throughout her encounter with Bottom suggests sexual ravishment. Informing her servants to "Tie up my lover's tongue" and to "bring him silently" to her bower (3.1.201), Titania commands Bottom: "Out of this wood do not desire to go / Thou shalt remain here, whether thou wilt or no" (3.1.152–53). Unbeknownst to Oberon, Bottom has successfully penetrated his coterie theater.

Because the ass-headed Bottom represents a nightmarish montage of both the "players' theater" and the "authors' theater," this scene of unbridled social miscegenation also suggests a parody of the latter's aspirations to gentility. Promising to purge Bottom of his base beginnings, the swooning Queen Titania is determined to outfit Bottom with the trappings of aristocracy, exclaiming:

> I'll give thee fairies to attend on thee;
> And they shall fetch thee jewels from the deep,
> And sing while thou on pressed flowers dost sleep.
> And I will purge thy mortal grossness so,
> That thou shalt like an aery spirit go.

> (3.2.157–61)

This scene quite literally makes light of the nonplayer-authors' weighty desire to bypass the "mortal baseness" of the theater; the reigning fantasy is that their poetry will assume an "aery spirit" and rise above its own conditions of production, garnering aristocratic privileges for its "authors" without the gross mediation of players' bodies. This desire materializes when Titania weaves a garland of flowers for Bottom's mane—suggestive of the poet's laurel—and promotes him to the rank of "gentleman" (3.2.164). But Titania shortly discovers her error in judgment and loathes Bottom's visage, a discovery that exposes the "ass" in the aspirations of the nonplayer-authors, who believe that they too can become gentlemen by be-decking themselves with university degrees and weaving poetic fantasies of obscuring the "bottom" from which they came.

Compelled at last to intervene amidst Puck's composite maneuvers, Oberon emerges at this point to inquire about how his scripts have been performed. Proudly, Puck proceeds to inform him of Titania's infatuation with an "ass" of a "rude mechanical" (3.2.9), to which Oberon replies: "This falls out better than I could devise" (3.2.35). Given the fact that Oberon did not devise this plot, what choice does he have but to respond this way? Indeed, Oberon *can't* devise such a plot, for he is the maker of masques, a thoroughly aristocratic genre. Therefore, the only time he deigns to appear on stage to perform in his own intrigue drama is in the presence of royalty—when he anoints his Queen's eyes (2.2.27, 4.1.70)—a function befitting the later Jonsonian masque tradition of the author-king. Moreover, not only would it be beneath Oberon's social station to rewrite Apuleius's popular tale of *The Golden Ass* for cheap applause (as Puck does), but also, such a move would threaten his high position with the contagion of the low. In the absence of Oberon's controlling presence, then, it soon appears as though things have "fallen out" indeed, for Oberon indicates that he is uncomfortable, even jealous of Titania's "affair" with Bottom, explaining that

> meeting her of late behind the wood,
> Seeking sweet favors for this hateful fool,
> I did upbraid her, and fall out with her.

$$(4.1.48–50)$$

Oberon does not like the prospect of mixing his company with a "fool" who, as Helgerson reminds us, was the "central figure of the old players' theater" (223). Making it plain that Puck has improvised to a fault, Oberon repeatedly admonishes him: "This is thy negligence. Still thou mistak'st / Or else commit'st thy knaveries willfully" (3.2.345–46). Oberon raises a provocative point here; knowing Puck's history of willful knavery, it might be productive to think about him not as Oberon's budding understudy but as a kind of double-agent, engaged, for the moment, in revealing the illusionistic and manipulative aspects of the masque and, therefore, the mechanisms of its magic. As if suddenly overtaken by the need to flex his authorial muscles, Oberon proceeds to

expose the crude political trumpery of his magic, unwittingly demysti-
fying his own "illusion of power":

> When I had at my pleasure taunted her,
> And she in mild terms begged my patience,
> I then did ask of her changeling child;
> Which straight she gave me, and her fairy sent
> To bear him to my bower in fairy land.
> And now I have the boy, I will undo
> This hateful imperfection of her eyes.
> And, gentle Puck, take this transformed scalp
> From off the head of this Athenian swain,
> That he, awaking when the other do,
> May all to Athens back again repair,
> And think no more of this night's accidents
> But as the fierce vexation of a dream.

> (4.1.57–69)

Puck has forced this confession on Oberon's part by opening up for debate the question of who wears the real ass-head in this scene. After all,
it is Puck who delights in things "That befall prepost'rously" (3.2.121).

The construction of composite figures, according to Freud, "serves
various purposes in dreams: firstly to represent an element common to
two persons, secondly to represent a displaced common element, and
thirdly, to express a merely wishful common element" (357). I have already suggested how the linking image of the ass-head alternately paro-
dies the fears of both the "players' theater" and the "authors' theater."
What is of more interest to this analysis, however, is the role of the latter two components of Freud's paradigm for composite figures, namely,
the displaced and wishful elements, both of which converge in the
figure of Puck, the one figure in the play who operates within and between both the "players' theater" and the "authors' theater" but belongs exclusively to neither.

Perhaps the only Shakespearean character whose changes in title do
not signal a change in ontological status, Puck represents a montage effect in his own right, continually displacing the tokens of his presence in
the production process by changing shape and name. Indeed, he is the
ideal embodiment of the Foucauldian conclusion: "what matter who's

speaking?" (138). In his very first appearance, for example, Puck is addressed by the Fairy in four different ways: first as "lob" (2.1.16) as in Lob-lie-by-the-fire, a house-elf assigned menial labor; second as "Robin Goodfellow" (2.1.34), the popular practical joker of English lower mythology; third as "Hobgoblin" (2.1.40), a more menacing spirit; and fourth as Puck (2.1.40), a figure of still more "nefarious ancestry" whom Shakespeare converts to an "honest Puck."[15] Puck himself tells us that he is both a court fool and a free agent, explaining that he is Oberon's "servant" (2.2.268) and a "fear'd Goblin" (3.2.398–99). Although Puck often appears to be just a part of a larger apparatus of patronage and censorship embodied in the figure of King Oberon, we should resist viewing him as a prototype for the enslaved Ariel in Shakespeare's *The Tempest*. For it is clear that, with or without permission from the Monarch, Puck enjoys a fair amount of autonomy as an "auditor and actor" *and* as a kind of "author" in both the fairyland and rude mechanical productions. In fact, Puck's uncanny ability to mimic various identities and functions (as in 3.2, for instance, by alternately assuming the voices of Lysander and Demetrius) suggests not only the figure of the playwright who "im/personates another (many others) in the process of writing a play-text and thus refracts the supposed singularity of the individual in language" (Masten 368), but also the actor who disembodies himself to "shadow" the likeness of someone else. As Theseus reminds us: "The best in this kind are but shadows" (5.1.211). Consonant with this patronizing description of players, Theseus's assessment of the poet is no less condescending, as he describes the "poet's eye" which, "in fine frenzy rolling"

> Doth glance from heaven to earth, from earth to heaven;
> And as imagination bodies forth
> The forms of things unknown, the poet's pen
> Turns them to shapes, and gives to aery nothing
> A local habitation and a name.

> (5.1.12–17)

But there is something more in heaven and earth than in Theseus's philosophy, something distinctly "Puckish," and this is where Freud's wishful component enters Shakespeare's *Dream*.

---

15. See Winfried Schleiner's note in *Shakespeare Quarterly* titled "Imaginative Sources for Shakespeare's Puck" for a discussion of the radically different valences of this folkloric figure.

A Midsummer Night's Dream, as one critic observes, is "an 'exposition' of our best sleeps, including its author's" (Stewart 53). But *Dream* is more fundamentally an exposition of its "author's" worst nightmares. Whether deemed an "aery nothing" or a "kind of nothing," Shakespeare could not have rested easy with the dubious status allocated to the early modern dramatic "author" and, particularly, the early modern player-author in the 1590s. Accordingly, the "wishful element" embedded in Puck's dream-like composite of Oberon and Bottom is also decidedly linked to Shakespeare and is articulated, appropriately, by the rude mechanicals, who utter the following lament when they believe their show will not go on: "If our sport had gone forward, we had all been made men" (5.1.17–18). Becoming "made men" is what both Oberon's and Bottom's performances are all about. If Bottom *had* written his dream that "hath no bottom" (4.2.216), it would most certainly have revealed that, for his impersonation of Pyramus, he hopes to get a *raise* of "Sixpence per day" (4.1.23)—enough to buy a seat in a lord's room in the public theater and the minimum cost of entry to the semi-private venues like Blackfriars. Similarly, Oberon hopes to heighten his own authority by acquiring the Indian boy as the pièce de résistance of his "company," as well as by maintaining his shadowy subjects in obedience to his script. Thus, we might conclude that both Bottom and Oberon share a common wish to remove the ass-head from the word "author" by endowing it with semantic stability and ontological legitimacy in an historical moment wherein authorship is at best a "structure of feeling." By virtue of its sheer shock value, then, the collision between Bottom's and Oberon's theaters is intended to defamiliarize the hostilities on both sides just long enough for Puck to forge a montage of this common wish—and, in so doing, to facilitate the recognition that perhaps neither an exclusively "player"-oriented theater nor an exclusively "author"-oriented theater can guarantee that their dramatic "sports" will go forward.

Dream's peculiar resolution to this crisis of theatrical authority emerges in its internally staged performances, which generate one final collision between the two theaters of influence at stake in Shakespeare's play. Theseus sets this montage effect into motion when he chooses the popular play of *Pyramus and Thisbe* over the more sophisticated intrigues promised by the Athenian eunuch, the Bacchanalian revels, and the scholarly lament for the "death of Learning, late deceas'd in beggary" (5.1.45–53). Significantly, Theseus rejects this final option most vehemently, exclaiming: "This is some satire, keen and critical / Not sorting with a nuptial ceremony" (5.1.54–55). This line suggests a target beyond the play, issuing an overdue correction to the indiscrete criticism of Shakespeare's university wit rivals, whose second generation would create satires not sorting with any occasion other than the brief theatrical imbroglio which would, before long, consume itself with its own fire. Indeed, it never seemed to have occurred to the "authors" who scorned the adult companies that one day the boys who performed their learned scripts would grow up—no longer content, as Hamlet put it, "to exclaim against their own succession" (2.2.341). But if Shakespeare puts his learned, caustic competitors in their place, then he does the same to Bottom's company; for after the rude mechanicals receive the unprecedented honor of playing before a noble patron in an exclusive banqueting hall, they are forced to endure the audience's mockery and Theseus's veiled threat—precisely the one they sought to evade—of death-by-hanging. Swiftly rejecting Bottom's offer of an epilogue, Theseus exclaims:

> No epilogue, I pray you. For your play needs no excuse. Never excuse; for when the players are all dead, there need none to be blam'd. Marry, if he that writ it had play'd Pyramus, and hang'd himself in Thisbe's garter, it would have been a fine tragedy... (5.1.355–60).

If, earlier in this scene, Shakespeare alludes to the eventual "decease" of the scholarly contention showcased in the self-consuming "authors' theater," then here he evens the score, as Theseus employs the bawdy terms associated with popular tastes to threaten Bottom with the death of the player-author. Before comedy can devolve into tragedy, however, Oberon and Titania enter with their fairy trains to perform a masque-like vision of order restored, after which Puck calls an end to the petite wars *Dream* has staged—and perhaps even started: "Now to scape the serpent's tongue, / We will make amends ere long" (5.1.433–34).

The rude mechanicals' burlesque of *Pyramus and Thisbe* and, by association, *Romeo and Juliet*, suggests that the original structure of *auctoritas* that rendered Romeo's efforts at self-authorship tragic is no longer tenable—not only within the green world of romantic comedy into which Lysander and Hermia stumbled at the beginning of the play but also in the real world of "competitive social relations, which necessitated increasingly self-conscious care for one's presentation... 'on the market'" (Macrone 85). In such an unpredictable, metadramatic environment, the Puck-inspired impromptu performance—not the rehearsed readiness—"is all." And in this spirit, it seems apropos that the search for substitute textual formations begun in *Romeo and Juliet* ends with Puck's embodiment of the "auteur-function" in *A Midsummer Night's Dream*. Indeed, Puck's curious positioning in the play as the occasionally agential, often accidental, and ever-knavish "author" of and "player" among *Dream*'s extraordinary montage effects is reminiscent of Foucault's description of the author-function, which is "situated in the breach, among the discontinuities, giv[ing] rise to new groups of discourse and their singular mode of existence" (123). But like a dream, the *auteur*-function is located on the very edges of semantic availability, for it is a "structure of feeling" that emerges in the breach of an historical conflict between two modes of authorial production and, as such, it is only visible as a special effect. Born of the shifting alignments of the 1590s, the auteur-function relies upon the "collateral collisions" of montage in order to renegotiate notions of liaison and continuity at a juncture where no ends seem to meet, producing what Jameson refers to as "imaginary or formal 'solutions' to unresolvable social contradictions" (*Political Unconscious* 79). Shakespeare's theater was modeled on a very real composite vision of heterogeneous and often contradictory elements. We need only make a montage of Bottom's "players' theater" and Oberon's "authors' theater" to see the blueprint for the unprecedented event of 1603 when, following the conclusion of the War of the Theaters, Shakespeare's adult company players became "made men," indeed *gentlemen,* as The King's Men. Thus, the "auteur-function" does not revolve around "neutrality," as Gurr describes the positioning of Shakespeare's company during the War of the Theaters, but, rather, it depends upon a judicious and unmistakably "Puckish" eye for "noise"—between old and new, high and low, private and public, "authors" and "players," upstarts and asses.

⌀

> PUCK: Shall we their fond pageant see?
>   Lord what fools these mortals be.

After normalcy is restored in *A Midsummer Night's Dream*, Shakespeare's warning that a theater divided cannot stand was ignored in

favor of a declaration of War. In its aftermath, neither the "authors' theater" associated with the boys' companies nor the "players' theater" associated with the Henslowe companies survived for long, at least not in
their pure forms. Accordingly, if *A Midsummer Night's Dream* fails to
prevent the War of the Theaters and if dreams are, in fact, about wish-
fulfillment, then what wish *is* fulfilled by this play? What "third term,"
to return to Eisenstein's formula, is produced by *Dream*'s montage effects? Earlier in this analysis I alluded to a relationship between
Dream's wooded theater and the wooden theater of the Globe, a commercial venture begun in 1597 and christened by the performance of *Julius
Caesar* in 1599. What appears to have been a gamble by Shakespeare in
1597, namely, to become one of five "housekeepers" contracted to hold
shares in the Globe, was not really risky at all, for Shakespeare had already begun testing the viability of an *auteur's* theater, predicated on
constitutive collisions, in *A Midsummer Night's Dream*. Emerging as a
most profitable "material trace" born of the play's magnificent montage
effects, the Globe transaction not only maintained Shakespeare as an
"author" *and* a player in the company of the Lord Chamberlain's Men
but also granted him a partial share, if not the lion's share, of his labor
in both capacities, entitling him to a modicum of creative control that
his contemporaries could, in fact, only dream about. By 1599, then, the
War of the Theaters began for the "authors' theater" and the "players'
theater" and ended for Shakespeare, whose auteur's theater, embodied
in the totality of the Globe, guaranteed the singular success of Shakespeare's company all the way through the closing of the playhouses in
1642.[16] Thus, while Shakespeare left no traces of the hand that was engaged in the uncertain task of lending "aery nothing a local habitation
and a name" (5.1.16–17), his midsummer night's dream cast a most
substantial "shadow."

16. Shakespeare later threatened in *The Tempest* to abandon "the great Globe itself,"
perhaps in favor of the new fashion for masques, *tromp l'oeil*, and *deus ex machina* associated with venues like Blackfriars. However, as in *Dream*, this threat, too, is swiftly
"rounded with a sleep" (*Tempest*, 4.1.153, 158).

3

The Machine in the Ghost

Hamlet's Cinematographic Kingdom

Who is to deny that there is something rotten in our cinematographic kingdom? But why?

—Bazin et al., "Six Characters in Search of Auteurs"

That is the question.

—Shakespeare, *Hamlet*[1]

In 1957 the editorial board of the pioneering French film journal *Cahiers du Cinema* announced its desire to "create a new soul for French cinema" (Bazin et al. 34). Professing their dissatisfaction with the stagnant academicism, stylistic cowardice, and thematic complacency of post–World War Two film production, these "six characters" turned to Shakespeare's *Hamlet* to articulate their experience of aesthetic purgatory, finding themselves doomed for a certain time to walk the night in search of an "auteur film" (38). But is an auteur cinema to be or not to be? That is the question *Cahiers du Cinema* implicitly asks of Shakespeare's play and protagonist. Searching *Hamlet* for an answer to this question is curiously appropriate to the play's temporal logic, wherein "Time is out of joint" (1.5.188) and "anachrony," as Jacques Derrida suggests, "makes the law" (7). In conjuring Shakespeare's play

---

1. All citations of *Hamlet* are from Susanne Wofford's edition, Bedford Books, 1994. This version of the play is derived from the First Folio edition, but Wofford includes brackets to indicate disagreements raised by the First and Second Quarto editions.

to convey their own liminal state of cinematic being, then, the French cinephiles imply that they share a common "hauntology" with Hamlet and the state of Denmark.[2] Indeed, I will take them at their word and up the ante by exploring the implications of anachrony in the *opposite* direction. Roland Barthes has argued that film theory began in the eighteenth century with Diderot; I will argue that it begins in the seventeenth century with *Hamlet*.[3]

In his fascinating book *Like a Film: Ideological Fantasy on Screen, Camera and Canvas*, Timothy Murray investigates how cultural preoccupations and productions become legible as "cinematic 'happenings'" (5). According to Murray, the fundamental mechanisms of cinema—such as projection, shot selection, and montage—generate perceptual analogies that reveal the workings of ideological fantasy, so that what appears to be symbolized "inside" the film is always "what it would have symbolized outside of the film—that is to say, within culture" (Metz, qtd. in Murray 3). Because "the universality of ideological fantasy can make itself known only in symbolically specific ways," Murray contends that cinematographic analogy can be used to illuminate personal and communal traumas "from the Renaissance of Shakespeare and Caravaggio to…modernity" (4).[4] In this spirit, I will read Shakespeare's play "like a film." Focusing on Hamlet's cinematographic strategies for dealing with trauma, as well as the Ghost's presence as a "phantasmatic precursor" of cinema,[5] I will argue that the ideological fantasy at stake in Shakespeare's play is, paradoxically, an *escape* from theater. In keeping with Hamlet's cryptic admission that he has "that within which passes show" (1.2.76–86), I will explore the ways in which Shakespeare's play symbolizes—from within its own theatrical form— a nascent cultural preoccupation with the idea of "passing show" as that which *surpasses* theater, generating, in the process, what I will refer to as "the desire called cinema."[6] Rather than relying on a particular school of cinematic theory or practice, then, my appropriation of the cinematic metaphor invokes the earliest and broadest possible vi-

2. Derrida 10.

3. See Barthes's "Diderot, Brecht, Eisenstein" in *The Responsibility of Forms*.

4. Murray explores crises of representation and reality pertaining to sexuality, feminism, ecology, and postcoloniality, among many other specific cases of traumatic "cinematic happenings."

5. The term "phantasmatic precursor" is from Murray's *Like a Film* (5).

6. I borrow the phrase "the desire called" from Jean-François Lyotard and Fredric Jameson. In *Libidinal Economies,* Lyotard invokes "the desire called Marx" which Jameson

sion of cinema as a "wonder apparatus" capable of surpassing theatrical constraints and offering a window on the psychological interiors of
individuals.

In *Like a Film*, Murray traces the development of "phantasmatic precursors" of cinema ranging from painting and photography to the medi-
cal discourse of the gynaeceum. In *Hamlet*, the most obvious example of
a "phantasmatic precursor" of cinema is the Ghost. Calling into question the efficacy of theatrical representation, the Ghost "passes show"
by destabilizing the narrative continuities of space, time, and causality.[7]
As "the concretization of a missing presence, the sign of what is there
by not being there" (Garber 129), the Ghost poses a fundamental challenge to the representational space of the stage. As Robert Weimann explains of the Elizabethan theater: "the general absence of scenery on the
large acting area of the Elizabethan platform stage placed rigorous de-

---

in *The Geopolitical Aesthetic*, appropriates as "the desire called cognitive mapping." Both
theorists use the phrase "the desire called..." to invoke a cultural phenomenon—a space
of praxis—that exists prior to receiving a name.

7. The paradigm for this narrative logic is of course derived from the Aristotelian insistence on continuities of space, time, and action, which specifically conform to the narrative
structure of ascending action, climax, reversal, and denouement. Though Shakespeare,
the Russian constructivists, and Brecht (to name a few) attempted to defy these conventions through epic narration, the Elizabethan platform stage nonetheless demands a narrative logic defined by similar constraints of space, time, and action. Destabilizing these
continuities, the Ghost consistently interrupts the narrative sequence in *Hamlet*. For example, when the Ghost emerges during Barnardo's account of the preceding night's
watch, Marcellus commands Barnardo: "Peace, break thee off! Look where it comes
again!" (1.1.40). Similarly, in the midst of Horatio's attempt to theorize the Ghost's
meaning, the specter returns and Horatio responds by silencing himself: "But soft, be-
hold! lo where it comes again!" (1.1.126). Indeed, the Ghost produces a fracture point in
the "logico-temporal" (Barthes, "Third Meaning" 57) that not even Horatio, "the
scholar," can bridge (1.1.42). Driven to desperation, Horatio resorts to bullying the Ghost
into discourse:

> HORATIO: I'll cross it though it blast me. Stay, illusion!
>
>   ...stay and speak! (*The cock crows.*) Stop it, Marcellus.
>
> MARCELLUS: Shall I strike it with my partisan?
>
> HORATIO: Do, if it will not stand.
>
> BARNARDO: 'Tis here!
>
> HORATIO: 'Tis here!
>
> MARCELLUS: 'Tis gone!   [*Exit Ghost.*]
>
>   (1.1.127, 139–42)

Demanding a mode of intellection that exceeds such histrionic efforts to arrest its meaning and its image, the Ghost, like Hamlet, has that within which "passes show."

mands on the dramatist's use of language, the actor's use of gesture, and the audience's attentiveness and imagination" (*Shakespeare and the Popular Tradition* 215–16). Under such conditions, the Ghost's ontological difference from any other actor on stage could only be conveyed indirectly—in the harrowed reactions or special affects of other characters rather than through the technological special effects necessary to represent the Ghost's horrifying status as an absent presence. Similarly, with respect to time, the Ghost emerges as a symptom of the play's skewed or "rotten" logic of succession, indicating that the state of the monarchy—and temporality in general—are "out of joint." Citing Marcellus's famous remark about the "rotten" state of Denmark, Jacques Derrida explains this skewed temporality as follows: "Here again what seems to be out in front, the future, comes back in advance from the past, from the back. 'Something is rotten in the state of Denmark,' declares Marcellus at the point at which Hamlet is preparing, precisely, to *follow* the ghost" (10). In other words, ghosts demand a kind of "double-time" which, despite the occasional use of prophecy and retrospective narration in Shakespeare's plays, cannot be synchronized on the Renaissance stage. After his encounter with the Ghost, then, Hamlet may *tell* us that "Time is out of joint" (I.v.188) but he cannot *show* us. Not even the use of epic construction in Shakespearean drama can compensate for the fact that exits and entrances on the Renaissance stage mark narrative breaks only in a single direction.[8] Ultimately, then, as Hugo Munsterberg concludes, theater "can move only forward and not backward," for it is "bound by the fundamental principle of real time" (358). Finally, if we add space and time together, we arrive at the third component of narrative logic: causality. As we shall see, the Ghost offers Hamlet multiple causes for his return from the dead, splicing together a primary reason ("revenge") with a conflicting intention ("remember"), forcing Hamlet himself to become "out of joint" like the Ghost or, indeed, "like a film."

---

8. Not even the tutelage of the most expert Chorus, such as the one that prompts the audience in *Henry V*, can take us two places at once, for it is difficult enough to move convincingly in even one direction, as *Henry V*'s Chorus suggests:

> I humbly pray them to admit th' excuse
> Of time, of numbers, and due course of things,
> Which cannot in their huge and proper life
> Be here presented.

(Ch. 5.3–6)

In its capacity for disrupting the "logico-temporal," the Ghost serves as a useful hermeneutic for approaching *Hamlet* as a play that gestures beyond the representational technologies of early modern England.[9] This suggestion accords with Derrida's provocative contention in *Specters of Marx* that ghosts return from the future, that is, as signs of "the future-to-come" (xix).[10] However, before we can explore the extent to which Shakespeare's play resonates as a "parable of cinematic thinking," we must consider Hamlet's own attitude toward the existing modes of expression at his disposal, all of which correspond to what Marshall McLuhan calls "alphabetic thinking."[11] Unlike cinematic thinking, alphabetic thinking is confined to the demands of referentiality and the dictates of narrative continuity. In Shakespeare's play, the three principal modes of alphabetic thinking—scribal, typographic, and theatrical—all fail to represent that which "passes show" in Hamlet.

Like *Romeo and Juliet*, *Hamlet* demonstrates a considerable reliance upon the scribal mode of alphabetic thinking in the interests of trans-

9. I borrow the expression "logico-temporal" from Roland Barthes's essay on "The Third Meaning," in which he explores the capacity of photographic stills to disrupt narrative continuity. In *The Avant-Garde Finds Andy Hardy*, Robert Ray extends Barthes's paradigm to the film still and, more specifically, to the work of avant-garde filmmaking which, he explains, is preoccupied with "interruption" and strategies of "fragmentation designed to defeat a given continuity's ideological effect" (105).

10. Against the more conventional idea that ghosts return from the past, Derrida argues that ghosts "come back," paradoxically, "from the future" in order to rectify a fault "of time and of the times" (120). This idea is particularly suggestive with respect to *Hamlet* since, in this play, it is the future that is "rotten," for this future has been usurped by Claudius. Significantly, upon his very first sighting of the Ghost, Hamlet connects this specter with the status of his own future, exclaiming: "My fate cries out" (1.5.82). Agreeing to follow the Ghost wherever it leads, Hamlet tacitly consents to some kind of transaction between his body and his father's spirit. And now Marcellus's initially perplexing remark provides us with a more substantial gloss on the "rotten" state of Denmark, for as he watches Hamlet exit following the Ghost—a movement that recapitulates the appropriate line of succession from father to son—Marcellus suddenly realizes the extent to which the structure of inheritance has been corrupted in Denmark. Though Horatio assures Marcellus that regardless of what comes of the specter's visitation with Hamlet, "Heaven will direct it" (1.5.90–92), Marcellus knows that there is something more than the divine right of kingship at stake in the Ghost's summons of his heir, retorting: "Nay, let's follow him" (92). Marcellus's decision to follow Hamlet suggests that once the ghostly transaction takes place, it is not Heaven but Hamlet who will "direct" the future-to-come. And in more ways than one, "direct" is the operative word here.

11. In *The Avant-Garde Finds Andy Hardy*, Robert Ray explores what he calls "parable of cinematic thinking" in stills and films that allegorize "cinema's radical break with alphabetic culture" (114). See particularly Ray's chapter on "Fetishism as Research Strategy" (94–119).

ferring *auctoritas* from one generation to the next. Scribal communication revolves around "the shared texts, shared experience, shared culture, and shared ideological assumptions of medieval and early Tudor humanism that are understood by both speaker and audience" (Ayers 430). In *Hamlet*, the chief representative of this kind of thinking is Polonius, the character who utters the famous commonplace: "to thine own self be true." Because the transmission of scribal precepts is based on the "direct" inscription of *auctoritas* onto the memory, Polonius begins his famous speech to Laertes with the following instruction: "these few precepts in thy memory / Look thou character" (1.3.58–59). Polonius's use of the verb "character" here is a term derived from scribal culture meaning "to write," and more specifically, to copy. Whereas Laertes and Ophelia do, for the most part, "copy" or abide by their father's *auctoritas*, Hamlet stands out among the play's younger generation for his resistance to scribal authority. For example, upon receiving the Ghost's injunctions, Hamlet rejects the entire scribal regime of copying with a single gesture, as he vows to "wipe away" from the tablet of his memory "All saws of books, all forms, all pressures past / That youth and observation copied there" (1.5.99–101). In so doing, as P. K. Ayers explains, Hamlet "wipes away" the "basic structures of scribal education, the compressed summaries of all fields of knowledge which function as the cues needed to retrieve and employ the larger corpus already filed in the mind" (430). Indeed, at this point Hamlet has found a "corpus" more worthy of "copying."

Perhaps more than any other Shakespeare play, *Hamlet* employs books as props in the playing space to comment on the pitfalls and potentialities of the new typographic form of alphabetic thinking. And though we cannot know if the books referred to in the play exist in manuscript or printed form, it is likely that the latter is the case in Hamlet's scenes involving books. As Walter Ong observes, print culture produced books that were smaller and, therefore, more portable than those associated with manuscript culture (130–31); as such, printed books were ideally suited to the developing concept of personal privacy so noteworthy in Hamlet's character. However, despite Hamlet's auspices as a disciple of Wittenberg and the Guttenberg revolution associated with it, he appears plainly disinterested in the brave new world of the printed word. For while print had the advantage of "mechanically as well as psychologically lock[ing] words into space and thereby establish[ing] a firmer sense of closure than writing could" (Ong 48), this ideological fixity suggests precisely the kind of existence that Hamlet finds too, too "solid" (1.2.130).[12] Indeed, Hamlet's dissatisfaction with the innovations associated with the typographic transmission of ideas is implied in act two, scene two, where he enters the playing space reading a book. Asked by Polonius, "What do you read, my lord?" (2.2.190), Hamlet responds indifferently: "Words, words, words" (191), as if mimicking the proliferation of infinitely repeatable, identical texts made possible by the invention of moveable type. Unmoved by the possibilities of the printed word, Hamlet appears "locked into" a world that is too fixed, too repeatable—until, that is, he meets the Ghost.

Just as the Ghost implicitly challenges the ability of theater to represent aberrations in space, time, and causality, Hamlet, too, exposes the limitations of theatrical representation—through both his perceptions and productions.[13] Although it has long been argued that *Hamlet* is Shakespeare's most metatheatrical play and, therefore, an homage to the stage, I will argue that *Hamlet*'s meditations on the theatrical form expose its limitations and, in so doing, assume the search for a new technology of representation altogether. While theatrical representation embodies and animates the comparatively flat and confining forms of alphabetic thinking discussed above, it is bound to a grammar even more restrictive than scribal or typographic modes of communication—namely, the aforementioned continuities of space, time, and causality dictated by theater's reliance on "live" action. Perhaps, then, we should not be surprised by the fact that Hamlet, a character long-criticized for his failure to act according to the conventions of revenge tragedy, appears to situate himself beyond even theatrical communication. For example, in his first full speech to the Danish court, Hamlet defends his habit of mourning in stridently anti-theatrical terms, as Gertrude asks him "Why," when the death of fathers is so common,

12. A textual crux, "solid" is also glossed as "sallied" and "sullied." I have chosen to quote "solid" here rather than using Wofford's choice "sallied."

13. Offering specific commentary on the theater of Shakespeare's day, *Hamlet* provides us with a mimetic theory of acting during Hamlet's instruction to the players (3.2), a discussion of/intervention in the "War of the Theaters" in Hamlet's conversation with Rosencrantz and Guildenstern (2.2), and the most extensive play-within-a-play of any work in Shakespeare's oeuvre, in Hamlet's "The Mousetrap/The Murther of Gonzago" (3.2). *Hamlet*'s intervention in the War of the Theaters is extremely complicated and differs depending on which version of the play (Q1, Q2, F1) is consulted. For a provocative reading of *Hamlet*'s three texts in relation to the War, see Rosalyn L. Knutson's essay "Falconer to the Little Eyases: A New Date and Commercial Agenda for the 'Little Eyases' Passage in *Hamlet*."

"seems it so particular with thee?" (1.2.75). Seizing on the word "seems," Hamlet replies:

> Seems, madam? nay, it is, I know not "seems."
> 'Tis not alone my inky cloak, [good] mother,
> Nor customary suits of solemn black,
> Not windy suspiration of forc'd breath,
> No, nor the fruitful river in the eye,
> Nor the dejected havior of the visage,
> Together with all forms, moods, [shapes] of grief,
> That can [denote] me truly. These indeed seem,
> For they are actions that a man might play,
> But I have that within which passes show,
> These but the trappings and the suits of woe.
>
> (1.2.76–86)

Rejecting all the modes of expression available to him, Hamlet laments the inadequacies of the "inky" inscriptions of written grief, the dull "denotative" forms and shapes of typographic communication and, of course, the "dejected" moods of theatrical representation—none of which can adequately represent what he has "within."

> When everything feels like the movies
> You bleed just to know you're alive.
> —The Goo Goo Dolls, "Iris," from *Dizzy Up the Girl*[14]

Michael Almereyda's millennial film of *Hamlet* (2000) offers a stunning contemporary vision of *Hamlet* as a play poised on the verge of a new technology of expression. Like Shakespeare's Hamlet, who, as I shall argue, cannot represent that which he has within except through cinematic analogy, Almereyda's Hamlet (played by Ethan Hawke) unsuccessfully strives for a means of accessing his own feelings in an increasingly virtualized, "hyperreal" world. Almereyda conveys this

---

14. This song is from the movie soundtrack for *City of Angels* (Brad Silberling 1998), a remake, significantly, of Wim Wenders's *Wings of Desire* (1987). Both films are about the crisis of the undead.

message through the grainy, intimate medium of 35-millimeter film and its "indie" style production values, as well as through Hamlet's own independent productions as an aspiring filmmaker. Using the camera as an apparatus for projecting that which he possesses within onto the outside world, Hamlet relies on film as an arbiter of the onslaught of images and affects that characterize the "schizophrenic" experience of postmodern consumer culture—wherein, Žižek explains, the subject is compelled to search for images which "regulate the excess" of stimuli (*Tarrying* 210).[15] The most striking example of Hamlet's attempt to locate an image that will unify his internal and external reality occurs when he delivers his "to be or not to be" speech while walking down the "action film" aisle of a Blockbuster video store. Prompted to his revenge by the infinitely recyclable products of postmodernity, Hamlet struggles to sift through the barrage of surfaces that urge him to take action as he ponders the irony of his predicament: for what indeed can it mean to act—let alone "to be"—in a world "transformed into sheer images of itself" through "pseudo-events and 'spectacles'" (Jameson, "Postmodernism" 74)? That is the question implicitly raised by the film playing on the store monitor, *The Crow II* (Tim Pope 1996), which offers an additional gloss on Hamlet's metaphysical musings. Like Hamlet's own status as a "sequel" to his father, this sequel to *The Crow* (Alex Proyas 1994) relentlessly invokes the father-film which, significantly, is not only about revenge but also about the capacity of postmodern technology to restore a dead actor to virtual life—in the very real event that an action-film actor dies "in action." In an uncanny "cinematic happening," the star of *The Crow*, Brandon Lee, was killed on the set, leaving the filmmakers with no other choice but to recycle and manipulate previous footage of Lee in order to complete the film. The spectacle surrounding this tragedy-within-the-tragedy made *The Crow* a financial success, but Lee never got his share of the returns, nor could he return to revenge his "foul and most unnatural murther" (1.5.25). Akin to Shakespeare's melancholy Dane, then, this Hamlet is exhorted to his revenge by heaven and hell, but he cannot "make it a Blockbuster night" with a revenge sequel of his own. Like all the little lives that call out to him from beyond their videocassette graves, Ham-

15. In his essay on "Postmodernism and Consumer Society," Jameson contends that "schizophrenia" is one of the dominant cultural pathologies of postmodernity. This pathology is born of the confusing stimuli of postmodern consumer culture which, as Jameson explains, lead to the "schizophrenic experience" of "isolated, disconnected, discontinuous, material signifiers that fail to link up into a coherent sequence" (195).

let remains locked in the hyperreal purgatory of "to be or not to be," unable to translate these surreal promptings into a message that is real to him.

Perhaps this is because the only thing that is real to Hamlet *is* the reel. Indeed, Hamlet's unnatural, almost umbilical attachment to his handheld camera suggests that he replaced real family relations with reel ones long ago. When Hamlet is not shown watching movies in Almereyda's film, he is engaged in making and, in effect, re-making films, as he rifles through footage from home movies of his parents, Ophelia, and himself, hoping to find the perfect take on his own past. Almereyda's representation of Hamlet as a filmmaker thus offers a particularly compelling illustration of how "the screens of cinema and psychoanalysis converge with a charged likeness" (Murray 45), as the "cinematic happenings" of Hamlet's home life become—like the Ghost in Shakespeare's play—"virtual constructs related to the plane, screen, or mirror of [his] personal and communal projections" (5). Using film as a revisionary medium, this quintessentially postmodern Hamlet seems to operate under the assumption that by playing back these primal scenes, he can edit and, ultimately, master them, as he zooms in on particular frames—freezing and manipulating them in time and space. But like his photographer-girlfriend Ophelia, who tosses snapshots of her dead father in a frantic, final gesture of filial duty, Hamlet's filmic acts of remembrance—akin to his metacinematic musings about revenge— can only expose his family ties for what they really are, that is, *never real* in the first place. Nor can Hamlet's short film, "The Mousetrap," get him closer to the affective regions and relations he seeks beyond the virtual. As Lisa S. Starks observes, Hamlet "can only create a pastiche of images from various media, he cannot, in a modernist sense, create original art. Moving from silent film to classic Hollywood cinema, TV and advertising, Hamlet's short film fails to do much more than chronicle the history of the image."[16] As both a vehicle and a victim of this virtualized world, Hamlet ultimately has only one true course of "action," which lies in the act of choosing his simulacra. For the question is no longer "to be or not to be" but, more simply, *how* to be in a world in which *everyone* is a ghost. And like Shakespeare's protagonist, this

---

16. This quotation is from Lisa S. Starks's forthcoming essay on Almereyda's *Hamlet*, titled " 'Remember me': Psychoanalysis, Cinema, and the Limits of Modernity," which will appear in a special issue of *Shakespeare Quarterly* (Summer 2002).

Figure 1. All the world's a screen: Hamlet (Ethan Hawke) and Ophelia (Julia Stiles) at the movies in Michael Almereyda's millennial *Hamlet*. Miramax Films, 2000. Photo: Larry Riley. Courtesy of Photofest.

Hamlet will rise to the challenge by taking virtual matters into his own hands, getting his revenge by becoming, ironically, a real ghost.

Both Shakespeare's early modern protagonist and Almereyda's postmodern prince are in search of a medium of expression that lies somewhere beyond the affective technologies of the cultural moment in which they find themselves. However, quite unlike the many filmed *Hamlet*s that precede Almereyda's version, this millennial film realizes what Shakespeare's *Hamlet* merely gestures toward: that this family drama is—at least from Hamlet's perspective—really more of a "home movie." For just as Almereyda's Hamlet uses the camera to project his interior psychological states from multiple angles and in different exposures, Shakespeare's Hamlet employs his "mind's eye" like a cinematic apparatus, generating the equivalent of zooms, fades, pans, and jump cuts in an effort to create an external reality that matches the disruptions in the logico-temporal he carries within. Similarly, while Almereyda's Hamlet tries unsuccessfully to make the virtual "real," Shakespeare's Hamlet works in vain to make the theatrical "cinematic." Indeed, in Shakespeare's play, Hamlet's production of "The Mousetrap" reveals only the failure of theatrical representation to accommodate the demands of his mind's eye, signaling a crucial turning point in the development of his cinematic thinking. As we shall see, if, prior to "The Mousetrap," the shots generated by Hamlet's cameratic gaze suggest the work of *decoupage,* or shot-construction before production, then after the failure of the play-within, Hamlet's cinematic thinking moves in the direction of montage, or editing performed during post-production.[17] It is almost as if, through Hamlet's obsessive playing out and replaying of scenarios of remembrance and revenge, Shakespeare imagines a mode of authorial intervention that bypasses the provisionality of performance, extrapolating, from Hamlet's acts of memorial reconstruction, the opportunities for perfection associated with the invention of recording technology. Of course, Shakespeare's Hamlet has neither a camera nor a cutting room, but Almereyda's film enables us to imagine what Hamlet's home movies might have looked like—if only he had the technology to represent "that within which *passes* show."

Citing Abel Gance's famous remark that "Shakespeare, Rembrandt, Beethoven will make films," Marjorie Garber explains that in a sense "we can say Gance's prediction has come true. 'Shakespeare'—Shakespeare's works—has made films. But in another sense, Gance's words describe what Shakespeare had already achieved, in furnishing his plays with...ghosts who demand to be written" (18). What distinguishes *Hamlet* from Shakespeare's other plays featuring ghosts is that Hamlet has a ghost in his machine—a ghost "within" which, like the Ghost without, demands to be written. But given Hamlet's complaint that all existing avenues of expression prove "[weary], stale, flat and unprofitable" (1.2.133–34), he necessarily struggles to represent that which he has within—except through cinematic analogy. In fact, Hamlet could be credited with the invention of the close-up, creating its early modern equivalent in his obsessive exploitation of the soliloquy form. Designed to surpass "show" or theatrical gestures, the soliloquy offers a verbal simulation of an approach shot that resembles the close-up in its focused attempt to represent the interiorized feelings of a character. Of course, the declamatory, exaggerated style of delivery featured in

---

17. I refer here to montage in the broadest sense as "editing" and, more specifically, editing as continuity rather than editing as collision.

the soliloquy will become unnecessary with the invention of the movie camera; but Hamlet cannot wait, for as early as his first soliloquy he attempts to convert his own body into an apparatus of projection in an effort to break out of his depressing two-dimensionality. Making a "virtual construct" of his own flesh, Hamlet commands it to "melt, / Thaw, and resolve itself into a dew!" (129–30).[18] However, such a radical and selective contraction of space is possible only through the "partial and preselected" perspectives of camerawork (Aston and Savona 101) or, as Hamlet's musings suggest, through suicide. Like Abel Gance, then, Hamlet's projections forward "writ[e] history backward" (Garber 18), as he imagines a new use for his world-weary flesh that will materialize some four-hundred years later, when the phenomenon of cinematic projection enables "the massive outer world [to lose] its weight" and to be "clothed in the forms of our own consciousness" (Munsterberg, qtd. in Tibbets 218).

Hamlet's unconventional reflections on the uses of space are clothed in his painful consciousness of his mother's unconventional abuses of time—specifically, the time separating mourning from remarriage. Continuing his first soliloquy, Hamlet engages in an increasingly frantic inquiry into his mother's indiscretion, simulating a cinematic "chase tempo" which, as Sergei Eisenstein explains, employs rapid cutting to convey the "expressive sharpening of [an] idea" (*Film Form* 12). Lamenting his mother's "o'er hasty marriage" to Claudius (1.2.57), Hamlet sharpens his focus as follows:

> That it should come [to this]!
> But two months dead, nay, not so much, not two....
> Must I remember?...and yet, within a month—
> Let me not think on't! Frailty, thy name is woman!—
> A little month, or ere those shoes were old....
> Within a month...
> She married—O most wicked speed: to post
> With such dexterity to incestious sheets...

$$(1.2\ 137-38,\ 145-47,\ 156-57)$$

Attempting to reduce his mother's mourning period to a size commensurate with his anger, Hamlet "cuts" the two months separating his fa-

---

18. Murray describes "cinematic happenings" as *virtual* constructs related to the plane, screen, or mirror" of "personal and communal projections" (5).

ther's funeral from his mother's re-marriage down to "not quite" two months, to "within a month," to a "little month," and at last to the split-second utterance "ere these shoes were old." In so doing, his chop-logic conveys a blatant disregard for the sense of "real time" on which live theatrical action relies, creating an illusion more akin to the cinematic jump cut. Such temporal compression was one of the principal ways in which early cinema sought to distinguish itself from theater, featuring race scenes and chases in an effort to showcase the unique temporal possibilities of cutting. Provocatively, it was cinema's ability to create incisions in the logico-temporal that led theorists such as Walter Benjamin to liken the work of the cameraman to that of the surgeon, a metaphor that suggests the distinctly morbid component of Hamlet's own capacity to "cut." Indeed, Hamlet's penetrating inquiries will be subject to further sharpening, as he learns to render cuts not only in words but also in flesh.[19]

The frenzied spatial and temporal illusions that Hamlet produces in his first soliloquy ignore the Renaissance innovation of fixed perspective, resembling instead the dollying motion of a movie camera. In his ensuing encounter with Horatio, however, Hamlet adds freeze-frames to his repertoire of cinematic thinking. Like Almereyda's postmodern prince, who zooms in on and freezes selective moments of his family history in order to analyze and revise them, Shakespeare's Hamlet suddenly conjures a static image of his deceased father:

> HAMLET: My father—methinks I see my father.
> HORATIO: Where, my lord?
> HAMLET: In my mind's eye, Horatio.
> HORATIO: I saw him once, 'a was a goodly king.
> HAMLET: 'A was a man, take him for all in all.
>
> (1.2.184–87)

What is significant about this scene is the work of Hamlet's mind's eye *after* Horatio proceeds to inform him that his father's Ghost has, in fact, returned to haunt the battlements of Elsinore, for Hamlet's gaze does not "take him for all in all," but rather, nervously takes him *apart* bit by bit:

19. Hitchcock's films tend to represent this cinematic death-drive through their obsession with scenes of "cutting" (i.e. murder with a sharp weapon) which mirror the directorial "art of film editing or cutting per se.…It is as though, for Hitchcock, filmmaking were an art of murder, of killing off the living body on and as the strip of celluloid that would render it cinematic" (Peucker 45).

HAMLET:	[Was he] Arm'd, say you?[20]
[MARCELLUS, BARNARDO]:	Arm'd, my lord.
HAMLET:	From top to toe?
[MARCELLUS, BARNARDO]:	My lord, from head to foot.
HAMLET:	Then saw you not his face.
HORATIO:	O yes, my lord, he wore his beaver up.
HAMLET:	What, look'd he frowningly?
HORATIO:	A countenance more
	In sorrow than in anger.
HAMLET:	Pale, or red?
HORATIO:	Nay, very pale.
HAMLET:	And fix'd his eyes upon you?
HORATIO:	Most constantly....
HAMLET:	Stay'd it long?
HORATIO:	While one with moderate haste might tell
	a hundreth.
[MARCELLUS, BARNARDO]:	Longer, longer.
HORATIO:	Not when I saw't.
HAMLET:	His beard was grisl'd, no?
HORATIO:	It was, as I have seen it in his life,
	A sable silver'd.
HAMLET:	I will watch to-night,
	Perchance 'twill walk again.

(1.2. 226–33, 236–43)

Unable to represent Hamlet's fetishistic approach shot toward his dead father's visage, this scene must settle for capturing Hamlet's growing anxiety through relentless verbal inquiry, offering an excellent example of the play's impossible attempt to articulate "the desire called cinema." Underscoring the fear that Hamlet's fetishistic desire encodes, Derrida observes: "Hamlet gets to the head, to the face, and especially the look beneath the visor. As if he had been hoping that, beneath an armor that hides and protects from head to foot, the ghost would have shown neither his face, nor his look, nor therefore his identity" (8). Indeed, not even Hamlet's methodical, zooming inventory of his father's features can create the special effects necessary to explain the cause of the Ghost's return.

20. The brackets around "Was he" are mine as opposed to the editor's and are implemented in the interest of clarity.

The corporealizing activity of Hamlet's mind's eye in this scene offers him a proleptic vision of his pending encounter with his father's Ghost, leading Hamlet into a series of anxious reflections on the third component of the narrative triumvirate: causality. In an essay titled "From Logos to Lens," Yves de Laurot explains that proleptic visions are central to cinematic productions: "the important point to make here," de Laurot contends, "is that this vision has to exist *before* creation: in fact, were it not for this vision, there would be no creation...Because a work of art *is* the man's projection beyond the real—it is the inevitable *praxis* that stems from his moral needs" (582). Projection was a concept that was very much on the mind of the Renaissance, as demonstrated by the perspectival projections of Italian Renaissance painters, whose work was later revisited as one of the original models for the camera lens (Baudry 304). Much later, of course, Freud likened the phenomenon of psychological projection to the complicated mechanisms of cinematic camerawork (Baudry 300). But what exactly is the cause linking Hamlet's cameratic vision of the Ghost to the psychological projection of his "moral needs"? Appropriately, in the very next scene, Hamlet engages in a distinctly moralizing discourse that provides some clues into this relationship. While denigrating the Danish custom of excessive drinking in the course of a conversation with Horatio, Hamlet abruptly begins a diatribe on the faults of "particular men" who,

> for some vicious mole of nature in them,...
> Or by some habit,...
> Carrying, I say, the stamp of one defect,...
> Shall in the general censure take corruption
> From that particular fault.

> (1.4.23–24, 29, 31, 35–36)

It is significant that this often overlooked speech occurs immediately after Horatio has informed Hamlet of the Ghost's visitations, for the Ghost is precisely such a baffling "particularity," resonating—in cinematic terms—as a "Hitchcockian blot," a "mysterious detail that 'sticks out,' that does not 'fit' into the symbolic network of reality and that, as such, indicates that 'something is amiss'" (Žižek, *Looking Awry* 116). However, Hamlet's investigation into "particularities," "moles," and "defects," stops short of linking these blots directly to the Ghost; for if "something is amiss" with the father, then there must also be something wrong with the son.[21] Is it possible, then, that the cause of the Ghost's return is related to a particular defect in Hamlet's own nature?

Hamlet's particular fault, his symptom, is the unnatural degree of filial obligation he feels toward his dead father. When we first encounter Hamlet in the social setting of the Danish court, he is being admonished by Gertrude for wearing his black mourning garb well beyond the dictates of custom. According to his mother, Hamlet stubbornly insists on searching "for [his] noble father in the dust" (1.2.71), a behavior that she identifies, significantly, as "particular" to Hamlet. And indeed, against the standard explanation that Hamlet's symptom stems from the collective Oedipal trauma of his father's death and his mother's speedy second marriage, I will argue that Hamlet's excessive mourning masks a "particular fault" in *him*. In other words, might Hamlet's fastidious obsequies be intended to compensate for his failure to pay enough attention to his father *when he was living?*[22] Is Hamlet, in other words, a bad son?[23] The scant information the play

21. In his chapter of *Primal Scenes* titled "Shakespeare in the Ear of Hegel," Ned Lukacher performs an extensive reading of the "mole" as "a figure of the flaw in Hamlet's own character" (205); however, he takes this reading in the standard Oedipal direction of Hamlet's fascination with his mother's desire.

22. This suggestion reverses the traditional psychoanalytic reading of Hamlet's "mourning and melancholia," a reading Lukacher summarizes as follows: "Claudius and his court, along with the audience, assume that Hamlet's problem is excessive mourning...[and that it is] attributable to the depth of Hamlet's sorrow over his father's death. Hamlet's first soliloquy makes it unmistakably clear, however, that what 'passes show' in the depths of his inwardness is precisely the opposite of excessive mourning. As Jacques Lacan argues in his essay 'Desire and the Interpretation of Desire in *Hamlet*,' the problem of 'central importance' in the play is that of 'insufficient mourning.' *Hamlet*, writes Lacan, 'is a tragedy of the underworld,' an underworld of sexual loathing and Oedipal guilt" (213). I prefer, however, to read Hamlet's behavior following his father's death in less cynical and less Oedipal terms. Rather than arguing with what the play actually says to an apparently naïve audience (i.e., Hamlet is genuinely disturbed by his father's premature death), I wish to take the play at its word and fill in the blanks where the play doesn't offer any explanations—that is, concerning the nature of Hamlet's relationship with his father before his death. It is in this gap, I will speculate, that insufficient obsequies *to the living* have occurred. However, like all Shakespeare's plays, and particularly a play with a complex textual history like *Hamlet*, the text(s) will accommodate multiple readings.

23. In a provocative unpublished paper titled "The Mousetrap," Stephen Greenblatt suggests that in the Jewish tradition, Hamlet might be considered the "Wicked Son." During the Passover ritual of the Seder, the Wicked Son "refuses to incorporate the memory of enslavement and the exodus from Egypt; he refuses to swallow the story as his own" (3). Greenblatt takes as his point of departure for this reading *Hamlet*'s own dramatization

offers concerning Hamlet's life reveals that he spends most of his time at school and, despite his mother's wishes, he does not look upon Denmark "like a friend" (1.2.69). We also know that Rosencrantz and Guildenstern, "being of so young days brought up with him" (2.2.11), will be called in on a special mission to gain access to Hamlet's "mystery," as if Hamlet's own family were a stranger to him. The only other view into Hamlet's past is provided by the grave-digging scene, wherein we learn that the king's jester, and not the king himself, was Hamlet's playmate of choice as a child. In short, we know nothing about Hamlet as a son; the play makes no effort to establish a special relationship between Hamlet and his father in the past that would explain Hamlet's excessive grief in the present. Could it be, then, that Hamlet's solemn commitment to (by)passing "show" stems from a lifelong refusal to show up? Has the "heir apparent" not been "apparent" enough? Why else does an *apparition* in the likeness of Hamlet's father return to seek him out? I would suggest that Hamlet's "symptom," the "inky cloak" of mourning he wears inside and out, is his own way of denoting his particular fault as the "black sheep" of the family, and the Ghost's return from the dead resonates as proof positive of this conclusion. Thus, perhaps what the Ghost is "presumed to know" as he enters Hamlet's picture is the fact that young Hamlet—like Almereyda's celluloid Prince—has always already been a ghost, that is, a ghost *son*.[24]

This possibility materializes in the split-causality that the Ghost offers Hamlet for his return from the dead. It is a famous Lacanian axiom that the dead return because they were not properly buried; and while this is, in fact, one of the causes that the Ghost discloses, Hamlet appears to expect a different explanation. Indeed, when the Ghost exclaims, "If thou didst ever thy dear father love—" (1.5.24), Hamlet cuts him off and cries: "Oh God!" (25), as if he were anticipating a thundering paternal rebuke of the "bad" son. But Hamlet is quickly forced to relinquish this drama of his own making when the Ghost proceeds to charge someone else with wrongdoing, ordering Hamlet to revenge

---

of the ingesting of "leftovers" based on the play's participation in the Eucharistic controversies of the sixteenth and seventeenth centuries.

24. Throughout the play, the Ghost emerges as a screen for Hamlet's projections and, more specifically, as the subject of Hamlet's transferential desire. Consequently, the Ghost becomes a kind of analyst-figure for Hamlet. In the psychoanalytic dynamic, the analyst is positioned as the subject "presumed to know in advance...the meaning of the analysand's symptoms" (Žižek, *Sublime* 185).

his uncle's, not his own, crime. While this injunction may bring with it a sigh of relief, it does not satisfy the moral needs to which Hamlet's proleptic vision of the Ghost is bound. In fact, Hamlet's desire for punishment is not satisfied until the Ghost fades from view, his last words forming the mandate Hamlet has been waiting for: "Adieu, adieu, adieu! remember me" (1.5.91). If the Ghost serves, in part, as a "virtual construct" or screen for Hamlet's "personal and communal projections," then in this scene, the Ghost is positioned as a kind of analyst figure who is "presumed to know" the meaning of Hamlet's symptom. This presumption is reinforced by the injunction to "remember," which is perfectly attuned to Hamlet's symptom of *excessive* remembrance of the dead. But why "revenge" *and* "remember"? Elaborating on the Lacanian explanation of why the dead return, Zizek suggests that the "return of the dead is a sign of a disturbance in the symbolic rite, in the process of symbolization; the dead return as collectors of some unpaid symbolic debt" (*Looking Awry* 23). If, as I have speculated, young Hamlet has misrepresented Old Hamlet by being a "bad" or "ghost" son—by rendering insufficient obsequies to the living— then perhaps the Ghost's injunction to "remember" is intended to register a disturbance in the process of symbolization that characterized Old Hamlet's *life,* while the more obvious injunction to "revenge" reveals the disturbance (murder) that led to the improper symbolization (natural causes) of Old Hamlet's *death.* Appropriately, the double-bind generated by this split injunction can only be resolved with recourse to the cinematic thinking that Hamlet has been practicing—thus far in vain—all along.

"Revenge" and "remember" inscribe more than a conflict of actions and words, for they also demand opposing temporalities which, as suggested at the outset of this discussion, only a ghost—or a film—can occupy. While "revenge" designates a future action (destined to restore the integrity of the future line of the Danish monarchy), "remember" designates a return to the past (designed to restore the integrity of the dead king's living memory). Despite the apparent impossibility posed by the Ghost's injunctions, this double-bind is actually custom-made for a "bad" son like Hamlet, for it invests his symptom with meaning and endows his formerly morbid penchant for cinematic thinking with new life. Significantly, cinema itself emerged as the bad offspring of

theater. As "a hybrid medium that emerge[d] amid the ruins of traditionally sanctioned cultural forms" (Peucker 55), cinema played havoc
with time, space, and causality in a way that led its early critics to de-
nounce it as a "monstrous birth" (63). But cinema, like the Ghost in
Hamlet, maintains the capacity to "revenge" its dubious past through its
ability to edit or, in the Ghost's terms, "re-member," its own history, as
Susan Sontag explains:

> This youngest of arts is also the one most heavily burdened with memory.
> Cinema is a time machine. Movies preserve the past, while theatres—no matter
> how devoted to the classics, to old plays—can only "modernize." Movies res-
> urrect the beautiful dead; present intact vanished or ruined environments...
> solemnly ponder irrelevant or naive problems...[they are] saturated with a
> kind of pathos. (370)

Like the pathos that "passes show" in Hamlet, cinema maintains privileged access to forgotten affective regions, remembering them for the
sake of the living and the dead. In this spirit, then, Hamlet is commanded by the Ghost to "resurrect the beautiful dead" and to damn the
wicked living and, in so doing, he is given the opportunity to remember himself as a "good" son, as his ecstatic response to the Ghost's injunctions implies:

> Remember thee!
> Ay, thou poor ghost, whiles memory holds a seat
> In this distracted globe. Remember thee!
> Yea, from the table of my memory
> I'll wipe away all trivial fond records,
> All saws of books, all forms, all pressures past
> That youth and observation copied there,
> And thy commandement all alone shall live
> Within the book and volume of my brain,
> Unmix'd with baser matter. Yes, by heaven!
>
> (1.5.95–104)

By "wiping away" all the learned precedents of alphabetic culture,
Hamlet suggests that the Ghost is communicating in an altogether different language—one that, as Robert Ray explains of cinematic thinking, "inevitably interrupts the story he already knows, [leading him to]
tak[e] time to inspect details, follow leads, imagine other outcomes"

that lie beyond alphabetic logic (109). The question thus becomes, once Hamlet has inscribed "the logic of the ghost" directly onto his brain (Derrida 63), how exactly does he pursue this new lead?

In response to this question, Linda Charnes likens Hamlet's predicament to that of the *noir* detective who finds himself trapped in a universe defined only by the impossibility of narrativization, wherein every potential clue or lead generates, quite literally, a dead end. As Žižek explains, in the *noir* universe, "narrativization becomes possible only when the subject is, in a sense, already dead" (*Enjoy* 151). Because the *noir* sensibility refuses linearity, order, and consistency, it requires a different kind of logic, one that can accommodate the ontological impossibilities that inhere in it; and indeed, it is no coincidence that *noir* detective fiction and cinema emerged in the same historical moment. Accordingly, what makes the anti-logic of *noir* so suggestive with respect to *Hamlet* is the fact that its chaos and contingencies derive from a crucial mutation in the status of authority and, more specifically, paternal authority. In contrast to the logic-and-deduction universe of classical detective fiction, wherein the symbolic authority or Law of the Father is stable, benign, and fundamentally absent, in the *noir* universe, the Father is obscenely present and, therefore, can no longer function as the guarantor of the symbolic prohibitions—juridical, ethical, filial, and sexual—that are ascribed to him (Charnes, "Dismember me" 2). In Shakespeare's play, the Ghost is a product of precisely this kind of mutation in paternal authority, returning as "the obscene, uncanny, shadowy double of the [Law] of the Father" as the *"father who knows"* (Žižek, *Enjoy* 158–59). More than the subject presumed to know the "particular fault" of the son, the Ghost harbors scandalous knowledge about the father, revealing a figure who died stuffed with sin, "full of bread / With all his crimes broad blown, as flush as May" (3.3.80–81). The knowledge that the Ghost purveys "is therefore a very special kind of knowledge, a knowledge of enjoyment, i.e., the knowledge which is by definition excluded from the Law in its universal-neutral guise" (Žižek 159). Functioning on a level beyond the symbolic operations of language and paternal Law, *Hamlet*, Charnes ingeniously observes, "is the first fully *noir* text in Western literature, and Prince Hamlet is the first *noir* detective" (4).

I would argue, however, that Shakespeare's Hamlet has more in common with an aspiring *film noir* director than he does with the reluctant detective of *noir* fiction, and that Shakespeare's play is, therefore, not "like *any* film," but more specifically, like *film noir*.[25] For if, in the *noir* universe, narrativization becomes possible only when the subject is, in effect, already a ghost, then Hamlet, as we have begun to see, experiences this logic not as a trap, but as a triumphant means of escaping his boredom with the dull linearity of his own existence. Moreover, the skewed temporal logic fully realized in *film noir*—wherein every forward movement leads only backward—suggests the ideal cinematic analogy for fulfilling the Ghost's split injunction to revenge *and* to remember. But why, then, doesn't the play end with Hamlet's *noir* production of "The Mousetrap"? Critics have long wondered why Hamlet fails to seize this "live" opportunity to carry out the Ghost's demands. Such a feat could actually be accomplished during a stage performance, for early modern records indicate several performances involving sword-play that did, "accidentally," turn lethal. This connection between theatrical spectacle and death is also suggested by the fact that "real life" events such as executions were often performed as though they were plays—on a scaffold before a crowd.[26] And within the play of *Hamlet*, the conditions for actualizing the Ghost's demands during "The Mousetrap" are made possible by Hamlet's clever creation of Lucianus, the avenger, as nephew to the king, paralleling Hamlet's own relationship to his murderous uncle. Thus we are led to expect that either the actor playing Lucianus or Hamlet himself will take revenge against Claudius when the remembrance of the regicide is staged. Why does this fail to happen? Perhaps because Hamlet's oft-cited hang-up over revenge is just a decoy for his real problem of remembrance. As Charnes explains, "the Ghost commands Hamlet to 'Remember me' even as he makes the task impossible, speaking the paternal mandate from a corrupted enunciatory site that splits the integrity of the Law

25. Roy Armes explains that the director emerged when "stage production was transformed by mechanisation and the introduction of electric lighting" (44). I should also point out that a study titled *Shakespeare the Director* examines in great detail Shakespeare's use of gestural language, but the author, Ann Pasternak Slater, focuses exclusively on the mechanics of "directorial" language as opposed to investigating the ideological and historical implications of designating Shakespeare as a "director" when we can't even designate him an "author." Significantly, Robert Weimann observes that in the course of "The Mousetrap," "Hamlet as *actor-character* revitalizes, on the dramatized plane of stylized art, the legacy of the Vice actor as director and Master of ceremonies theatrical" ("Mimesis" 285). I wish to demonstrate, however, the ways in which Hamlet is more of a Master of ceremonies "cinematic."

26. See James Shapiro's essay " 'Tragedies naturally performed': Kyd's Representation of Violence."

open to reveal its kernel of obscene enjoyment" ("Dismember me" 5). Beautifully conveyed in Almereyda's film, Hamlet is, in effect, torn between making the action film and editing—if not enjoying—all the "dirty stills" along the way.[27] After all, he has been saddled with the task of "setting things right" (1.5.189), which is not the same thing as merely getting the job done. Consequently, following his failure to execute the Ghost's desired performance through his "live" acts of *decoupage*, Hamlet turns to the possibilities of montage, as a means of reconciling revenge and remembrance through cinematic "cutting."

In his debut production of "The Mousetrap," Hamlet employs the "logic of the ghost" to his advantage, as his cinematic thinking gravitates toward the *noir* techniques of skewed framing, disembodied voice-over narration, and chiaroscuro effects, all of which conspire to generate a *coup de théâtre*.[28] Hamlet's first challenge as an aspiring director is to insure that the audience views the performance exactly as he sees it developing in his mind's eye. But this effect is easier to imagine than to create, for the principal disadvantage of the Elizabethan platform stage lies in the fact that no two sections of the audience have precisely the same perspective on the action. By the end of "The Mousetrap," then, "no one in the theatre, on stage or in the audience, will have 'seen' its action completely—nor...authoritatively" (Shurgot 6). In an effort to circumvent this problem, Hamlet, in an extraordinary act of *de-*

---

27. I borrow the phrase "dirty still" form Timothy Murray, who explores one dirty still in particular from Olivier's portrayal of Othello, which captures a shot of Desdemona's cheek, accidentally smeared with the residue of Olivier's blackface, emerging as the "trac[e] of nothing less than the Eurocentric horror of miscegination, a horror often glossed over by a criti-cal overinvestment in the humanist theme of the enigma of moral darkness" (110).

28. Hamlet's instructions to the players set the stage for this *coup de théâtre*, for his instructions are more appropriate for film than stage actors:

Speak the speech, I pray you, as I pronounc'd it to you, trippingly on the tongue, but if you mouth it, as many of our players do, I had as live [lief] the town-crier spoke my lines. Nor do saw the air too much with your hand, thus, but use all gently, for in the very torrent, tempest and, as I may say, whirlwind of your passion, you must acquire and beget a temperance that may give it smoothness....I would have...a fellow whipt for o'erdoing Termagant, it out-Herods Herod, pray you avoid it. (3.2.1–7, 12–13)

Hamlet's obsessive instruction-giving is noteworthy not only for its distinct portrait of a director unilaterally providing verbal and gestural cues but also for the sense that even here, Hamlet is expressing the desire to "pass show," for the subtlety he demands from the players is difficult to reproduce in a theater, particularly in a platform-stage venue like the Globe, which requires the exaggerated projection of voice and gesture.

coupage, attempts to operate multiple "cameras," hoping to skew the audience's perspective to match the bent of his mind. Positioning Horatio as a "steadi-cam," Hamlet instructs him to observe Claudius in the act of watching the performance "[w]ith the very comment of thy soul" (3.2.75). In contrast to Horatio's stationary gaze, Hamlet assumes a perspective on the action that simulates mobility. Despite his assertion that "I must be idle" (85), Hamlet's frenetic verbal intrusions on the diegesis betray this claim, suggesting instead the tremulous bias of hand-held camerawork as he pre-selects revealing angles for capturing the onstage action—while still attempting to maintain a stable, "objective" perspective through Horatio's gaze. Hamlet soon discovers, however, that because this is a "theatre event," something "always 'live,'" as Susan Sontag explains, "The Mousetrap" will "not admit a comparably exact integration of effects" (369) to meet the demands of his cinematic thinking.

After only two exchanges between the Player King and Queen, Hamlet attempts to generate the verbal equivalent of establishing shots through the ghostly *noir* technique of voice-over narration, beginning a series of intrusions upon the diegesis in an effort to direct both the onstage and off-stage drama into a single vision of revenge and remembrance. The problem with voice-over, however, is that it is a mode of communication traditionally identified with the "failure of meaning" in a world in which voice and image are radically heterogeneous, resonating as "proof of the faltering of the hero's knowledge, his inability to control or comprehend the image which then often seems to belie what he says" (Copjec 185). In the case of "The Mousetrap," such incompatibilities between image and voice emerge in the gap between the spectacle occurring on stage and the drama developing in Hamlet's mind. Increasingly agitated over the audience's failure to respond to this latter "plot," Hamlet steadily compromises his status as an invisible, controlling presence. For example, in response to the Player-Queen's couplet: "In second husband let me be accurs'd! / None wed the second but who kill'd the first," Hamlet utters: "That's wormwood!" (3.2.167–69). Later, he will echo this sentiment when the Queen repeats her vow, interrupting anxiously: "If she should break it now!" (212). In both cases, Hamlet employs the classic gambit of voice-over narration to elicit a response from the audience attuned to that which *passes* show, urging them to look beyond the obvious. As Joan Copjec might argue, Hamlet's speech-acts convey the entreaty: *"Don't read my words; read my desire!"* (187). Privy to knowledge that the audience lacks, Hamlet hereby attempts to draw attention to the pending irony of the Queen's words; but this is a subtlety made impossible by the conditions within which he must work. And because Hamlet cannot simultaneously show the audience the equally important plot that is developing among off-stage actors such as Claudius and Gertrude, Hamlet engages them in the midst of the performance, approximating the effects of shot-reverse-shot camera work:

> HAMLET: Madam, how like you this play?
> QUEEN: The lady doth protest too much, methinks.
> HAMLET: O but she'll keep her word.
> KING: Have you heard the argument? is there no offense in't?
> HAMLET: No, no, they do but jest, poison in jest—no offense
>   i' th' world.
> KING: What do you call the play?
> HAMLET: "The Mouse-trap." … 'Tis a knavish piece of work,
>   but what of that? Your Majesty, and we that have
>   free souls, it touches us not. (3.2.217–28)

Following this certain breach of theater decorum, Lucianus, the revenger, enters the scene and Hamlet directs him to "Begin, murtherer, leave thy damnable faces and begin. Come, the croaking raven doth bellow for revenge" (237–39). But Hamlet's Poe-like croaking only widens the gap between image and voice, damnable faces and damning words, as he exclaims aloud: "'A poisons him i' th' garden for his estate. His name's Gonzago, the story is extant, and written in very choice Italian. You shall see anon how the murtherer gets the love of Gonzago's wife" (246–50). Though the audience fails to comprehend the meaning of Hamlet's desire, Claudius rises immediately and cries: "Give me some light. Away!" (254). Echoing the king, Polonius exclaims: "Lights, lights, lights!" (255). But there is no "action" to follow this call for lights, for the play is "given o'er" (253) and Hamlet has directed it right through to its sabotage.

Though we cannot know the extent to which Claudius's response is a register of his guilty conscience, we can discern an important and often overlooked detail about Hamlet's production: the fact that "The Mousetrap" employs chiaroscuro effects. Quite distinct from the natural daylight productions of the Elizabethan outdoor theater, Hamlet's production simulates, or appears to take place within, the more controlled environment of a dimly lit castle interior. The absence of lights in Hamlet's production functions much in the same way as a darkened movie theater does, heightening the audience's sensibilities and priming them for the suspense and suspicion-filled environment of the *noir* universe. Such a setting also creates the ideal forum for Hamlet's voice-over narration which, coming from the darkened space of the audience, generates the verbal equivalent of rear projection. Significantly, it was precisely this kind of experimentation with light and shadow that led to the birth of the modern stage director in the second half of the nineteenth century, for the introduction of electric lighting created the conditions of possibility for the director to emerge as a controlling presence in production. Yet what "The Mousetrap" demonstrates is quite the opposite: clearly, Hamlet is a very bad theater director and an even worse detective, ever-compromising his undetectability as a behind-the-scenes figure. Indeed, Hamlet's regular intrusions upon the diegesis are the exclusive prerogative of the *film* director, whose ghostly presence shapes the film product at various stages without being seen by the film audience. And it is this particular "logic of the ghost" that prompts Hamlet to embrace a different cinematic strategy for piecing together revenge and remembrance: montage.

Unable to exert total control over the performance and reception of his live production, Hamlet turns to the post-production practice of montage or, more appropriately, editing, as a means of executing—to perfection—the Ghost's commands. Along with the creative control offered by the invention of the movie camera, editing is the other critical development that led to cinema's break with theater, for through editing, cinema "passes show" by piecing together a final picture without relying on live or continuous action. And as Robert Ray astutely observes in a chapter titled "Fetishism as Research Strategy," if the movies' "relentless unrolling [from reel to reel] prevents your noticing anything except the narratively underscored details, then the only response is to stop the film" (103). After "The Mousetrap," Hamlet's increasingly fetishistic practice of "stopping the film" of his own making—in order to research the *noir* details of the Ghost's narrative—generates another cinematic analogy, this time resembling what Timothy Murray calls "filmic retrospection." Significantly, Murray cites the editorial enterprise of Heminge and Condell as one precedent of filmic retrospection: "in gathering together Shakespeare's many texts as a monument to be looked back on, they [Heminge and Condell] tamed the temporal and generic disorderliness of the plays, printed texts, and performances.... Indeed, the editorial enterprise of Heminge and Condell froze Shakespearean textuality into...[a] monument of unified representation" (105). From this Shakespearean precedent, we can surmise the two critical functions of filmic retrospection: one is a formal, economic function of removing any excess that threatens the coherence of the representation, while the other revolves around the act of recuperation, which means creating a narrative "of a past safely negotiated and reappropriated" (Heath, qtd. in Murray 106). In *Hamlet*, these two functions correspond to "revenge" and "remembrance," respectively.

Explored through the lens of filmic retrospection, the scene following "The Mousetrap" in which Hamlet passes up an opportunity to kill Claudius makes far more sense. Stealing upon Claudius in the act of prayer, Hamlet whispers: "Now might I do it [pat], now 'a is a-praying; / And now I'll do't—and so 'a goes to heaven, / And so am I [reveng'd]" (3.3.73–75). But Hamlet doesn't do it "pat" at all. A textual crux, "pat" is occasionally rendered "pah," and the latter is more appropriate at this particular moment, since Hamlet claims with disgust that to act now would mean sending Claudius "fit and seasoned for his passage" to heaven (86). Consequently, Hamlet turns from the acting of revenge to the contemplation and compilation of alternative scenarios for fulfilling the Ghost's command:

> Up, sword, and know thou a more horrid hent;
> When he is drunk asleep, or in his rage,
> Or in th' incestious pleasure of his bed,
> At game a-swearing, or about some act
> That has no relish of salvation in 't—
> Then trip him, that his heels may kick at heaven,
> And that his soul may be as damn'd and black
> As hell, whereto it goes.
>
> (3.3.88–96)

Hamlet's act of filmic retrospection not only buys him yet more time to "set things right" but also enables him to "cut" the otherwise perfect revenge scene in which he finds himself. Rather than killing Claudius "pat," then, Hamlet will return to scenes such as this, gathering fragments of footage in hopes of re-membering them when the time is *exactly* right for setting his deadly montage into motion.

Hamlet's hesitation in this scene reinforces the traditional conclusion that he is incapable of revenge. But as Almereyda's film poignantly reveals, Hamlet's *reel* problem is remembrance, and Shakespeare's early modern prince is no exception to this postmodern rule, for he, too, remains trapped in the virtual reality of his own over-active imagination. What Almereyda's film makes strikingly clear is that Hamlet *enjoys* the act of remembrance, rendering visible the point at which the *noir* father's knowledge of enjoyment returns to corrupt the son. For on one level, the Ghost's injunction to remember is a commandment to edit the filthy edges of his father's memory—to send him fit and seasoned for his passage to heaven. But on another level, the commandment to remember is, unavoidably, a commandment to enjoy, an inducement to ponder the father-king in all his obscene glory. Hamlet's ensuing confusion between excising and enjoying his father's faults is brilliantly represented in Almereyda's depiction of Hamlet as an obsessive editor of his own home movies. Similarly, in his above encounter with Claudius, Shakespeare's Hamlet is the victim of a comparable ambivalence; but what distinguishes this scene from Hamlet's earlier voice-overs is that here Hamlet protests too much—that is, too much *pleasure* in the act of "stopping the film" and delaying revenge. Indeed, there is more at stake in Hamlet's voice-over narration than a simple divergence "from the *truth* of the image" (Copjec 185). Rather, what emerges in this scenario which, to all appearances, presents Hamlet with the perfect revenge by calling the bluff of Claudius's penitence, is nothing less than the truth of enjoyment, for "the destiny of [Hamlet's] voice-over seems not to be exhausted by its function as message. An excess of pleasure, a private enjoyment, seems to adhere in the act of speaking as such" (Copjec 186). Clearly, Hamlet's obsessive shots of Claudius engaged in drunken, angry, gaming or, worse, "incestious" exploits contain precisely this residue of private enjoyment and an excess of pleasure—neither of which Hamlet appeared to experience prior to the Ghost's visitation in act one of the play. Whereas before Hamlet was a solemn student from Wittenberg who engaged in moralizing discourses about Danish over-indulgence, after the Ghost's visitation, Hamlet's musings appear to be contaminated by the licentious side of the father-king. Accordingly, the longer Hamlet delays his performance of revenge, the more he gets to "enjoy his symptom" of remembering his father's dirty stills.

Perhaps this explains why in the final third of the play, Hamlet seems inclined to kill everyone *but* Claudius. For in killing this living substitute for the obscene father, Hamlet removes the screen onto which he can project "the pleasure of illusions and the fetishistic preservation of the residues of trauma" that the Ghost, in its fleeting appearances, has both awakened and frustrated in Hamlet (Murray 5).[29] With the help of other screens, however, Hamlet can engage in editing his father's tarnished memory without sacrificing his enjoyment. Polonius is the first victim of Hamlet's new-found capacity to "cut," and it is particularly significant that just prior to his death, Polonius offers to take Gertrude's place as a "screen" between Hamlet and his antics, advising her as follows:

> Tell him his pranks have been too broad to bear with,
> And that your Grace hath screen'd and stood between
> Much heat and him. I'll silence me even here;
> Pray you be round [with him].... [*Polonius hides behind the arras.*]

> (3.4.2–5)

Discounting the phenomenon of the Ghost itself, it would be hard to locate a more proto-cinematic scene in Shakespearean drama than the murder of Polonius, for he is killed at the very moment that he projects sound and movement onto the two-dimensional screen behind which he hides. But while cinema "passes show," Polonius cannot; accidentally sending a tremor through the arras, Polonius is stabbed by Hamlet, who disingenuously inquires as to whom he has slain. "Is it the King?" (3.4.26), Hamlet asks, knowing very well that he has just left the king praying. Subsequently, having used Polonius's live body as a screen for the rehearsal of revenge, Hamlet appropriates Polonius's dead body as a screen for the projection of remembrance, as he proceeds to orchestrate a flashback sequence designed to remember his father, quite literally, in a better light.

"I took thee for thy better" (3.4.32), exclaims Hamlet upon discovering Polonius's dead body behind the arras. Yet the word "better" is fraught with ambiguity here; for is it possible that rather than mistaking Polonius for Claudius, Hamlet mistakes this "cinematic happening" for the Ghost, whose better days have been all but eclipsed by the revelation of his foul disports? Indeed, in the act of deliberating over whether or not to kill Claudius in the previous scene, Hamlet admits

---

29. This is the fetishistic function, according to Murray, not only of cinema, but also of ideology.

for the first time that his father was not the man he took him for in his mind's eye:

> How his audit stands who knows save heaven?
> But in our circumstance and course of thought
> 'Tis heavy with him.

(3.3.82–84)

And in the Ghost's own words, Old Hamlet's last moments were, in effect, overexposed—the final snapshot capturing a figure "[c]ut off even in the blossom of [his] sin ...With all [his] imperfections on [his] head" (1.5.76, 79). But Hamlet knows that the best way to take revenge against this recent memory is to remember his father as the better of the two father-kings. Consequently, Hamlet begins this process of filmic retrospection by taking out a portrait of his father, which he proceeds to compare with that of his uncle in an effort to reverse the ontological status of these two brothers, converting Claudius into a ghostly unknown quantity while rolling his father's credits.[30] Once again assuming a controlling perspective, Hamlet directs Gertrude's gaze at the portraits as follows:

> Look here upon this picture, and on this,
> The counterfeit presentment of two brothers.
> See what a grace was seated on this brow:
> Hyperion's curls, the front of Jove himself,
> A station like the herald Mercury
> New lighted on a [heaven-]kissing hill,
> A combination and a form indeed,
> Where every god did seem to set his seal
> To give the world assurance of a man.
> This was your husband. Look you now what follows:
> Here is your husband, like a mildewed ear,
> Blasting his wholesome brother. Have you eyes?
> Could you on this fair mountain leave to feed,
> And batten on this moor? ha, have you eyes?

(3.4.53–67)

---

30. This portrait functions as a "perspectival object" intended, along with Hamlet's ensuing narration, to "concretiz[e] the perception of the unknown through visual and linguistic perspectives that aim to make visible or plastic what is not" (Murray 108).

Relying on "the visual machinery of orderly perspective, framing, and mirroring" (Murray 107), Hamlet removes Old Hamlet's imperfections and restores the sanctimony of his image through this idealizing sequence of film-like stills. The problem is, however, Hamlet doesn't simply "stop the film" here, for in the act of excising from memory his father's crimes, Hamlet's fascination with them is triggered and he turns to projecting their foul residue onto Claudius. This is why Zizek contends that the central problem of the *noir* universe is that there are always *two* fathers. Indeed, once the *noir* father splits the Law in half, the subject becomes caught between a fundamentally absent paternal ideal and the excessively present obscene "father who knows." For Hamlet, then, this problem of two fathers translates into the production of two "films": one emerges from Hamlet's ongoing attempt to erase the presence of obscene information about his father, restoring him to the absent and, therefore, ideal figure of memory, while the other film stems from Hamlet's projection of this perverse "psychoaesthetic waste and excess" onto Claudius (Murray 106), a figure whose lechery and treachery require little embellishment. Knowing, however, that these two films—and fathers—cannot coexist, Hamlet's act of remembrance must culminate in revenge, that is, in permanently cutting Claudius from the picture. The problem this presents for Hamlet is that his directorial energies appear to be far more invested in and aroused by this other "film" and, indeed, his other "father."

Pasolini argues that in every film there is always "the temptation to make another film" (554). Indifferent to pretexts of visual mimesis and plot, this underlying film emerges in stylistic "insistences" such as gratuitous "detail" and "digressions," as well as uncommon "framing" and "montage-rhythms" (554). As we shall see in Chapter Five, Kenneth Branagh's *Hamlet* (1996) offers a striking illustration of this temptation to make another film, as Branagh's extra-diegetic fascination with Derek Jacobi leads him to posit an unmistakable family resemblance between his Hamlet and Jacobi's Claudius, further skewing the filial dynamics of Shakespeare's play by suggesting that Claudius is Hamlet's *real* father. Similarly, in Shakespeare's play, Hamlet's acts of filmic retrospection too quickly leave his noble father in the dust to focus on Claudius. Continuing his diatribe against his mother's choice of a second husband, Hamlet casts his own fascination with Claudius in diversionary terms that position him as the "subject presumed to know" the meaning of *Gertrude's* desire. In so doing, Hamlet sets up Gertrude for her role in the *noir* universe as "traumatic Thing," the woman whose sexual appetite defies age, reason, and decorum:

HAMLET: You cannot call it love, for at your age
                   The heyday of the blood is tame, and it's humble,
                   And waits upon the judgment, and what judgment
                   Would step from this to this? ...
                   O shame, where is thy blush?
                   Rebellious hell,
                   If thou canst mutine in a matron's bones,
                   To flaming youth let virtue be as wax
                   And melt into her own fire. Proclaim no shame
                   When the compulsive ardure gives the charge,
                   Since frost itself as actively doth burn,
                   And reason panders will.

QUEEN: O Hamlet, speak no more!
                   Thou turn'st my [eyes into my very] soul,
                   And there I see such black and [grained] spots
                   And will [not] leave their tint.

HAMLET: Nay, but to live
                   In the rank sweat of an enseamed bed,
                   Stew'd in corruption, honeying and making love
                   Over the nasty sty!

QUEEN: O, speak to me no more!
                   These words like daggers enter in my ears.
                   No more, sweet Hamlet!

HAMLET: A murtherer and a villain!
                   A slave that is not twentith part the [tithe]
                   Of your precedent lord, a Vice of kings,
                   A curpurse of the empire and the rule,
                   That from a shelf the precious diadem stole,
                   And put it in his pocket—

QUEEN: No more!

Enter Ghost [*in his night-gown*]

HAMLET: A king of shreds and patches— (3.4.68–71, 81–102)

Coinciding with Hamlet's repeated refusals to cease his fetishistic prying into Claudius's sexual and political vices, the Ghost's entry serves

as a reminder that this other, action-packed home movie is threatening to usurp the more mundane, static picture of Old Hamlet that the young prince has just taken pains to construct. Significantly, Hamlet anticipates precisely this reason for the Ghost's return:

HAMLET: Do you not come your tardy son to chide,
That, laps'd in time and passion, lets go by
Th' important acting of your dread command?
O say!

GHOST: Do not forget! This visitation
Is but to whet thy almost blunted purpose.

(3.4.106–11, 115)

The real challenge this scene poses is determining whether or not the Ghost is just a figment of Hamlet's mind's eye or if it does, in fact, return to rebuke him for his delay. One clue toward unraveling this riddle is the fact that Gertrude cannot see the Ghost, for she accuses Hamlet of bending his "eye on vacancy" and holding discourse "with th' incorporal air" (3.4.117–18). Recalling that the members of the Watch *could* see the Ghost, this scene appears to represent the most dramatic discrepancy of image and voice in the play, suggesting that Hamlet's voiceover narration no longer even attempts "to describe the world that the narrator inhabits," but rather, "present[s] that world at the point where he is abstracted from it" (Copjec 186). In other words, through his discourse "with th' incorporal air," Hamlet "clings not to the community with which speech put him in touch, *but to the enjoyment that separates him from that community*" (186, emphasis added). Indeed, Hamlet's increasing resistance to performing his ghostly mandates is suggested by what the Ghost "says" to Hamlet:

But look, amazement on thy mother sits,
O, step between her and her fighting soul
Conceit in weakest bodies strongest works,
Speak to her, Hamlet.

(3.4.112–15)

Here "the Ghost" provides Hamlet with a diversionary mandate, adding further fuel to his deferral of revenge. But what is more interesting about the Ghost's command to step between Gertrude and her fighting soul is the way in which it positions her as a femme fatale. In his attempt to redefine the role of the femme fatale in *film noir*, Žižek argues against the traditional explanation that woman represents the "symptom" or fall of man; rather, he explains that the femme fatale is really the structural center of the *noir* universe, in that she exists to mask "the true traumatic axis of the noir universe, the relationship to the obscene father" (160). Thus, whether or not the Ghost actually materializes in the above scene is irrelevant. What is far more important is the fact that Gertrude is positioned as a screen onto which the ontological horror of the obscene father is projected, as the psychomachian struggle over his soul becomes *Gertrude's* problem. Even before Hamlet can "speak to her," then, Gertrude has served her purpose as femme fatale, for while the Ghost enters the scene as the punitive "father who knows," he exits as the benign father who knows *best*, offering Hamlet both the advice and the opportunity to remember himself as a "good" son by intervening in Gertrude's personal drama.

Signs of this treatment of woman-as-mask begin to emerge much earlier in the play in Hamlet's opening invective against Gertrude and, more explicitly, in his imputation of Ophelia. Not coincidentally, it is only *after* Hamlet's initial encounter with the Ghost that he turns his venomous accusations of Gertrude toward Ophelia, tacitly revealing the fact that "what is ultimately at stake in the *noir* universe," as Žižek explains, is the impossibility of "a viable, temperate relation with a woman; as a result, woman finds herself occupying the impossible place of the traumatic Thing" (*Enjoy* 160). Positing Ophelia as "traumatic Thing," Hamlet famously instructs her to get to a "nunnery," punning on the double meaning of "nunnery" as "whorehouse":

> Get thee to a nunn'ry, why wouldst thou be a breeder of sinners? I am myself indifferent honest, but yet I could accuse me of such things that it were better my mother had not borne me: I am very proud, revengeful, ambitious, with more offenses at my beck than I have thoughts to put them in, imagination to give them shape, or time to act them in. What should such fellows as I do crawling between earth and heaven? We are arrant knaves, believe none of us. Go thy ways to a nunn'ry. Where's your father? (3.1.120–29)

What is so fascinating about Hamlet's misogynistic tirade against Ophelia is that its real destination is not Ophelia but her father Polonius—and all fathers for that matter—just as when Hamlet similarly imputes Gertrude, purporting to pluck out "what's the matter" with his mother, his anger is really directed at what's amiss with the father. But as in *film noir*, in *Hamlet*, not even the repudiation of the woman can restore the lost relationship with the father; neither the death of Ophelia nor the rejection of Gertrude can screen Hamlet from the truth that once the Ghost fades from view, there is nothing there—and, as in Almereyda's *Hamlet*, there may have been nothing there to remember in the first place. Thus, the only "thing" that Hamlet's incessant voice-overs make visible is "no thing"—"the void as such, contentless and nonsensical" (Copjec 188).

As a would-be director torn between enjoying his symptom and giving up the Ghost, Hamlet's real problem is, clearly, remembrance. For the fact that Hamlet has no qualms about killing Polonius, nor with speaking "daggers" to Gertrude and Ophelia, not to mention sending Rosencrantz and Guildenstern "without debatement" to their death, is no subtle indication that Hamlet is capable of rendering cuts in flesh even as he sutures gaps in memory.[31] And yet there can be no doubt that the play's most spectacular "cinematic" events—the sea mutiny, the sabotage of Rosencrantz and Guildenstern, Hamlet's boarding of the pirate ship—all take place off-stage, underscoring the fact that Hamlet does, in fact, lack a medium for his message. His "desire called cinema" can, in other words, only be realized through surrogate screens. The most striking illustration of Hamlet's deadly ability to perform another off-stage variation on the theme of revenge and remembrance occurs when he uses Rosencrantz and Guildenstern's commission in the same way he used Polonius's arras, that is, as a screen for rehearsing the fulfillment of the Ghost's mandates. Revising the royal commission for his own death, Hamlet writes an order for Rosencrantz and Guildenstern to be "put to sudden death, / Not shriving time allow'd" (5.2.45–47)—an act of filmic retrospection that materializes in the actual cutting of Rosencrantz and Guildenstern beneath the Sexton's axe. And revenge is not the only agenda fulfilled by Hamlet's invisible hand, for as in the earlier scene with Polonius, Hamlet splices revenge and remembrance together, informing Horatio that he sealed Rosencrantz and Guildenstern's fate with his "father's signet" (5.2.49)—a memory in miniature of Old Hamlet's reign. It is most curious, then, that despite being exhorted to action by the success of this

---

31. At this point, we might add to our consideration of the ways in which *Hamlet* reads "like a film" the notion that film narrative "leaves behind a trail of corpses" (Corrigan, qtd. in Peucker 38). Paraphrasing Timothy Corrigan, Brigitte Peucker explains that in film, "a series of little murders" takes place "as each frame in the sequence is replaced by another" (Peucker 38).

latest test-run, Hamlet still desires the approval of a test-audience, as he suggests to Horatio:

> Does it not, think thee, stand me now upon—
> He that hath kill'd my king and whor'd my mother,
> Popp'd in between th' election and my hopes,
> Thrown out his angle for my proper life,
> And with such coz'nage—is't not perfect conscience
> [To quit him with this arm? And is't not to be damn'd,
> To let this canker of *our nature* come
> In further evil?
>
> (5.2.64–70, emphasis added)[32]

What is evident from this speech is that Hamlet would rather continue to mourn the loss of his ideal father-king than face the reality that the other, cankerous king is just a symptom of the obscenity that is endemic to the "rotten" state of Denmark. But Hamlet's words ultimately signal his understanding that what is rotten in the state of Denmark is the state itself—the Law—and, as a result, the cankers that once emerged in the "particular faults" of "particular men" are now ubiquitous, indeed, an indelible part of "our nature." Thus, in this speech detailing his motives for killing the king, Hamlet's rationale for revenge is no different than it was at the beginning of the play; what *is* different is his recognition that, in this distinctly *noir* universe, "perfect conscience" does not exist—for anyone.

It is appropriate that the final scene of the play is staged as a fencing match, for here, in a most literal fashion, all the other takes imagined by Hamlet during his process of filmic retrospection are brought to bear on a single moment of decisive editing. But the events fail to go according to Hamlet's plan, for the moment that he resolves to act, crying upon the Queen's death by poison, "O villainy! Ho, let the door be lock'd! / Treachery! Seek it out" (5.2.293–94), his directives are undermined by Laertes, who informs him that the sought-after treachery

---

32. For clarification, the end bracket for this passage does not occur until line 80.

> ...is here, Hamlet. [Hamlet,] thou art slain.
> No medicine in the world can do thee good;
> In thee there is not half an hour's life.
> The treacherous instrument is in [thy] hand,
> Unbated and envenom'd. The foul practice
> Hath turn'd itself on me. Lo here I lie,
> Never to rise again. Thy mother's pois'ned.
> I can no more—the King, the King's to blame.
>
> (5.2.295–302)

Laertes's repetition of "the King, the King" once again begs the question: *which* king is to blame? But the answer is no longer a source of anxiety for Hamlet, who realizes that the only way to fill in the void in the Law is to use his own body as a suturing mechanism. Having experimented with a variety of different screens for the projection of this final performance, Hamlet now understands that the sole means of combining revenge and remembrance into a unified representation is to *incorporate* them himself, by converting his own body—as he imagined doing earlier in the play—into a screen for this fatal montage effect.[33] Accordingly, Hamlet responds to Laertes's prompting with revenge, killing the king in a setting that indeed has no relish of salvation in it; and, in so doing, Hamlet satisfies the Ghost's desire for remembrance as well, for young Hamlet remembers his father in the flesh, becoming the acting king until the venom claims him too. Having thus restored the proper line of succession from absent father to "good" son, Hamlet performs the ultimate act of creative control by directing his own death:

> Horatio, I am dead.
> Thou livest. Report me and my cause aright
> To the unsatisfied.
>
> (5.2.320–22)

Emulating the ontological prerogatives of a ghost—whose spirit comes back from the dead with a report from the future—Hamlet's final voice-

---

33. Here Hamlet arrives at his *noir* destination of the "in-between-two-deaths." Charnes cites Zizek's explanation of this phenomenon as follows: "the narrativization of his [the hero's] fate, becomes possible only when the subject is in a sense already dead, although still alive, when 'the game is already over,' in short: when the subject finds himself at the place baptized by Lacan 'the in-between-two-deaths' (*l'entre-deux-morts*)" (Zizek, qtd. in Charnes, "Dismember me" 1).

over is no longer the continuous, insistent voice of his earlier attempts at narration but merely "the grain of the voice," the ghostly remainder that "issu[es] from the point of death" (Copjec 188). As Copjec explains, the grain of the voice "marks not some ideal point where the subject would finally be absorbed into his narrative, used up; it materializes rather that which can never be incorporated into the narrative. Death becomes in *film noir* the positivization of the narrator's absence from the very diegetic reality his speech describes" (188). At last having exorcised the ghost in his machine, Hamlet insists once more, "O, I die, Horatio, / The potent poison quite o'er-crows my spirit" (5.2.334–35), knowing that it is the *spirit*, and not the poison, that o'er-crows him.

Since spirits return from the future, it is fitting that Hamlet's final speech contains a prophecy about the future-to-come. In his last effort to set things right, Hamlet informs Horatio:

> I do prophesy th' election lights
> On Fortinbras...he has my dying voice
> ...the rest is silence.
>
> (5.2.337–38, 340).

The rest is silence indeed. Hamlet's body is picked up off the cutting room floor and placed "[h]igh on a stage" (5.2.360), resting there for some three-hundred years until that which "passes show" in Hamlet crystallizes in a formal challenge to theatrical representation: the silent film. But there will be sound in this future, too, as Horatio suggests in this "trailer":

> So shall you hear
> Of carnal, bloody, and unnatural acts,
> Of accidental judgments, casual slaughters,
> Of deaths put on by cunning and [forc'd] cause,
> And in this upshot, purposes mistook
> Fall'n on th' inventors' heads...
>
> (5.2.363–67)

Appropriately, the figure whose name implies both "oratory" and "rationality," Horatio is charged with remembering young Hamlet, implying that alphabetic thinking, time, and narrative in Elsinore have been "set right" indeed. But this report is not entirely honest to Hamlet's memory, and perhaps this is why the "strong arm" of the law, Fortinbras, enters the picture at this moment to acknowledge Hamlet's legacy of cinematic thinking. After all, following Hamlet's call for "lights" and Horatio's call for "action," Fortinbras, in the play's last word, cries "camera!": "Go, bid the soldiers *shoot*" (5.2.385, emphasis added).

Like *Romeo and Juliet*, the textual history of *Hamlet* uncannily acts out its protagonist's battle against the established regimes of alphabetic thinking and narrative logic, scrambling the play's time, space, and causality across three distinct versions (Q1, Q2, F1). Perhaps it was this insistent sense of haunting that caught the eye of the French cinephiles back in 1957, when they turned to *Hamlet* in hopes of being inhabited by the spirit of an "auteur film." Indeed, if the phase of auteur theory most appropriate to understanding Shakespearean authorship is the period *following* the death of the Author, then *Hamlet* helps us to understand the ways in which this theory of the future comes back, as it were, from the past. Recent work by James Naremore, Timothy Corrigan, and Dudley Andrew testifies to the persistence of "author"-centered criticism in film studies today, based on what Corrigan astutely calls "the historical adaptability" of the auteur as an agent of cultural mediation (101).[34] I wish to stretch this notion of historical adaptability further by suggesting that the defining feature of the auteur—in all its incarnations—has always been an *undead* quality, a spirit or distinctive mark that haunts an oeuvre. For auteur theory is, fundamentally, a theory of haunting, an attempt to give this spirit a local habitation and a name. In this context, then, *Hamlet* redefines the ontological status of the "author" in early modern culture by privileging rather than "giving up" the ghost, initiating a search for a mode of representation that mobilizes *spirits* over letters and, for that matter, bodies. But we know that this mode of representation is not yet meant "to be." Thus, in the breach between a ghost "author" and the inadequate machinations of the theatrical apparatus, Hamlet emerges as an auteur—a ghost in the machine—bequeathed only the dubious afterlife of these irreconcilable

34. See James Naremore's article, "Authorship and the Cultural Politics of Film Criticism," Timothy Corrigan's book *A Cinema without Walls* (and particularly the chapter titled "The Commerce of Auteurism"), and Dudley Andrew's essay "The Unauthorized Auteur Today."

tensions. But this is, as Derrida concludes, "the insignia trait of spirit, the signature of the thing 'Shakespeare'" (22).

Perhaps this curious insignia can be explained by the "mark" that the Ghost left on Hamlet in his first and remarkably overlooked injunction:

> GHOST: Mark me.
> HAMLET: I will.

(1.5.1)

In consenting to mark the Ghost, Hamlet, too, becomes a marked or destined man. Like a ghost, a mark purveys a meaning which, while always already there, only arrives later. The Ghost's injunction, "mark me," is delivered from an enunciative position on a threshold between alphabetic and cinematic thinking, as well as between theater and that which "passes show." Indeed, in its verb form, "to mark" is "to direct," and I would argue that this is the future meaning toward which this overlooked injunction gestures: the figure of the director as a nascent preoccupation of early modern culture. Though the figure of the director will not materialize on stage or screen until the latter half of the nineteenth century, *Hamlet* points to the "insignia trait" of this figure as precisely a haunting, undead quality. Rather than describing the director in more historically accurate terms as unborn, then, the idea of being undead draws attention to the sense of unrest that marks this figure, a sense of being unfinished, forced to return again and again to "set things right." Akin to a ghost but not reduced to one, the director is a figure who "passes show," producing a body of work without showing the body beneath. What could be a more apposite metaphor for Shakespeare, whose prolific hand likewise passes show within the very corpus that bears his name? But the words and actions of *Hamlet* do not "cry out" for just any director. This play, as suggested at the outset of this discussion, points specifically to the figure of the film director; for what else can it mean to mark a ghost—to produce an inscription upon an "aery nothing"—if not to engage in cinematographic articulation? Had Marcellus's prediction that Hamlet will direct the future-to-come materialized, then, perhaps Hamlet would be admitted to Andrew Sarris's pantheon of auteurs based on what he defines as the "ultimate premise of the auteur theory": "interior meaning," which is "extrapolated from the tension between a director's personality and his material" ("Notes" 586), or, in Hamlet's (and Shakespeare's) case, immaterial.

෨෴෭

The fact that many French critics had small English and less American actually aided them in discovering the visual components of a director's style.

—Andrew Sarris, "Towards a Theory of Film History"[35]

More important for the French cinephiles than Hamlet's individual struggle with his material was the possibility of collective identification with Hamlet's status as a "bad" son, which could be put to two—not surprisingly, conflicting—purposes. On the one hand, the allusion to *Hamlet* in 1957 reflects a residual desire that was part of auteur theory's founding effort to raise cinema's reputation from a second-rate or bad offspring of theater to a legitimate art form. Such a citation thus expresses the French cinephiles' desire to infiltrate the transcendent cultural status of Shakespeare, basing their logic on the notion that Hamlet may have started off being rotten, but (like their own hopes for cinema) he didn't wind up that way. On the other hand, this same allusion betrays a very different, emergent desire, for after having obtained a certain degree of respectability by the end of the 1950s, many of the French cinephiles had reinvested themselves in the business of being "bad." Under the banner of the *nouvelle vague,* classic considerations of time, space, and causality were radically destabilized with the use of hand-held cameras, elliptical story-lines, and deliberate efforts to be unfashionable. The "new wave," then, was perhaps the "new soul" that the six characters went in search of in *Hamlet.* And if it is true that Shakespeare himself played the Ghost in this play, then this new soul was very old indeed. Little did Shakespeare's contemporaries know that somewhere among the shreds and patches of small Latin and less Greek were the makings of a cinematographic kingdom. They should have had more respect for the undead:

Mark me.
I Will.

35. Here, Sarris puns on Ben Jonson's famous "encomium" to Shakespeare in the First Folio, in which Jonson clarified for posterity that Shakespeare had a minimal education, including "small Latin and less Greek." See Jonson's "To the memory of my beloued, the AVTHOR Mr. William Shakespeare."

4

Strictly Shakespeare?

Dead Letters, Ghostly Fathers, and the Cultural
Pathology of Authorship in Baz Luhrmann's *William
Shakespeare's Romeo + Juliet*

Man can create only in continuity, by making the potential
actual, he is excluded, by his nature, from originality and innovation. But this difference is an adaptation.

— Pierre Macherey, "Creation and Production"

"I've always wanted to do *Romeo and Juliet*," writes Baz Luhrmann. "Shakespeare," he claims, was a rambunctious, sexy, violent, entertaining storyteller. We're trying to make this movie rambunctious,
sexy, violent, and entertaining the way Shakespeare might have if he
had been a filmmaker" ("Note" i). Intent on realizing Shakespeare's
ghostly legacy of cinematic thinking as a full-bodied film, Luhrmann—
perhaps even more than Hamlet—has his work cut out for him, for in
adapting a play that is simultaneously a legend, he, too, must contend
with ghosts. Indeed, long before it was a play by William Shakespeare,
Romeo and Juliet was a legend, a genre which, as Linda Charnes argues, fosters the desire to "escap[e] prior encoding" even as it exposes
the dead letter at the core of this authorial ambition (*Notorious Identity*
99). In titling his film *William Shakespeare's Romeo + Juliet*, however,
Luhrmann appears to have no qualms with "prior encoding," a gesture
which is perfectly in keeping with the cultural pathology of postmodern aesthetic production. According to Fredric Jameson, one of the "essential messages" of the postmodern aesthetic involves, paradoxically,
"the necessary failure of art and the aesthetic, the failure of the new,
[and] the imprisonment in the past" ("Postmodernism and Consumer

Society" 190). Yet even the past remains recalcitrant to representation, for "we seem condemned to seek the historical past through our own pop images and stereotypes about that past, which itself remains forever out of reach" (194). Missing this "essential message," critics have been quick to dismiss Luhrmann's film as "postmodern tomfoolery" (Welsh 152), mourning losses in the name of Shakespearean textuality and early modern history without realizing the extent to which the film itself mourns these "losses" as symptomatic of the madness of its *own* mode of production.

The authorial stakes of *William Shakespeare's Romeo + Juliet* are best understood by situating Luhrmann's film within the dynamics of the legendary, a genre that has received significantly less attention from critics than other narrative genre such as myths, fables, and folktales.[1] Because legends confront would-be authors with the paradox of their belated arrival at the very scene of the narratives they presume to originate, legends offer a particularly compelling case study of the pathology of postmodern aesthetic production. In the absence of more extensive and specific treatment of legends in narrative theory, I find Roland Barthes's concept of *déjà-lu*—the already read—to be particularly useful in the case of the Romeo and Juliet legend, which is distinguished by a long line of almost exclusively literary, rather than oral, transmission.[2] Without specifically referring to legends, Peter Brooks explains the narrative pathology of *déjà-lu* in terms of what he calls the "anticipation of retrospection":

> If the past is to be read as present, it is a curious present that we know to be past in relation to a future we know to be already in place, already in wait for us to reach it. Perhaps we would do best to speak of the *anticipation of retrospection* as our chief tool in making sense of narrative, the master trope of its strange logic. We have no doubt forgone eternal narrative ends...yet still we read in a spirit of confidence, and also a state of dependence, that what remains to be read will restructure the provisional meanings of the already read. (23)

---

1. In referring to the Romeo and Juliet story as a legend, I wish to distinguish it, for example, from myths, which maintain a focus on the supernatural, and fables, which are dependent on a moral. For an extensive analysis of the distinct components of these and other narrative genres, see Vladimir Propp's *The Morphology of the Folktale* and Peter Brooks's *Reading for the Plot: Design and Intention in Narrative*.

2. Barthes explores the concept of *déjà lu* throughout *S/Z*.

Offering a variation on this theme, Shakespeare's Romeo and Juliet, as I have argued in Chapter One, operate under the assumption that what remains to be *written* will restructure the tragic fate that they have *already read* in the stars. And if we continue to read forward from the early modern to the postmodern, we find a similar authorial gambit at stake in recent cinematic re-makes of stories such as *The Legend of Sleepy Hollow* (Tim Burton 1999) and *The Legend of Bagger Vance* (Robert Redford 2000), as well as retakes on legendary films such as *Psycho* (Gus Van Sant 1998), all of which suggest the peculiar—if not pathological—lure of always already "authorized" material for aspiring auteurs who, like Luhrmann, seem to welcome the challenge of leaving their stylistic stamp on widely known stories with predictable plots and predetermined outcomes.

But can there be any such thing as a *postmodern* auteur? Is this a contradiction in terms, or might this concept offer a local habitation and a name for another unspeakable ghost in the machine of cultural impossibility? Baz Luhrmann's *William Shakespeare's Romeo + Juliet*, with its fetishistic appropriation of the plus (+) sign, offers a vision of authorship as something more than a site of negation in postmodern culture, even as it signals the added and, in fact, defining challenge of the postmodern auteur, who is exhorted to deploy "dead styles," as Jameson describes them ("Postmodernism and Consumer Society" 190), without becoming dead again.[3] Rather than taking note of the provocative crisis of representation staged in *William Shakespeare's Romeo + Juliet*, however, critics take Luhrmann's adaptation to task for not being "Shakespearean" enough, reading the film's title too literally. "*William Shakespeare's Romeo & Juliet* is deceptively titled," writes one reviewer, because "it is really Baz Luhrmann's *Romeo & Juliet*" (Welsh 152). *Rolling Stone* critic Peter Travers observes, "It's a good thing that Shakespeare gets his name in the title, or you might mistake the opening scenes for Quentin Tarantino's *Romeo and Juliet*" (123). Yet another review echoes this sentiment quite precisely: "Good thing Shakespeare's name is included in the title. Otherwise, you might mistake this audacious version of his tale of star-crossed teen lovers for an extended music video" (Jones E1). What is so striking and, in fact, symptomatic about these critical remarks is that they protest too much—that is, too much in common with each other. For in going to the same linguistic well to describe the film's titular strategy, these critics not only testify to

---

3. I appropriate the phrase "dead again" from Kenneth Branagh's 1992 film title.

the uncanny power of the legendary, which subsumes their purport-
edly "original" angles on the film's "postmodern razzmatazz" (Johnson 74) within a narrative form of repetition compulsion, but more importantly, their comments act out the problems of authenticity and
authority embedded in the very cultural logic they set out to critique.
William Shakespeare's Romeo + Juliet is unabashedly replete with "postmodern razzmatazz." However, the critical reception of Luhrmann's
film tends to rest too easy with this complex cultural category, drowning any discussion of the film's provocative negotiation of its own historical dilemma in a self-indulgent, hipper-than-thou inventory of its
aesthetic failures. A more productive project would involve calibrating
the degree to which Luhrmann's film resists easy insertion into this
postmodern "legend" which, as we shall see, brings us back to the authorial struggle embedded in William Shakespeare's own *Romeo and
Juliet.*

ᐠᐟ

Before exploring how Luhrmann's film facilitates this provocative
historical intersection of postmodern and early modern, it is first necessary to establish how *William Shakespeare's Romeo + Juliet* qualifies as
specifically postmodern, since this is a label that the film's detractors
have taken for granted. From its opening moments, Luhrmann's film
announces its apparent overdetermination by the modus operandi of
pastiche, the quintessential signifier of the postmodern aesthetic. For
what indeed is the alternative in "a world in which stylistic innovation
is no longer possible"? (Jameson, "Postmodernism and Consumer Society" 190). In such an environment, as Jameson observes, the new is replaced with the "neo" and "personal style" is replaced with "the random cannibalization of all the styles of the past," leading to "the
well-nigh universal practice today of what may be called pastiche"
("Postmodernism" 73–74).[4] The formal consequence of the postmodern preoccupation with pastiche is the "emergence of a new kind of flat-
ness or depthlessness, a new kind of superficiality in the most literal
sense" (68). Not surprisingly, the most striking formal feature of
Luhrmann's so-called "neo-*Romeo*" (Johnson 74) is its barrage of incon-
gruent surfaces that reproduce the complex textuality of Shakespeare's

4. I am working with several different versions of Jameson's work on postmodern culture because each of them offers a slightly different perspective on his theory of aesthetic
production.

play at the level of mise-en-scène, generating the pastiche visual night-mare known as "Verona Beach"—itself a curious hybrid of Shakespeare's Veronese setting, LA's Venice Beach, and the film's on-location shots of Mexico City. The opening scene of Luhrmann's film builds on this sense of rupture by calling into question not only the film's location but also the spectator's. Declaring open season on the viewer's visual loyalties, the cinematic frame yields to a television screen as a news anchor-woman delivers Shakespeare's prologue in bleak monotones. This unique interpretation of a dramatic Chorus is quickly eclipsed by an-other shift of medium as a violent montage of newsreel footage, news-paper headlines, and prime-time drama shots of the awestruck faces of Capulets and Montagues collectively document the ongoing war in Verona Beach. The prevailing feel of this bizarre opening sequence is pure pastiche: evening-soap fiction meets evening-magazine "real life," but the lines separating titillation from truth, melodrama from docu-drama, are fuzzy at best. True to postmodern form, Luhrmann intro-duces us to *William Shakespeare's Romeo + Juliet* in a manner wholly at-tuned to a "consumers' appetite for a world transformed into sheer images of itself and for pseudo-events and 'spectacles'" (Jameson, "Postmodernism" 74).

By the time we arrive at the first scene of Shakespeare's play involv-ing the confrontation between the Capulets and the Montagues, the spectator's sense of being unstuck in space and time suffers further dis-placement in the midst of the bizarre ethnic mix created by Luhrmann's cast.[5] One critic sizes up the cultural differences between the Capulets and the Montagues as follows: "The Montagues are a motley crew with a kind of Apocalypse Now dress code, army surplus Hawaiian shirt and semi-punk hair. The Capulets are smooth, sleek, groomed and fe-line, Latin cowboys in close-fitting black, accessorized with silver trim-mings and images of the Virgin Mary" (Hawker 6). Essentially, the south-of-the-border-*cum*-spaghetti-western Capulets are characterized by an excess of ethnicity, while the pasty-faced Montague boys sport a

---

5. For an illuminating discussion of the intersection of ethnicity and postmodernity in Luhrmann's film, see Barbara Hodgdon's essay *"William Shakespeare's Romeo + Juliet:* Ev-erything's Nice in America?" especially 96–98. In a paper given at the 1999 Shakespeare Association of America meeting, Peter S. Donaldson offered a fascinating analysis of the film's politics of ethnicity from the standpoint of Luhrmann's status as an Australian and, therefore, postcolonial subject. See "Baz Luhrmann's *Romeo + Juliet:* Media, Spectacle, Performance."

lack of ethnicity, becoming, in effect, "beastie boyz" as they rap, grind, and signify in classic wanna-be style. The stereotypes operative in both the Capulet and Montague gangs offer pointed testimony to the post-modern loss of "personal style" and the compensatory predominance of pastiche. But this loss extends beyond the diegetic reality to encom-pass the film itself, which creates a visual vernacular for audiences weaned on popular film through a relentless cinematic intertextuality. The opening scene alone "is filled with glancing references to and overt borrowings from the cinema of violence: the Western, the gangster movie, the kung-fu pic, the urban drama, the crime thriller, the action comedy" (Hawker 6). Such borrowings keep the spectator's gaze hostage to the shifting, shimmering surfaces of Luhrmann's film, demonstrating the extent to which, as Jameson argues of the "remake" film, intertextuality has become "a deliberate, built-in feature of the aesthetic effect" designed to tap into "our awareness of the pre-existence of other versions" ("Postmodernism" 76).

Playing on the audience's awareness of Franco Zeffirelli's lusty, busty, flower-girl version of *Romeo and Juliet* (1968) starring Olivia Hussey, Luhrmann stages several intertextual echoes of and overtly parodic gestures toward Zeffirelli's film. While Lady Capulet is intro-duced primping and preening in Zeffirelli's film, in Luhrmann's "re-make," she becomes a monstrous crossbreed of Southern debutante and Hollywood diva. And where Zeffirelli shows Lady Capulet and Tybalt merely dancing together at the ball, Luhrmann heightens this erotic suggestion in the direction of incest, as they become "kissing cousins" on the dance floor. Similarly, while Zeffirelli only hints at Mercutio's homoerotic attachment to Romeo, Luhrmann's Mercutio is a black-skinned, white-sequined, drag queen who seems desperately disturbed by Romeo's heterosexual awakening. Less problematic and more clever is Luhrmann's revision of Zeffirelli's famous morisco dance at the Capulet ball, which involves a dizzying interweaving of hands, gazes, and bodies; in Luhrmann's film this motif is revisited in the form of an ecstasy trip designed to mimic the frenzied whirl and hum of love-at-first-sight. Finally, whereas Zeffirelli showcases the song "What Is a Youth?" as the memorable (and now clichéd) centerpiece of his film, Luhrmann not only installs musical performances ranging from gospel to disco throughout his version but also develops a music video and MTV special to promote the film. Thus we glimpse the postmodern confrontation between Shakespeare, Zeffirelli, and Luhrmann's sex, drugs, and rock-and-roll rendition of star-crossed love through the magnifying glass of a consuming intertextuality, which now becomes, as Jameson observes, "a constitutive and essential part of the film's structure…as the operator of a new connotation of 'pastness' and pseudo-historical depth, in which the history of aesthetic styles displaces 'real' history" ("Postmodernism" 76).

☙

In what sense, then, does this film live up to its title as *William Shakespeare's Romeo + Juliet?* And, for that matter, to what extent does Shakespeare's own play deserve this attribution? As an initial response, I will argue that *Romeo and Juliet,* in both its dramatic and filmic incarnations, materializes the blank-parody function of early modern *and* postmodern authorship. "Blank parody" is the phrase Jameson uses to describe the pastiche nature of postmodern aesthetic production which, as I shall demonstrate, offers a surprising analogue to the equally vexing practice of early modern authorship. Unlike traditional parody, which maintains an affective or critical edge, blank parody is "speech in a dead language…without any of parody's ulterior motives, amputated of the satiric impulse, devoid of laughter and of any conviction that alongside the abnormal tongue you have momentarily borrowed, some healthy linguistic normality still exists" ("Postmodernism" 74). This unhealthy linguistic environment, in which the only available mode of articulation is "speech in a dead language," marks the point at which the pathologies of early modern and postmodern authorship merge. For just as the postmodern "author" is doomed to circulate like a dead letter postdating its own ideological demise, its early modern precursor emerges prior to the historical birth of the Author. Consequently, early modern authorship must take its cues from the medieval ideology of *auctoritas* which, as we have seen, reduces the figure of the author to a pastiche ensemble of "speech in a dead language"—quite literally, the words of ghostly fathers, or *auctores,* whose authority is preserved through cultural regimens of repetition.[6] Thus, whereas early modern

6. Although the phrase "ghostly father" invokes the description of Friar Lawrence in Shakespeare's *Romeo and Juliet,* it is a particularly apt description of the *auctor* which, as Mary Carruthers reminds us, designates a reiterative, text-centered mode of production that bases its promulgation of *sententiae* on the authority already contained in other texts. Representing this tradition of authority, Friar Lawrence is a figure who is always spouting aphorisms and sententious phrases; and despite the fact that he briefly acts upon his

authorship emerges in the spirit of adaptation to the still culturally dominant demand for *purposeful* cannibalization of past styles and pre-existing authority, postmodern authorship is fueled by the more *random* cannibalization, or pastiche, of precedents drawn from the past. In other words, the pathologies of early modern and postmodern authorship converge, provocatively, along the path of blank parody.

From this historical perspective, then, there appears to be no such thing as William Shakespeare's *Romeo and Juliet*, let alone a film claiming that authority. But in *practice*, specifically, dramatic practice, there are opportunities to articulate new or emergent "structures of feeling" toward authorship and authority, as W. B. Worthen argues. In contrast to the ideological strictures that govern the production of nondramatic texts, dramatic texts do not engage in the mere blank parody of preexisting authority; rather, in their "surrogate" existence as performances, they engender an authority of their own. Dramatic performance, as Worthen explains, should not be conceptualized as a straightforward "performance *of* the text but as an act of iteration, an utterance, a surrogate standing in that positions, uses, signifies the text within the citational practices of performance" and which, as a result, achieves at least a semi-autonomous existence *apart from* the text ("Drama, Performativity, and Performance" 1101). What Worthen identifies as "surrogation" is the capacity of performance to utilize the multiple citational practices of the stage in order to transform the potentially "dead language" of the text. Surrogation can even transform fundamental notions of priority and origins, for it is an "act of memory and an act of creation [that] involves not the replaying of an authorizing text, a grounding origin, but the potential to construct that origin as a rhetorically powerful effect of performance" (1101). Worthen's emphasis on the transformative as opposed to the merely translative power of surrogation stresses the liberating provisionality of performance without simply reverting to the incapacitating dialectic of the text-versus-performance paradigm. However, Worthen's analysis redirects this contentious energy toward the straw man of the "always-absent author," reinscribing this figure within the fabric of historical omissions and ambiguity that plagues our understanding of early modern and postmodern author-

---

own authority in helping Romeo and Juliet, he ultimately concedes to the "greater power" or *auctoritas* of law and religion which, he tells Juliet, "hath thwarted our intents" (5.3.153–54).

ship (*Shakespeare and the Authority* 37). While it is certainly true that in the context of theatrical production, the idea of the dramatist as "author" is even less appropriate than it is to considerations of nondramatic literature, there is a certain risk involved in always positioning the figure of the Author as the rigid designator of a regulative, hegemonic, and simultaneously "mystified" function.[7] Therefore, I wish to complicate as well as to complement Worthen's argument by considering the possibility that "authors" engage in counter-hegemonic performances themselves. However, I will also argue that this contestatory presence may be traced back to Shakespeare's play only by way of its surrogates, which are activated by the provocative citational practices of performances such as Baz Luhrmann's *William Shakespeare's Romeo + Juliet,* a film that wages resistance to the legend, both postmodern and early modern, that reduces authorship to a blank parody of the past.

Luhrmann's aspirations to authorship are complicated by the fact that he chooses to adapt not only a play by William Shakespeare but also one of Shakespeare's legend plays. Legends count on the fixed nature of their citational power regardless of changing historical contexts, the exigencies of genre, or the subjective predispositions of authors and audiences. Proceeding through a kind of cultural repetition-compulsion, legends are driven by the force of inevitability, ultimately leading to widely known and infinitely recyclable conclusions. Every "new" articulation of a legend, in other words, is more or less destined to be a blank parody of its precursor. What makes the legend of Romeo and Juliet such a peculiar choice for Luhrmann's authorial intervention in this pathology is that, atypical of legends as a genre, the Romeo and Juliet story reflects "a long line of almost purely literary transmission," and

7. The idea of the "rigid designator" is particularly appropriate to a discussion of Shakespeare's hegemonic status and function as an "author." The rigid designator, according to Slavoj Žižek, masquerades as a "'pure' signifier which gives unity and identity to our experience of historical reality itself," despite the fact that "every symbolization is in the last resort contingent" (*Sublime* 97). Similarly, even though we know that Shakespeare's status as an "author" is radically contingent, we nonetheless ascribe to him a mystified sense of authority. For a detailed illustration of Worthen's take on the "phantom author" and the way this figure is alternately appropriated by the "politics of performance" and the "hegemony of literature," see chapter one of Worthen's *Shakespeare and the Authority of Performance,* 1–43.

"is only remotely connected with oral tradition and folklore" (Moore viii). In contrast to other legendary characters, then, Romeo and Juliet do not achieve legendary status through "word of mouth" but rather through the written word and, consequently, the cultural authority, or *auctoritas*, that inheres in it.

Stories of star-crossed love, replete with plot-lines involving sleeping potions and arranged marriages, may be traced back as far as ancient Greece and, of course, to *Pyramus and Thisbe* in Ovid's *Metamorphoses*, but it is not until the late Italian Renaissance that this theme becomes widely popular, materializing in the legend of "Romeo and Giulietta." This legend has its origins in the historical feud of the Montecchi and the Cappelletti, two political factions that eventually became associated with two hostile families. Though knowledge of the "ancient grudge" between the households had virtually passed from Italian popular memory by the end of the thirteenth century, Dante revived interest in the Cappelletti and the Montecchi by invoking them in his *Purgatorio* as an example of the destructive nature of civil strife. As a consequence of Dante's somewhat cryptic explanation of the families' relationship, "a series of misinterpretations arose, which became crystallized into one of the most famous legends of literature" (Moore 15). Accordingly, in his exhaustive analysis, Olin H. Moore traces the development, transmission, and popular reception of this tragedy of star-crossed love from mere sketches in Dante, Bocaccio, and anonymous fifteenth-century novellas to more complex treatments by Masuccio (1476), Da Porto (1530), and Bandello (1554) and, finally, to the legend's importation to England through Boiastuau's French collection of tales (1559), translated by William Painter in his *Palace of Pleasure* (1567) and adapted by Arthur Brooke in *The Tragicall Historye of Romeus and Juliet* (1562).[8] The "final and decisive stage" of this peculiar process of literary accretion, as Moore concludes, is none other than "the transition from Brooke to Shakespeare" (vii).

Precisely because the legend of Romeo and Juliet is distinguished by a literary as opposed to oral history, it is a particularly useful source for exploring the legends that accrue to authorship in the age of blank parody. Like Hamlet, Luhrmann seeks to overcome the citational clutches of

8. In addition to Moore's extensive work on the legend of Romeo and Juliet, a useful source containing the texts of the legend's Italian transmitters, Masuccio, Da Porto, and Bandello, is Adolph Caso's edited volume on *Romeo and Juliet*.

preexisting textual authority with the creation of a distinctly cinematographic language. In creating a contemporary screen adaptation, however, Luhrmann is not only faced with the sedimented *literary* history of
the legend but also with the legendary status of Shakespeare's own
play in contemporary popular culture—a status that is perpetuated by
the standard inclusion of *Romeo and Juliet* in high school curriculums,
the success of adaptations such as *West Side Story*, and the rising star of
Leonardo DiCaprio, whose popular reception as the ultimate "Romeo"
uncannily culminates in his star-crossed "sequel" to *William Shakespeare's
Romeo + Juliet: Titantic*.[9] Thus, as Shakespeare's play-ending couplet inscribing "Romeo" and "woe" triangulates all too easily to include "Di-
Caprio," we are reminded that the legend—despite its reworking in the
predominantly visual medium of cinema—returns as a dead letter to
inscribe even the most powerful performances in its consuming textuality. And though Luhrmann seizes every opportunity to convert the
potentially "dead language" of Shakespeare's *Romeo and Juliet* into a
distinctly cinematic visual language, such repressions of the text, as
Geoffrey Nowell-Smith argues, return as "hysterical" moments in the
mise-en-scène.[10] Remarkably, it is the abundant baptismal-water imagery, unanimously considered by critics to be the most innovative aspect of Luhrmann's film, that exposes the steady encroachment of the
legendary and, specifically, of Arthur Brooke's own poetic imagery on
Luhrmann's cinematic tour de force. Rife with images of fish, water,

---

9. In her essay on Luhrmann's film, Philippa Hawker observes that

the figures of Romeo and Juliet are already inscribed into contemporary high and popular
culture, in contexts ranging from *West Side Story* to Ashton's ballet, from Bugs Bunny car-
toons to the Everclear song on the film's soundtrack. How many countless times has the
balcony scene been the subject of parody and homage? How many overt references are
there in popular songs to the figure of Romeo? (And, for that matter, isn't it interesting
how the word has acquired a pejorative, dismissive meaning: a 'Romeo' is a gigolo, a
Latin lover of unreliable disposition. Juliet, however, has disappeared from view, re-
membered by little more than the bridal accessory known as the Juliet cap.). (9)

Additionally, in *Unspeakable ShaXXXspeares: Queer Theory and American KiddieCulture*,
Richard Burt observes that *Romeo and Juliet* has become something of a sexual legend in
the porn industry, spawning a distinctly X-rated cult following.

10. For a discussion of an unacknowledged precedent of Luhrmann's aggressive at-
tempt to pit image against word, see Douglas Lanier's brilliant exploration of Peter
Greenaway's *Prospero's Books*, titled "Drowning the Book: *Prospero's Books* and the Textual
Shakespeare." The concept of the hysterical return of the repressed is invoked throughout
Nowell-Smith's extensive work on mise-en-scène criticism.

and baited hooks, Brooke's Tragicall Historye contains a lure that not even Luhrmann can resist—so strong is the pull of this "ghostly father" reluctantly entombed in Shakespeare's play.

ख़ें

> Every artist is a cannibal, every poet is a thief.
> All kill their inspiration and sing about their grief.
>
> —U2, "The Fly," from *Achtung Baby!*

In discussing *William Shakespeare's Romeo + Juliet*, Luhrmann has rather oddly asserted that Shakespeare "did not write *Romeo and Juliet*, he stole it," a remark that undermines the fidelity to Shakespeare advertised in the film's title ("An Interview" 13). In virtually the same breath, however, Luhrmann implies that his filmic realization of the Romeo and Juliet legend *is* based exclusively on Shakespeare's version of it, for he admits only a vague familiarity with the fact that Shakespeare's play was based on "a long poem" that was in turn derived from "an Italian novella" (13). The connection between Luhrmann's film and Brooke's poem therefore seems to be a coincidence but, as we shall see, it is a coincidence so provocative as to be classifiable only as "uncanny." Another curiosity related to the film's title and its apparent privileging of Shakespeare is Luhrmann's cutting of more than one-third of Shakespeare's play from his screenplay; more significantly, when pressed to discuss the film's distinctly "Shakespearean" qualities, Luhrmann somewhat disdainfully indicated that the standard quota of "witty epigrams" and "speaking in perfect sonnets" is hard to find in *William Shakespeare's Romeo + Juliet*" ("An Interview" 13).

As we enter Luhrmann's distinctly postmodern mise-en-scène, then, it is tempting to read what remains of Shakespeare's *Romeo and Juliet* in the bleak spotlight of blank parody. Signs representing the "Globe Theatre Pool Hall," "The Merchant of Verona Beach," and "Out Damned Spot Cleaners," as well as advertisements for consumable goods such as "Pound of Flesh" fast food, "Rosencrantzky's" restaurant, and "Prospero's whiskey" refigure the high-cultural status of Shakespearean verse as an homage to postmodern consumer culture. But what is most striking about Luhrmann's conversion of these Shakespearean hallmarks into sites of consumption is his literalization of the aesthetic cannibalism that links the pathology of postmodern authorship to the early modern blank-parody function of imitating *auctoritas*—a function that would-be "authors" such as Ben Jonson uncannily defined in terms of the metaphor of *digestion*:

> The third requisite in our *Poet*, or Maker, is *Imitation*, to bee able to convert the substance, or Riches of another *Poet*, to his owne use. To make choise of one excellent man above the rest, and so to follow him, till he grow very *Hee*: or, so like him, as the Copie may be mistaken for the Principall. Not, as a Creature, that swallowes, what it takes in, crude, raw, or indigested; but, that feedes with an Appetite, and hath a Stomacke to concoct, divide, and turne all into nourishment. (*Timber,* 8:638)

Similarly, Luhrmann "feedes with an Appetite" on Shakespeare's words, seeking to "concoct and divide" them into a kind of cinematic mincemeat. And where his camera fails to commodify and consume Shakespearean verse, Luhrmann adopts an ironizing, literalistic approach to the language. For example, at the Capulet ball, Luhrmann playfully converts Juliet into Romeo's "bright angel" (2.2.26) as she emerges decked out in an angel costume. Luhrmann has even more fun with Shakespeare's memorable account of Paris as a "precious book of love" that only "lacks a cover" (1.3.87, 88); in the film, Paris is given a literal cover when "Dave Paris" is introduced to us as a coverboy, featured as *Timely Magazine*'s "Bachelor of the Year." In the spirit of Jonsonian imitation, then, these tongue-in-cheek visual variations on a Shakespearean theme encode Luhrmann's more serious, indeed carnivorous desire to authorize a version of the legend that occupies a distinctly cinematic register—not the tragic registry of "sour misfortune's book."

This desire is not without precedent, however, for Shakespeare's play attempts to authorize a new version of the legend in its own terms by staging an escape from referentiality in Romeo and Juliet's language. As I suggested in Chapter One, Shakespeare's lovers are in search of a properly poststructuralist universe in which signifier and signified exist in arbitrary relation to each other—where Romeo, for example, is neither "hand, nor foot, nor arm, nor face, nor any other part" (2.1.82–83) belonging to the deadly inscription of his legendary name. Thus what distinguishes Shakespeare's play from its source in Brooke's poem is the fact that

while Brooke had told his story in a mercilessly prolix succession of poulter's measure couplets, Shakespeare now gave voice to the most various linguistic range of any play that had yet appeared on the English stage. Colloquial prose, rhymed and unrhymed blank verse, Petrarchanism both sincere and parodic, stichomythia, epithalamion, aubade, bawdy, song, pun, lament, soliloquy, epistle, flyting, gnomic "sentence," the conceits that clownage keeps in pay, and even an elegant embedded sonnet are among the many rhetorical styles that vie for center stage in the course of the two hours' traffic. (Pearlman 23)

This extraordinary if not paranoiac flurry of stylistic, metrical, and linguistic innovation is a far from subtle indication of Shakespeare's desire to keep the dead letter at the core of Brooke's poem "in sufferance."

Whereas Shakespeare keeps the dead letter of Brooke's *Tragicall Historye* in sufferance by filtering it through an extraordinary range of poetic styles, Luhrmann continues this game of cat-and-mouse through a radically fluctuating cinematic rhetoric. As Luhrmann's comments on the film imply, although *William Shakespeare's Romeo + Juliet* does not claim an explicitly textual debt to its Shakespearean source, it does reveal a textural debt to Shakespeare in its cinematic language:

Let's talk about that cinematic language. You get a lot of people saying, "Oh my god, you change style every 5 minutes. How MTV." Well, have you ever seen a Hindi movie? Please. That idea of low comedy one minute, a song, then *Rebel Without a Cause*, is aligned with Shakespeare's need to keep changing style, to keep clarity, to keep surprising the audience, to keep ahead of them. ("An Interview" 14)

As far as Luhrmann is concerned, then, what qualifies as "strictly Shakespeare" is strictly pastiche. But Luhrmann's stylistic investment in pastiche is distinctly *not* aligned with the dead language of blank parody. For what is most striking about his commentary is its invocation of the life-infusing, transmigratory mystique of Hindi culture and cinema, which Luhrmann manipulates as a means of linking the metamorphoses of Shakespearean verse to his own ever-changing cinematic language. But why is Luhrmann so concerned with the principle of dynamic change in the first place? Is it possible that the somewhat peculiar "needs" he ascribes to Shakespeare—the need, for example, "to keep changing style" and "to keep ahead of the audience"—expose his own sensitivity to the pull of the legendary? Despite his occasionally flip remarks about Shakespeare's potentially out-of-date rhyme schemes, Luhrmann's film really does live up to its title as *William Shakespeare's Romeo + Juliet*, uniquely transmitting both the authorial audacity *and* anxiety embedded in Shakespeare's own attempt to cheat the *auctoritas* of the legend. Indeed, Luhrmann's innovative camerawork and editing techniques alone suggest his aspirations to originality even as the film's frenetic pacing encodes a coexisting fear—as if Luhrmann's ability to keep one step ahead of the audience really were a matter of life or death. Simply put, there is an unmistakable urgency in *William Shakespeare's Romeo + Juliet* that does not exist in Luhrmann's earlier work; and this urgency, I would argue, stems from the fear that Luhrmann may, in fact, fall one step *behind* the audience or, more importantly, the legend, having exhausted his quota of new steps in *Strictly Ballroom*.

As my title implies, Baz Luhrmann's *William Shakespeare's Romeo + Juliet* is perhaps better described as *Strictly Ballroom* meets *Romeo and Juliet*. Luhrmann's first commercial release film, *Strictly Ballroom* (1992) serves as a provocative prequel to his tango with the Romeo and Juliet legend. Particularly illuminating are the parallels between this earlier film's principal character, Scott Hastings, and Shakespeare's Romeo. Like Romeo, whose every move is circumscribed by literary conventions, Scott Hastings (Paul Mercurio) is a dance legend in the making who remains "boxed-in" by the rules of the Australian Dance Federation. "Maybe I'm just sick of dancing someone else's steps all the time," exclaims Scott, eager to authorize new moves expressly forbidden by the Federation and the cultural dictates of "strictly ballroom" dancing. Defying the will of his parents, Scott partners up with a girl from the wrong side of the tracks and together they break the cycle of convention and corruption that has plagued the Pan Pacific Dance Championships for generations—by dancing, quite literally, out of bounds. Subsequently, the generation-long feud between rival households is ended when universal enthusiasm for Scott's fabled "new steps" proclaims victory against the old guard. Replete with Luhrmann's signature death-defying camera angles, *Strictly Ballroom* is *Romeo and Juliet* with a happy ending. Noting the striking likeness between *Strictly Ballroom*'s dance-duo and DiCaprio and Danes's Romeo and Juliet, one reviewer observes that "[t]hey would be just a slight variation on the romantic couple in *Strictly Ballroom*, if only the film-makers weren't stuck with Shakespeare's downbeat ending" (Mathews 55). Indeed, in one of *Strictly Ballroom*'s particularly "downbeat" moments, we are reminded of a theme that applies more strictly to *Romeo and Juliet*: "You can dance any steps you like," says a Federation Judge to Scott, "[but] that doesn't mean you'll win." Defying the *auctoritas* of tradition comes with a price. If *Strictly Ballroom*'s vision of defiance *without* consequence succeeds temporarily in keeping the letter of Federation law "in sufferance," then the letter's debt returns in *William Shakespeare's Romeo + Juliet* with a vengeance.

William Shakespeare's Romeo + Juliet thus marks a return to a primal scene for Luhrmann, who seems at once drawn to legendary themes and intent on modeling alternatives to their debilitating logic. Having successfully thwarted the legend of star-crossed love in his *Romeo and Juliet* spin-off, Luhrmann ups the ante, attempting to do something original with Shakespeare's "original" as the ultimate test of his auteurist aspirations. Consonant with Alexandre Astruc's watershed conception of the auteur as a film artist who uses the camera as a figurative "stylus" or pen, Luhrmann invents a whole new language to encompass the twists and turns of his own need to keep one step ahead of the Romeo and Juliet legend, as the filmic action unfolds through Luhrmann's signature whip pans, lightning cuts, super macro slam zooms, static super wide shots, tight on point-of-view shots, and other vertigo-inducing camera angles.[11] This highly texturized, frenzied mise-en-scène is the trademark, or, in keeping with the name of Luhrmann's production company, the "Bazmark" of his cinematic language. And according to longtime set designer and fellow collaborator Catherine Martin, Luhrmann succeeds in leaving his mark on a film whose title insists only on the mark that "William Shakespeare" has left on the Romeo and Juliet legend: "Whether you love or hate the film, it's completely unique and very much a director's film—it has Baz's vision stamped all over it" (qtd. in Hallet 7). Martin is not alone in her assessment of the film's auteurist innovations. For example, one critic observes that "[f]rom its first image...Baz Luhrmann's new version of *Romeo and Juliet* proclaims its origins and originality" (Hawker 6). But isn't this a paradox? How can something proclaim both its "origins" *and* its "originality"? As Linda Charnes would argue, these comments about Luhrmann's film bespeak an unwitting complicity in the ideology of the legendary, for

a legend is a cultural product which depends upon the naturalizing or "forgetting" of its own history as a manufactured thing. Always read as a paradigm for

---

11. These camera movements are representative of Luhrmann's stylistic repertoire and are recorded throughout the screenplay by Pearce and Luhrmann. Even before the pioneering work of journals such as *Cahiers du Cinema,* the earliest articulations of what would become auteur theory came from figures such as Alexandre Astruc, who was writing, along with Roger Leenhardt, for *L'Ecran Francais* in the early 1940s.

some authoritative reality, the legendary elides the space that originally existed between its own constructedness and that "reality" to which it refers, imposing both its values and its authority as *originary* rather than derivational. (2)

Simply put, the "authoritative reality" to which both Shakespeare and Luhrmann's versions of the Romeo and Juliet legend refer is a *reality without authors*. By the same token, however, in their stylistic innovations alone, Shakespeare's play and Luhrmann's film participate in the fantasy of eliding the gap between source and adaptation—between, in Ben Jonson's terms, "Copie" and "Principall"—by aspiring to produce "original" versions of this legend of star-crossed love. But if, as the proverb implies, it is a wise character who knows his author, then it is a wise auteur who knows the character of his source: Luhrmann's "quarrel" is not with Shakespeare but with Shakespeare's "master," that is, *his* source. Ironically, then, in attempting to baptize the Romeo and Juliet legend anew by recontextualizing the tragic referentiality of Shakespeare's language within the new citational protocols of cinematic language, Luhrmann misses the mark, paying his outstanding debt to the legend by reproducing Arthur Brooke's *imagery* "to the letter." And in this sense *William Shakespeare's Romeo + Juliet* is "strictly Shakespeare."

> Sticks and bricks *might* break our bones but words will most certainly *kill* us.
>
> —Hortense Spillers, "Mama's Baby, Papa's Maybe: An American Grammar Book"

Luhrmann's passing reference to the "long poem" that serves as Shakespeare's principal source for *Romeo and Juliet* clearly indicates that his desire to understand or represent the complex history of the Romeo and Juliet legend is quite secondary to his desire to place his own "Bazmark" on it. The relationship between Luhrmann and Brooke that emerges in *William Shakespeare's Romeo + Juliet* must, therefore, be considered in light of what Freud classifies as "uncanny." According to Freud, the experience of the uncanny stems from precisely this kind of vague or seemingly "neutral" knowledge which, having been "estranged only by the process of repression," returns in the form of a very real menace, often as a "morbid anxiety" that serves as a harbinger of death. More important for our understanding of the signifying operations of the legendary, Freud explains that, whatever the repressed content is, this psychic and semiotic terrain cannot be traversed "without preserving certain traces of it which can be reactivated" ("Uncanny" 46–47). As we have seen, Luhrmann reimagines *Romeo and Juliet* through the invigorating lens of his cinematic language—repressing, in the process, the primacy of Shakespeare's language. In so doing, however, Luhrmann activates a force far more potent: the uncanny return of the legend and its tragic inevitability, which materializes in the correspondences between the film's cinematic innovations and their source in the death-devoted imagery of Brooke's poem. Thus, *William Shakespeare's Romeo + Juliet* really is William Shakespeare's *Romeo and Juliet* in more ways than Luhrmann could have anticipated, for Luhrmann inherits Shakespeare's own battle with Brooke, taking on the early modern *and* postmodern legend that reduces authorship to the blank-parody function of (re)iterating speech in a dead language.

Even before we explore Brooke's impact on Luhrmann's visual language, our first indication that this ghostly father is traversing *William Shakespeare's Romeo + Juliet* is suggested by the fact that the film's spoken language is, in fact, dominated by the familiar rhythms of rhymed couplets. Though rhymed couplets may seem to be the most comprehensible form of Elizabethan dialogue and, therefore, most user- and audience-friendly, Luhrmann's cast members—with the exception of Claire Danes's Juliet—articulate the couplets in a way that draws attention to their forced, artificial, and constraining nature. Not only does this most conventional of poetic forms suggest the encroaching itinerary of the legend's signifying chain in its contrived, premeditated logic of succession, but also, these rhymed couplets bypass Shakespeare's stylistic deviations and reproduce the monolithic cadence of Arthur Brooke's poem, which is composed *exclusively* in rhymed couplets. And lest we forget, the alienating predictability of witty epigrams and perfect sonnets is precisely what Luhrmann claims to avoid in his film. Further evidence of the possibility that Luhrmann is dealing with an itinerary more potent than his own directorial vision emerges in the prevailing image of Romeo as a knight in shining armor. While the film's depiction of Juliet as Romeo's "bright angel" derives from Luhrmann's clever conversion of Shakespearean metaphor into cinematic pun, the parallel image of Romeo as Juliet's "knight" is only implicit in the "night's cloak" that panders to the lovers' clandestine affair in Shakespeare's play (2.1.117). However, in Brooke's poem, Romeo is repeatedly referred to and described as a "knight." This powerful but derivative image of Romeo-as-knight suggests Luhrmann's grail-like battle against the legend even as it inscribes the impossibility of originality on the shining surface of Romeo's body.

Other details of plot and character not contained in Shakespeare's play likewise seem to cue Luhrmann's film at crucial moments. For example, both Brooke and Luhrmann build scenes of foreshadowing into Romeo and Juliet's first encounter. Just before his first meeting with Juliet, Romeo, still in the throes of an ecstasy trip, suddenly exclaims "the drugs are quick"—precisely the line he will utter over his own dead body once he has swallowed poison in the Capulet tomb. This example of foreshadowing remarkably reproduces Brooke's early indication of the fatal bent of Romeus's love for Juliet, as Romeus gazes upon her and proceeds to "swallo[w] down loves sweete empoysoned bait"—lured into a love for which there is no remedy, as Brooke concludes: "so is the poyson spred throughout his bones and vaines" (10). However, the fact that in Luhrmann's film, Romeo oddly announces his "empoysoning" even *before* he meets Juliet, suggests the momentum that the legend has gathered since Shakespeare's own contention with Brooke four hundred years earlier. Another provocative correspondence between film and poem occurs immediately after Romeo and Juliet meet; before they are able to exchange words, the lovers' discourse is preempted with an invitation to dance. Brooke explains that just as Romeo is about to address himself to Juliet, another "comely" suitor "did fetch her forth to daunce" (l. 246); so, too, in Luhrmann's film, the "comely" figure of Paris kidnaps Juliet as his dance partner before she and Romeo can properly introduce themselves. Luhrmann and Brooke even agree on minor plot details involving the functions of secondary characters. At the lovers' nuptial, for instance, both Luhrmann and Brooke have the Nurse bear witness to the marriage ceremony, but in Shakespeare's play she is conspicuously absent from this scene. Similarly, whereas Paris is missing from the conclusion of Luhrmann's film and Brooke's poem, he *is* present at the end of Shakespeare's play, where he dies by Romeo's hand. Yet the ongoing irony of the film's title lies in the fact that Luhrmann's film, by virtue of its correspondences with Brooke, remains *William Shakespeare's Romeo + Juliet*, for in eliminating the mediation of his Shakespearean source, Luhrmann takes on Brooke "directly"—just as Shakespeare did.

In the spirit of *Strictly Ballroom*'s liberating embrace of the *passadoble*, *William Shakespeare's Romeo + Juliet* introduces a pair of new moves that delimit both the success and failure of Luhrmann's cinematic attempt to finish the business begun by his Shakespearean source. Sizing up these innovations, *People* critic Leah Rozen disparagingly notes that Luhrmann "piles on religious iconography and bathes the whole [film] in pointless water imagery" (21). But these two crucial innovations couldn't be more pointed, particularly when we consider the fact that the film's ubiquitous water imagery and cross iconography are inextricably linked through the rite of baptism—specifically, the new baptism demanded by Shakespeare's Romeo as a means of escaping the tragic referentiality of his name: "Call me but love, and I'll be new baptiz'd; / Henceforth I never will be Romeo" (2.1.93–94). In describing the significance of water in the film, Luhrmann explains that water serves as his motif of choice for escape. Romeo and Juliet "escape into water. They use water for silence, for peace and," he adds, "their 'there's a place for us' moments" ("An Interview" 14). Water, in other words, emerges as a distinctly cinematic substitute for the ebb and flow of language through which the lovers' relationship unfolds in Shakespeare's play. For example, Juliet is first introduced to us under water as she emerges, face-up, from submergence in the bath tub; later, Romeo undergoes a similar purifying ritual when an underwater camera frames his attempt to cleanse the ecstasy from his senses, as he plunges his head into a basin at the Capulet ball. Romeo and Juliet experience love-at-first-sight through the tropical waters of an aquarium—a twist to be topped only by Luhrmann's staging of the balcony scene in a swimming pool. And, finally, on the eve of the newlyweds' consummation, Romeo arrives wet with rain and leaves the next morning by way of the Capulet pool. Of course, the omnipresence of the ocean at Verona Beach locks the entire mise-en-scène into the tidal swings of Luhrmann's manic version of Shakespeare's depressing play. As in *Strictly Ballroom*, then, "the most telling, powerful moments between Romeo and Juliet are silent ones" (Hawker 11), suggesting at least a symbolic return to a pre-linguistic economy of representation, wherein image is anterior and, indeed, preferable to language. As Diana Harris speculates, ever since Australian director Jane Campion's pathbreaking film, *The Piano* (1992), "the associations of water with a pre-symbolic, pre-meaning, fluid and free state of ideal, non-fixed being have been absorbed...by the Western movie-going culture, especially Australasia."[12] But if the

12. I wish to thank Diana Harris for generously providing me with a copy of her unpublished conference paper, "Violent Delights, Violent Ends: Baz Luhrmann's *Romeo +*

Figures 2 and 3. Luhrmann's "two beautiful fish": Juliet (Claire Danes) and Romeo (Leonardo DiCaprio) court each other through the aquarium at the Capulet ball. Twentieth Century Fox, 1996. Photo courtesy of Photofest.

silent flow of water is Luhrmann's motif of choice for realizing Romeo and Juliet's desire to be "new baptiz'd" into a world without referentiality, then his recourse to the cliché "there's a place for us" suggests that the legend is already one step ahead of his attempt to liquidate it. For the source of this cliché is none other than that staple of Western movie-going culture, *West Side Story* (Robert Wise and Jerome Robbins), *the* contemporary incarnation of the Romeo and Juliet legend.

Though water is evoked in early versions of the legend through nautical references, in Brooke's poem, water imagery is deployed uniquely, serving as the singular metaphor through which he relays the "tragicall historye" of the young lovers. For example, descriptions of desire which connect "quenching" with "drenching," as well as images of the sea, ships, tempests, and fishing with baited hooks flow throughout the poem. In several instances it even seems as if Brooke's distinctive use of water imagery actually provides Luhrmann with stage directions. The most stunning example of this uncanny choreographic influence emerges in Romeo and Juliet's first meeting. In *William Shakespeare's*

Juliet," which was presented at the Centenary Conference of Shakespeare and screen scholars in Malaga, Spain, Sept. 21–24, 1999.

Romeo + Juliet, the lovers' meeting across the fish tank is the most technically brilliant, affectively engaging, and seemingly original sequence in the entire film. Luhrmann's camera focuses on Romeo and Juliet's eyes as they dart about in search of each other through the strobe-like glint of water, fish, and wonder that characterizes this surreal love-at-first sight sequence. At times the lovers blend so perfectly with the scenery that it is difficult to distinguish their flirtatious eyes from the flitting motion of the fish that both pander to and prevent Romeo and Juliet's face-to-face meeting. It is remarkable, then, to find that this stunning scene is virtually duplicated in Brooke's poem, which describes a similar dance of gazes between the lovers. This passage begins with Romeus experiencing the whirlwind emotions of love-at-first-sight, and bears quoting at length:

When Romeus saw himselfe in this tempest tost
Where both was hope of pleasant port, and daunger to be lost,
He doubtefull ska[r]sely knew what countenance to keepe;
In Lethies floud his wonted flames were quenched and drenched deepe,
Yea he forgets himselfe....
But onely seeketh by her sight to feede his houngry eyes.
Through them he swalloweth downe loves sweete empoysonde baite,
How surely are the wareless wrapt by those that lye in wayte?
So is the poyson spred throughout his bones and vaines,

That in a while, alas, the while, it hasteth deadly pains.
Whilst Juliet, for so this gentle damsel hight,
From side to side on every one did cast about her sight:
At last her floting eyes were ancored fast on him,
Who for her sake dyd banishe health and fredome from eche limme....
His whetted arrow loosde, so touchd her to the quicke,
That through the eye it strake the hart, and there the hedde did sticke.
It booted not to strive, for why, she wanted strength:
The weaker aye unto the strong of force must yeld at length.
The pomps now of the feast her heart gyns to despyse
And onely joyeth when her eyen meete with her lovers eyes.
When theyr new smitten heartes had fed on loving gleames,
Whilst passing too and fro theyr eyes ymingled were theyr beames,
Eche of these lovers gan by others lookes to knowe
That frendship in their brest had roote, and both would have it grow.

(9–10)

Unwittingly, and with extraordinary economy, Luhrmann's salt water aquarium captures the unspoken eloquence of Brooke's encumbered poetry.

Precisely in its *deviations* from Shakespeare, then, Luhrmann's film reveals its "primal baptism" as *William Shakespeare's Romeo + Juliet*, uncannily reproducing the Bard's head-on confrontation with Brooke's *Tragicall Historye*. Apropos of the film's peculiar repressions and displacements, Geoffrey Nowell-Smith has argued of the adaptation of literature into film that repressions of plot and dialogue return as hysterical moments in the mise-en-scène. So, too, I argue that *William Shakespeare's Romeo + Juliet* undergoes this process of hysterical conversion, for Luhrmann's repression of Shakespeare's language and details of plot return to haunt his mise-en-scène in the form of Brooke's increasingly sinister water imagery. Indeed, in Brooke's poem, water does not function in the same way as it does in Luhrmann's film. Far from signifying escape, water connotes entrapment, becoming a crucial accessory in the legend's quest to bait, ensnare, and hook its unwitting victims. Accordingly, as the volume of water steadily increases in Luhrmann's film, from establishing shots of Romeo and Juliet through the domestic waters of bath tubs and sinks, to their courtship by way of an aquarium and, finally, to Luhrmann's brilliant inversion of the balcony-as-swimming pool, the more we realize that what these images share is not only escape but also *enclosure*. Indeed, the fear that Romeo and Juliet may be drowning in the waters of their new baptism is implied by their frequent lunges under water to avoid the ubiquitous eye of the Capulet surveillance cameras. During the balcony scene, for example, as the guard dog barks and the security camera pans the rippling surface of the pool, Romeo and Juliet submerge themselves; with their hair streaming under water, they stare at each other—as Luhrmann directs them—"like two beautiful fish," suggesting a surreal but eerie sequel to their initial courtship through the aquarium (Pearce and Luhrmann 66). But Romeo and Juliet, while certainly beautiful, will drown if they cannot come up for air, despite the fact that Luhrmann makes it look as though they can breathe under water indefinitely through each other's mouths. This swimming-pool scene thus marks the beginning of the hysterical conversion of Luhrmann's mise-en-scène, as the film follows the flow of *The Tragicall Historye*'s scenery and staging from pleasure to "poyson." Consequently, the next image of fish under water is inflected with gratuitous violence, as Mercutio shoots fish with his gun while wading into the ocean—a proleptic vision, much like the earlier allusion to the "drugs" from which Romeo will die—of the gunshot with which Juliet, the "beautiful fish," will lay herself to rest at the film's conclusion.

It has long been acknowledged that in Shakespeare's play the tragic turning point occurs following the deadly clash between Tybalt and Romeo, which is also the scene that critics have traditionally identified as the structural knot or figurative navel of the Romeo and Juliet legend. In Brooke's poem the far-reaching effects of this pivotal encounter are registered in the chaos of the natural elements, as Brooke likens the fight to a meteorological disturbance:

> Even as two thunderboltes, throwne downe out of the skye,
> That through the ayre the massy earth and seas have power to flye,
> So met these two.

> (38–39)

In Luhrmann's film, this same image of thunderbolts crackling over the seas is produced through cinematic special effects, specifically, through an "optical insert" of a storm breaking over the ocean as Romeo and Tybalt fight. Following this fatal conflict in Luhrmann's film, Romeo gazes up into the sky and, as a mixture of blood and rain stream down his face, he sways deliriously from side to side, crying: "O, I am fortune's fool!" (Pearce and Luhrmann 111). In Brooke we find a parallel description of Romeus as a "broosed barke in cruell seas betost"

(l. 1363)—a personification not only of fickle Fortune but also of the
male body in pain—a spectacle that Luhrmann's camera fetishizes
throughout this sequence. Both poem and film proceed to describe the
storm giving way to a calm as Romeo arrives at Juliet's chamber soaked
with rain and weary from battle. Brooke's version of this scene could
easily provide the voice-over for Luhrmann's silent rendering of
Romeo and Juliet's bittersweet reunion and sexual consummation:

> In stormy wind and wave, in daunger to be lost,
> Thy steerless ship (O Romeus) hath been long while betost.
> The seas we new appeased, and thou by happy starre
> Art comme in sight of quiet haven and, now the wrackfull barre,
> Is hid with swelling tyde, boldly thou mayst resort
> Unto thy wedded ladies bed, thy long desyred port.

> (30)

But this calm after the storm is short-lived, for Romeo must speed to
Mantua as decreed by his banishment. In keeping with the seafaring
metaphors that predominate in *The Tragicall Historye*, Brooke's friar proceeds to assure Romeo that while he is gone, Juliet will remain the
"ancor of [his] blisse," for

> Unto a valiant hart there is no banishment,
> All countrys are his native soyle beneath the firmament.
> As to the fishe the sea.

> (40)

From the perspective of the film, however, there appears to be something fishy about this assurance, for as Luhrmann's Romeo departs
Juliet's bedchamber with a dramatic plunge into the pool, he sinks
under the weight of her "ill-divining soul," which proves to be anchored to the itinerary of the legend. Staring down at her "beautiful
fish" as the water folds ominously over him, Juliet's silent admiration is
suddenly usurped by Shakespearean verse and her own disembodied
voice, as she articulates this tragic itinerary through clenched teeth:

> O God...
> Methinks I see thee, now thou art so low,
> As one dead in the bottom of a tomb.

> (Pearce and Luhrmann 125)

At this moment all three versions of the Romeo and Juliet legend enter into alignment with each other, as Shakespeare's verse and Brooke's imagery conspire to convert Luhrmann's baptismal fantasy of rebirth into a watery tomb.

To describe this sequence as the structural knot of Luhrmann's film is also to imply its connection with hysteria, for what emerges in this scene is a revealing equation of "tomb" and "womb."[13] Long considered to be hysteria's mythical locus of origin, the womb is both a site and a symbol that inspires fantasies of self-creation and fears of mortality, encoding "a message about how we are haunted by the elusive and protean sense of vulnerability, implenitude, and fallibility, even while the mise-en-scène of desire created by phantasy work seeks to hide this traumatic knowledge" (Bronfen xv). Though no longer classified as a clinical phenomenon, the hysterical performance typically revolves around the conversion of psychic trauma into bodily symptoms that serve to camouflage the real source of the problem and, consequently, prevent the cure that would put an end to its protective fantasies of self-fashioning. In its dizzying subversion of origins, hysteria, as Freud frequently lamented, baffles not only diagnosis but also the fabled psychoanalytic "talking cure" and, in effect, language itself. It follows, then, that a film might simulate an hysterical performance by displacing a disturbance of its textual narrative onto its imagery or mise-en-scène. If so, our understanding of hysteria—with its self-conscious sense of performance, provisionality, and multiplicity—must be extended beyond the psychoanalytic to the realm of *cultural* pathologies. As Elisabeth Bronfen persuasively argues, in the context of contemporary culture, the hysterical performance has been most provocatively redefined as a powerful and quintessentially postmodern trope "for dissatisfied desire in general" (384). We might consider, therefore, how the seemingly pathological subversion of linguistic origins performed by Luhrmann's film might function *homeo*pathically to counter the dead language of the legendary, as well as to perform enabling alternatives to the theoretical diagnosis of and prognosis for authorship within postmodern culture. But the hysterical crux of *William Shakespeare's Romeo + Juliet*—the point at which its repressed legendary origin re-

13. In the psychoanalytic context of the subject's alienation into language, the navel and the knot are interchangeable signifiers for the knotted scar that closes off re-entry to the womb and with it, the possibility of returning to a pre-linguistic or "imaginary" universe.

turns to haunt the film's fantasy of escape—occurs when Romeo mouths the word "adieu" as he disappears beneath the dark surface of the Capulet pool, for this is an image that knots together Luhrmann's cinematic vision of new baptism with Brooke's tenacious inscriptions of death-by-drowning. At this moment Luhrmann's suggestive image of the pool-as-birthing-apparatus from which to create a new version of the legend undergoes a conversion from life to death, womb to tomb.

While this scene occurs just after the midpoint of Shakespeare's play, in Luhrmann's film fewer than twenty minutes of running time remain—a clear indication that the legend is gaining momentum en route to its destination. Luhrmann has one more visual trick up his sleeve, however, for the film's omnipresent cross imagery replenishes the promise of rebirth where the baptismal waters ran dry. But in this postmodern world filled with kitschified Mary and Jesus figurines, the crosses that appear on every surface from flesh to formica are all but emptied of their redemptive power. It is no wonder, therefore, that most critics have labeled Luhrmann's cross-laden mise-en-scène pointless, or worse, blasphemous. The real blasphemy lies in the fact that Luhrmann's exploitation of cross iconography is less concerned with exposing a religion bereft of devotion than it is with unveiling a whole new cult of the "Bazmark." Recalling the comments made by set-designer Catherine Martin, this "mark" emerges in her contention that *William Shakespeare's Romeo + Juliet* "has Baz's vision stamped all over it." Martin's comments invoke the classic and virtually obsolete conception of the auteur whose stylistic signature is unmistakably inscribed in the film and is capable of overcoming all barriers to its articulation. In its place are the Warhol-like spectacles of the "commercially conditioned auteur," as Timothy Corrigan has convincingly argued.[14] Corrigan claims that if there are any authors "alive" in postmodern culture, then they are to be found in film. Unlike their modernist counterparts, however, these commercially conditioned auteurs have no presumptions about becoming a controlling presence in film production; rather, today's would-be "authors" focus their creative energies on consumption generating "*commercial* strategies for organizing audience reception" (103). In this bottom-line environment, then, authorial originality is a by-product of supply and demand. But in Luhrmann's film this postmodern privileging of reception over production, commercial paratext over film-text, might prove to be the only means of escaping

14. See Corrigan's chapter "The Commerce of Auteurism," in *A Cinema without Walls.*

the itinerary of the legend. In other words, where Baz can't leave his mark on the legend, he leaves it safely outside its clutches, blazoning the cross trademark coined in the film's title on promotional trailers released before the film, an MTV special aired during the film, and videocassette covers manufactured after the film's commercial run. Thus, with the help of the Bazmark, Luhrmann emerges as a "brand-name vision that precedes and succeeds the film" (Corrigan 102), becoming a kind of legend in his own right.

This "+" or cross also marks one final point of resistance to the dead letter buried in Shakespeare's version of the legend, resonating as Luhrmann's most conspicuous attempt to replace word with image. In his effort to reach "the street sweeper" as well as "the Queen of England," Luhrmann recognizes that his marketing of the film must dispense with the high cultural mystique of Shakespearean drama ("Note" i). A particularly efficient means of announcing, if not accomplishing, this objective is to convert the "and" in Shakespeare's title to a simple "plus" sign, a commonplace of elementary math as well as a symbol of religious devotion. But as Pierre Macherey explains of such attempts to desublimate works that give rise to "the religion of art," before "disposing of these works...men have to *produce* them" (231). Paradoxically, he concludes, "creation is the release of what is already there" and, therefore, the "'creative process' is, precisely not a process, a labour, it is a religious formula to be found on funeral monuments" (232). There could be no more poignant literalization of this fatalistic philosophy than the conclusion of Luhrmann's film, wherein no amount of creativity can convert Romeo and Juliet's funeral monument into a reversal of what's "already in" the destination prescribed by the legend. Here, in the Capulet tomb, the redemptive force of Luhrmann's two "innovations"—the baptismal water imagery and the cross iconography—flow together in the spectacular image of the neon-blue sea of crosses. The force of this final image is so seductive that, if we just squint our eyes, we can imagine Romeo and Juliet floating, swimming in the bliss of their first rendezvous in the Capulet swimming pool. Luhrmann even delays the inevitable tragedy by having Juliet awake just before Romeo consumes the poison, dashing the vial from his lips after it is—barely—too late.[15] And when Juliet kills herself with Romeo's

15. It is important to note that even this seemingly innovative approach to the lovers' death has its origins in earlier performances of the legend, such as the eighteenth-century

gun, the camera cranes higher and higher to obscure any hint of blood. Significantly, Luhrmann's original plan for this scene was to have a "wash of deep red blood floo[d] across them both," but it seems as though he couldn't bear the finality of that image (Pearce and Luhrmann 160). Rather, the camera transports us from the sea of candles back to the swimming pool and a freeze-frame of Romeo and Juliet's underwater kiss. As the purifying baptismal waters rush over the lovers one last time, Luhrmann's remarks betray defeat: "That final image when they kiss under water," he says with chagrin, "it's just silence" ("An Interview" 14).

But this, too, is wishful thinking, for amid the faint aftershock of Juliet's fatal gunshot, we hear the whispers of ghostly fathers *other than* Shakespeare and Brooke chiding Luhrmann for his presumption in seeking to escape the inevitable, as he did so deftly in *Strictly Ballroom.* If, as Slavoj Žižek explains, "The letter which 'arrives at its destination' is also a letter of request for outstanding debts" (*Enjoy* 16), then while Scott and Frannie are able to overcome the ghostly agendas of deadbeat parents seeking to double-cross their best laid plans, Luhrmann's Romeo and Juliet must pay the debt left in their wake as the "original" star-crossed lovers. Accordingly, Lacan contends that the letter arrives at its destination when "the sender...receives...his own message in reverse form" ("Purloined" 52–53), and this is precisely what happens when we realize that the Bazmark—the insignia of Luhrmann's authorial agency—actually materializes the agency of the legend: the dead letter of star-*crossed* love. Not even Luhrmann's final attempt to thwart this tragic itinerary in the film's ending, wherein Romeo and Juliet are only a blink away from escaping double suicide, can thwart the momentum of the dead letter that seeks to settle outstanding accounts. For although this conclusion is nowhere to be found in Shakespeare's play or Arthur Brooke's poem, this ending is, ironically, a to-the-letter rendering of Matteo Bandello's conclusion—Arthur Brooke's principal source—and that of Bandello's source, Luigi Da Porto.[16] And so the

---

theatrical productions of David Garrick as well as nineteenth- and twentieth-century opera stagings. Luhrmann, whose career extends to opera, would certainly be familiar with several variations on the play's conclusion.

16. What we have here, as Žižek might conclude, "is an exemplary case of how 'a letter arrives at its destination' when, in a totally contingent way, it finds its proper place" (*Enjoy* 19).

slippery slope of the legend leads away from Brooke only to entrench Luhrmann's film in the echoes of more ghostly fathers. As Linda Charnes concludes, then, the legend, while "steadily leading us toward the 'promised end,'...promises absolutely nothing" (75).

Yet Luhrmann has delivered the end he promised: to make a movie "the way Shakespeare might have if he had been a filmmaker." Luhrmann's glib leap from the early modern to the postmodern brings this analysis back to the peculiar questions with which it began. Is the Shakespearean text always already postmodern? Is Luhrmann's film-making practice indebted to something indelibly early modern? Initiating this dialogue between the early modern and the postmodern through the mediation of the legendary does not merely satisfy the urge, as Stephen Greenblatt memorably put it, "to speak with the dead" (*Shakespearean Negotiations* i); rather, as in *Hamlet*, this double projection poses a challenge *from* the dead who *talk back*. In *William Shakespeare's Romeo + Juliet*, this image of the dead who talk back emerges in the burned-out movie house of Sycamore Grove, the specter, as Luhrmann describes it, of "a once splendid cinema" in ruins (Pearce and Luhrmann 17). In the futuristic landscape of Verona Beach, Sycamore Grove gestures bleakly toward the destination of cinema in the age of home theater, as it becomes the victim of its own "commercial conditioning" gone awry. It is almost as if, in staging the death of his own medium, Luhrmann takes his place as one more ghostly father calling out from the ruins for surrogate lives. But ruins imply an incomplete destruction—being at once degenerate and regenerate—and, as such, Sycamore Grove might be described as a monument to the difference between creation and adaptation. For if creation is "the release of what's already there," then adaptation is what occurs in its aftermath; contrary to the theoretical legends that explain it away as a compulsion to repeat the past, adaptation, in Leo Braudy's words, is "unfinished *cultural business.*"[17]

Luhrmann's title alone suggests a certain degree of unfinished cultural business in the "plus" sign it features. As Worthen concludes, the plus sign draws attention to what is lacking in the film: "*Romeo ' +' Juliet* makes visible what most performances work to conceal: that dramatic performance, like all other performance, far from originating in the

17. See Braudy's "Afterword: Rethinking Remakes," in *Play It Again, Sam. Retakes on Remakes.*

Figure 4. Sycamore Grove and the death of cinema in *William Shakespeare's Romeo + Juliet.* Twentieth Century Fox, 1996. Photo courtesy of Photofest.

text, can only cite its textual 'origins' with an additive gesture, a kind of '+'" ("Drama, Performance, and Performativity" 1104). But the plus sign, functioning simultaneously as the film's "Bazmark," does something even more important: it provides us with a crucial stage direction for rethinking authorship in the age of adaptation. For the plus sign is an "additive gesture" which reminds us that authorship in postmodern and early modern culture need not be conceived in terms of *negation*— just as this same sign, when viewed as a cross, insists that the road to hell *isn't* paved with authorial intention. Leaving its mark on these and other legends, *William Shakespeare's Romeo + Juliet* encourages us, above all, to adjust our (mind)sets in order to engage in an overdue process of adaptation ourselves, by accounting for provocative authorial practices that prove exceptions to our theoretical rules. Separated by four hundred years, Shakespeare's play and Luhrmann's film demand that we give up the ghost of the creative process to embrace the spirit of adaptation. Thus, as we sift among the ruins of their necessary failures, we might find that there's a place for...*authors*—not a pedestal, but perhaps a pool—wherein, amidst the whirl of historical contingency and cultural expectation that attends any act of adaptation, they have the opportunity to sink *or* swim.

5

Dead Again? Or, the Cultural Logic of Late Auteurism

Forging a vital link between the early modern and postmodern concerns of this analysis, Baz Luhrmann's *William Shakespeare's Romeo + Juliet* documents the elusive and allusive strategies that infuse authorship with life in two historical periods intent on burying the "author" without a trace. As its title alone suggests, *William Shakespeare's Romeo + Juliet* defines the unfinished cultural business of the postmodern auteur as the struggle to deploy "dead styles" without becoming dead again. Resisting the aesthetic nihilism of the cultural logic of late capitalism, Luhrmann's film challenges us to discern the differences between blank parody and pastiche, aligning the latter with "an emergent, still 'critical' postmodernism" that suggests at least a blueprint "for a new kind of intellectual activity in which many people could engage" (Naremore 19).[1] Indeed, Luhrmann's attempt to make Shakespeare accessible to the street sweeper as well as the Queen of England owes much to the cultural logic of *early* auteurism, which emerged as one of the first examples of the distinctly postmodern ethos of aesthetic populism.

---

1. There is an important distinction between auteur theory and auteurism. I am using a very specific version (post 1968) of auteur theory to explore the politics of authorial production in Shakespeare's plays. By contrast, "auteurism" refers to the entire cultural practice of auteur theory, which was largely concerned with the politics of reception and, more specifically, with cultivating a national-popular sensibility. I will be combining these approaches in order to explore the conflict of production and reception in Branagh's Shakespeare films. Additionally, as suggested in the preceding chapter, whereas Jameson uses the terms "blank parody" and "pastiche" interchangeably, I argue that pastiche is an enabling alternative to blank parody, as demonstrated by the work of postmodern auteurs such as Luhrmann and Branagh.

Though often misidentified with modernism and its fetishization of the figure of the artist, auteurism, as James Naremore explains, "belonged to a generation of people everywhere who would begin to use TV like a *cinemateque*, viewing films in no historical order, regarding the classic cinema as something distant or dying" (18). Coupling the sudden availability of old movies on TV with the burgeoning Pop sensibility articulated by figures like Andy Warhol, auteurism was first and foremost a theory of reception used to negotiate this brave new world of recycled images. With the help of pastiche, the early auteur critics combined the "lyrical, almost swooning language" of "high art" with praise for "certain 'pulpy' Hollywood auteurs" (Naremore 17, 18), articulating a crucial break with modernism's hostility toward mass culture even as they went "looking for what Andre Breton had called 'moments of priceless giddiness'" in B movies, *film noir*, and representations of *l'amour fou* (17). But what distinguished auteurism as a "still 'critical'" version of postmodernism was the fact that its most giddy deployments of pastiche were born of a common investment in articulating a "national-popular" sensibility.

A term coined by Antonio Gramsci in his *Prison Notebooks*, the "national-popular" is a structure of feeling capable of generating "expansive, universalizing alliances" among the "people-nation" (Forgacs 181).[2] Though Gramsci envisioned a political realization of this concept, his theory of the national-popular derives from his reflections on aesthetics and particularly authorship. Lamenting the failure of Italian literary culture to generate organic connections with the broad popular masses, Gramsci observed that in Italy, the "'writers' and 'people' do not have the same conception of the world...the feelings of the people are not lived by the writers as their own, nor do the writers have a 'national educative' function: they have not and do not set themselves the problem of elaborating popular feelings after having relived them and made them their own" (207). Significantly, some twenty years after Gramsci documented his disappointing forays through Italian literary culture, the French cinephiles lodged a remarkably similar complaint against the "tradition of quality" plaguing their national film culture. Arguing that French cinema lacked a rapport with the people, these

2. It should be noted from the beginning of this discussion, however, that in invoking Antonio Gramsci's concept of the national-popular, I am appropriating this term from Gramsci's reflections on culture, rather than his specifically political meditations on actualizing a class revolution.

early practitioners of auteurism complained that the elitism, academicism, and high seriousness of the "tradition of quality" was preventing French directors from "throw[ing] themselves into a film whose perspective is essentially that of their own culture" (Leenhardt, qtd. in Bazin et al. 35). Like Gramsci, who cited Shakespeare as a model of the "national educative function" of authorship, the French cinephiles also found in Shakespearean drama the rudiments of a national-popular sensibility in their quest to exorcise the "rotten" elitism from their cinematographic kingdom.[3] Such was the "still 'critical'" and uniquely postmodern sense of aesthetic populism that marked the cultural logic of early auteurism, a legacy that Baz Luhrmann's *William Shakespeare's Romeo + Juliet* invokes in its use of pastiche as an enabling approach to authorship in the age of blank parody. But the director whose work most provocatively resembles the "perturbed spirit" of late auteurism is Kenneth Branagh, the figure in whom the shreds and patches of auteurism's postmodern, Shakespearean, and national-popular legacies find an unlikely homecoming.

ᘓᨆᘒ

Perhaps the most critical distinction between the early modern and the postmodern auteur lies in the fact that while both are generated as an effect, indeed, a montage effect of the conflict between an "author" and an "apparatus," the postmodern auteur is endowed with a body. In other words, while a discussion of Shakespeare-the-auteur can lead only to the contested remains of a "corpus," the concept of the *Shakespearean auteur* poses an opportunity to localize these remains in *somebody*. And this body, as suggested in the preceding chapter, is fundamentally a performing body, one that engages in the possibilities of

3. These six characters in search of auteurs were not alone in pursuing the boomerang effect between their burgeoning notion of a national-popular cinema and the "perturbed spirit" of Shakespearean drama. Writing two years later in 1959, auteur-critic Luc Moullet looked to Shakespeare and Marlowe for cues in analyzing the "classic contradictions" that inhabit the directorial styles of Orson Welles and Sam Fuller, respectively (146). Shortly thereafter in 1965, Robin Wood launched an auteurist celebration of Hitchcock, comparing him with Shakespeare in an effort to cultivate a distinctly English national-popular sensibility. Even in the context of American cinema, Shakespeare emerged alongside the national-popular claims of auteur critics such as Andrew Sarris, who claimed that "no self-respecting American film historian should ever accept Paris as the final authority on the American cinema" (245).

"surrogation" as an antidote to the position of negation that postmodernism ascribes to authorship and agency alike. As Timothy Corrigan suggests, perhaps the principal way that the auteur keeps from becoming dead again is by locating a surrogate mode of production in reception. For Corrigan, authorship is a performance that is less concerned with the film-text than it is with the film's commercial paratext. Removing themselves from the textual *locus classicus* of authorship, Corrigan's "commercially conditioned" auteurs are situated along an *"extra*textual path" (105), as trailers, talk-show appearances, tie-ins, "the making of" books, and other promotional ephemera all conspire to reconstitute authorship as a pastiche strategy for organizing audience reception.[4] Clearly, then, we've come a long way from Andrew Sarris's swooning inscription of the auteur as a figure characterized by an *"élan* of the soul"* ("Notes" 587), for Corrigan's auteurs must sell their souls, "giv[ing] up their authority as authors and...communicat[ing] as simply figures within the commerce of that image" (136).

Corrigan's contention that authorship and auteurism today revolve around reception rather than production is a crucial intervention in poststructuralist theory, importantly recasting the banished specter of agency in a pivotal new role in consumer culture. But Corrigan's idea of the "commercially conditioned auteur" takes as too representative postmodernism's privileging of the commodity form—to the exclusion of other important aspects of the postmodern—among them, what Jameson identifies as postmodernism's struggle with modernism's remainders. A point that is often overlooked in theories of postmodernity is the fact that this historical period is characterized by its struggle with the modernist era that precedes it, resulting in a motley cultural moment wherein "[m]odernist styles...become postmodern codes" (Jameson, *Postmodernism* 17). Accordingly, I will argue that the postmodern auteur embodies a similar ambivalence, emerging as a *bricoleur* who attempts to resituate the high modernist notion of artistic *production* within a low postmodern mode of mass cultural *reception*. For to follow Corrigan's lead in completely depriving the contemporary meaning of "auteur" of its modernist ambitions—its investment in expressionist ideals and autonomous identity—is to forget that the very notion of the postmodern

4. Directors Spike Lee and Quentin Tarantino, and to a lesser extent Baz Luhrmann, are perfect examples of the auteur-as-star, vigorously marketing themselves—with the help of promotional venues such as MTV—as cult figures who write, direct, and—for Lee and Tarantino—star in their own films.

is a constitutive combination, even contradiction, of modernist motives and mass cultural means. Surely directors haven't stopped caring about personal expression just because academics say they have. Rather, their means of expression have changed and, to agree in part with Corrigan, what we find in the postmodern auteur is an attempt to construct a unique style and singular identity in the sphere of reception as opposed to production. The problem lies in the fact that the sphere of reception is itself a party to the fragmenting dynamics of commodity logic and consumer culture. Thus, like its early modern precursor, the postmodern auteur is also a third term—constituted as the inexorable residue of a collision between opposing historical and cultural forces.

Kenneth Branagh is a figure who stretches the limits of our thinking about postmodern authorship. In many ways, his work corresponds to Corrigan's formula for the commercially conditioned auteur, for Branagh envisions authorship as a practice that takes place within the sphere of reception as much as production, and his films consistently generate paratexts that focus on the "commercial performance of the business of being an auteur" (Corrigan 104). But Branagh challenges Corrigan's "giddy" definition of authorship, for as a postcolonial subject, he is simultaneously threatened by postmodernism's privileging of "the leveling, equalizing indifferent operations of the commodity form" which, as Terry Eagleton observes, "respects no unique identity [and] transgresses all frontiers" (36). Branagh's quest to achieve a unique identity is a quest that he articulates, ironically, in the name of Shakespeare. As I have argued in the preceding chapters, the Shakespearean corpus is, above all, a *contested* body—one that is at once enervated and energized by the equalizing, but far from indifferent, tensions between source and subjectivity, actor and "author," tradition and trespass. More than any other contemporary figure working with Shakespeare, Branagh *embodies* the dramatic tensions that constitute the Shakespearean corpus, exposing the tenacity of the Shakespearean remainder—the irreducible surplus that reveals a history of conflict beneath the "worked over," "smoothed out" surface of his shimmering adaptations. What makes Branagh's work even more valuable for analyses of Shakespearean authorship in the age of adaptation is the fact that this remainder assumes both personal and geopolitical dimensions. Taking Luhrmann's authorial interventions one step further, Branagh employs strategies of surrogation in order to reinvent not only his Shakespearean source material but also the sources of his own identity. In basing his authorial mission on the omission of his own site of origin, however, Branagh's work returns us to the empty search for Shakespeare with which we began, revealing the extent to which any authorial mission assumed in the name of "Shakespeare" is, like the cinematic specter of Sycamore Grove, a structure with a hole in the middle. But this void is also the space of possibility and, therefore, the landmark of the postmodern auteur's intervention in the cultural pathology of authorship. What most distinguishes Branagh from other directors working on Shakespeare, then, is how he uses this space to generate a singular confrontation between the postmodern and the postcolonial, the "national" and the "popular."[5]

∽⚬∾

HORATIO: There's no offense, my lord.
HAMLET: Yes, by St. Patrick, but there is, Horatio,
            And much offense too.

—Shakespeare, *Hamlet*

Describing the peculiar and distinctly politicized relationship between sacrosanct ideas of English heritage and postmodern consumer culture, Alan Sinfield observes that "the New Right subjects high culture to a market ethos in order to develop one part of its project, but

---

5. The history of filmmakers working on Shakespeare is as long as the history of cinema itself, but the two most prominent members of this tradition are Sir Laurence Olivier and Orson Welles. Yet neither of these extraordinary directors qualify as postmodern auteurs; Olivier is a thoroughly modernist figure, and Welles, who clearly anticipates some of the aesthetic and economic tensions endemic to postmodern cultural production, cannot be firmly identified with this historical period. For an elaborate discussion of Welles's positioning vis-a-vis modernism and postmodernism, see Michael Anderegg's *Welles, Shakespeare, and Popular Culture*. The title of this text is somewhat deceiving, however, for while Anderegg offers an extensive and fascinating assessment of Welles's popularizing approach to Shakespeare in mass media *other than film*, his analysis of Welles's Shakespeare films continually asserts and, in fact, laments their failure to connect with a wide popular audience. If we scan the more recent ranks of directors with Shakespearean credentials, we find an impressive list of avant-garde figures that includes Akira Kurosawa, Jean-Luc Godard, Derek Jarman, Gus Van Sant, Peter Greenaway, and, along more popular lines, Franco Zeffirelli, and, of course, Baz Luhrmann. However, the provocative, frequently obscurantist work of directors such as Greenaway and Jarman has more in common with the elitist productions of the "authors' theater" described in Chapter Two than

thereby undermines the mystique of cultural hierarchy and hence one of the convenient sources of state legitimation (the same thing has been happening to the UK royal family). One outcome is the determinedly inoffensive 'commercial' Shakespeare films of Kenneth Branagh; another is that dissident versions become more viable" ("Heritage and the Market," 271). Sinfield's remarks typify the academic response to Kenneth Branagh's "determinedly inoffensive 'commercial'" oeuvre—responses which, however perceptive, rarely accommodate considerations of the paratext that affects his work most of all: his experience as an internal émigré within the United Kingdom. When Branagh was ten years old, his parents decided to leave Belfast for Reading, England. Despite the fact that they were Protestants and, therefore, a political majority in Northern Ireland, Branagh's family experienced the chaos of the Troubles entering their own back yard, as Branagh recalls:

we heard the screams of my brother and his mates tearing up the hill towards us, yelling "Get inside, get inside!" They were being followed by a dark, clamorous mass which revealed itself to be a crowd of wild-eyed Protestants.... With the broken pieces of wrought iron they smashed a single window in each of the Catholic houses.... It meant, we know who you are and where you are, and if you don't move out, then next time we'll set the house on fire. (*Beginning* 19–20)

Branagh's response to this surge of street violence was confused complicity; he joined a local gang to loot a supermarket that had been bombed and, following the presentation of the spoils to his mother, his parents decided to move to England. But young Kenneth couldn't leave his troubles behind, for he quickly encountered a language barrier that threatened to single him out as an "enemy within" his new surroundings.[6] Fearful that his Belfast accent would make him an accomplice in the death of English soldiers, Branagh explains that he "was very careful when the subject of English casualties came up at school. It was another stage in the painful process of learning to keep my mouth shut" (24). The first stage was learning to speak in a new accent:

it does with the popular tradition central to Shakespearean drama. Similarly, the more commercially savvy adaptations of directors such as Zeffirelli and Luhrmann reflect an approach to the popular—itself a hotly contested term—that is popularizing rather than populist; they do not foster an explicit connection to the national-popular.

6. The phrase "enemy within" is drawn from Paul Gilroy's *There Ain't No Black in the Union Jack,* a study that will be cited throughout this discussion.

I was acutely aware of my speech at a school where it seemed to me everyone spoke like BBC newsreaders. The accent problem was already causing friction at home.... It was a traumatic period, for the whole family was undergoing an enforced change of personality.... The early 1970s were not a good time
to be Irish in Reading [England]. Many of the children at school had older
brothers in the [English] Army. Every death reported on the television news
made me try to change even further; I longed just to blend in. After a year or so
I'd managed to become English at school and remain Irish at home.... For as
long as I could, I kept up the double life, but my voice gradually took on the
twang of suburbia. (23–24)

This difficult period of adjustment crystallizes what Branagh describes as his lifelong affliction with an "Anglo-Irish sense of 'belonging nowhere'" (81). As a product of the infantilized Protestant population of Northern Ireland, Branagh, like his compatriots, suffers from an
identity in a state of arrested development. At once subject to the dis-
approving gaze of big brother England and the menacing disdain of the
Republic, the Belfast or Ulster Protestants are caught in a condition of
"double isolation." As Tom Nairn explains in *The Break-up of Britain*, the
Ulster Protestant's are not "'Irish,' in the sense that Catholic based
agrarian nationalism ha[s] established.... But they [are] not really
'British' either: they were always, and they still remain, profoundly and
embarrassingly different from the society they imagine they are a frontier of" (233–34). As documented in the work of many writers and
artists of the Irish Renaissance, this Anglo-Irish predicament of "double
isolation" can lead to a debilitating state of identity confusion; offering a
glib synopsis of this predicament, Oscar Wilde once observed that "'I
am Irish by race,... but the English have condemned me to speak the
language of Shakespeare'" (qtd. in Kiberd 35). But what exactly does it
mean to be *condemned* to speak the language of Shakespeare? For James
Joyce, the answer goes something like Caliban's rant in *The Tempest*:
"you taught me Shakespeare, and my profit on't, is that I have learned
how to curse." Shakespearean drama, according to Joyce, strikes a
chord of empathy with the Irish experience, for "the note of banishment, banishment from the heart, banishment from home, sounds un-
interruptedly from *The Two Gentlemen of Verona* onward till Prospero
breaks his staff, buries it certain fathoms in the earth and drowns his
book" (Joyce, qtd. in Kiberd 271). Shakespeare, in other words, has an
uncanny capacity to convey the problem historically faced by the Irish
as strangers in their own land, sounding the anomalous depths of the

"'mixed' experience of the Irish people, as both exponents and victims of British imperialism" (Kiberd 15).[7]

Yet this "mixed experience" can also be a locus of opportunity, a prompt to perform an enabling relationship to the sectarian dynamic through "surrogation." Posing a variation on this performative theme, Declan Kiberd begs the perennial question: "Was there ever an Irish man of genius who did not get himself turned into an Englishman as fast as he could?" Though such a conversion sounds like an act of national apostasy, this simultaneous alienation and theatricalization of the self is the trademark, paradoxically, of what Kiberd describes as the "authentic self-begetting Irishman" (121). In other words, in the absence of good English parenting, the Irish artist who hopes to avoid colonization by others must engage in *self*-conquest. Yeats was one of the most prominent proponents of this philosophy, embracing the precarious agency of self-conquest as a means of negotiating between a past and a putative self. Historically, then, the central preoccupation of the Irish artist

has been with a particular experience of what we may call *translation. By this I mean the adaptations, readjustments, and reorientations* that are required of individuals and groups who have undergone a traumatic cultural and political crisis so fundamental that they must forge for themselves a new speech, a new history or life story that would give it some rational or coherent form. (Deane 14, emphasis added)

The source of Kenneth Branagh's self-translation is, of course, Shakespeare, the figure in whom his cinematic and cultural processes of "adaptation" converge.

7. This connection to "the people" defines the appeal of Shakespeare to other artists associated with the Irish Renaissance and its legacy. Even before Gramsci and the French cinephiles explored the national-popular sensibility in Shakespeare, W. B. Yeats linked the Bard's appropriation of popular lore with the articulation of an emergent sense of nation in his plays, explaining that "'as in Elizabethan England,'" every "'national movement... has arisen out of a study of the common people, who preserve national characteristics more than any other class'" (qtd. in Kiberd 270). Following Yeats's cue, Jonathan Synge took this sentiment one step further, adding—to the equation of Shakespeare and the "national-popular"—Ireland: "It is probably that when the Elizabethan dramatist took his ink-horn and sat down to his work, he used many phrases that he had just heard, as he sat at dinner, from his mother or his children. In Ireland, those of us who know the people have the same privilege [.]...In Ireland, for a few years more, we have a popular imagination that is fiery, magnificent, and tender..." (qtd. in Kiberd 274). According to these artists, then, Shakespeare is equally at home in the English *and* the Irish Renaissance.

～✕～

"Hidden in the classic writings of England," Kiberd relates, "lay many subversive potentials, awaiting their moment like unexploded bombs. So the young Irish man and woman could use Shakespeare to explore, and explain, and even perhaps to justify themselves" (268). Seeking to escape the memory of real bombs, Branagh's appropriation of the Bard is, at first glance, subversive only to the extent that Shakespeare enables him to subvert his own Irish heritage. Caught in the debilitating adolescent role of being "English at school and Irish at home," Branagh's life and art have assumed a schizophrenic pattern of Yeatsian self-conquest, dominated by two conflicting principles, both of which may be coined from Shakespeare's name. The first half of this equation may be described as the "Will principle," or, Branagh's will to overcompensate for his Anglo-Irish lack of belonging by out-Englishing the English with the help of Shakespeare, the quintessential signifier of this "happy breed of men." The second half of this Shakespearean negotiation is the "Billy principle" which, by contrast, represents the return of Branagh's repressed Irish identity. A household name throughout Ulster, "Billy" signifies the name of Branagh's father, brother, countless friends, and ultimately, "King Billy," also known as King William of Orange, the folkloric hero of Northern Ireland's Protestant Community. These two conflicting modes of surrogation first began to clash when Branagh was a student at the Royal Academy of Dramatic Art in London, where he found himself having to choose between playing Hamlet for RADA and auditioning for Graham Reid's made-for-television *Billy* plays. Eventually a series comprised of four plays, the *Billy* dramas revolve around the story of an adolescent, working-class Ulster Protestant through whom the schizophrenic experience of sectarianism is represented. Not surprisingly, the casting announcement stipulated an "authentic Belfast accent"; but Branagh explains that, despite the fact that he was anxious for work and the prospect of an Equity card, he "resisted [auditioning], as I knew this ad would draw thousands of bogus Belfast backgrounds, and I'd have no chance. Anyway, *Hamlet* played from 24–28 October, the dates would never work out, RADA would never release me" (*Beginning* 74). Based on this confession it seems as though Branagh's devotion to the "Will principle" had convinced him that he, too, was a "bogus" Irishman. And though he eventually auditioned and landed the lead as "Billy," Branagh *did* have to persuade the di-

rector that "York street" where he grew up "was just below the surface" of his adopted English accent (74).[8]

What is particularly interesting about this episode is the clash it implies between high and low culture, reflected in the battle for center
stage between the RADA *Hamlet* and the Belfast TV *Billy*. Underscoring
this distinction with added disdain, Branagh rushed back to London
upon completion of the shooting schedule for the *Billy* plays, claiming
that the "BBC Ulster studio doubles as a cattle shed for half the year
and the cows were clamouring for the space" (82). Such gratuitous
slander barely conceals Branagh's painful experience of "double isolation," as the mutually exclusive coordinates of his identity vie for the
body of this self-described "Irishman in Ireland who lives in England
and speaks English, but who is making a living as an Irishman" (81).
Anxious to eliminate the obvious confusion embedded in this description, Branagh soon learned to suppress his Irish accent entirely by manu-
facturing what he describes as a "quintessentially English" identity
and, subsequently, by gaining approval for his performance from the
great arbiter and sculptor of English "character": the Royal Shakespeare
Company.[9] But Branagh was still not free from the grip of his double
life, for the "Billy principle" threatened to take over the "Will principle"
in his RSC debut as Henry V, assuming the contours of Branagh's
uniquely "Irish inheritance" of "original guilt" (58): "Henry was haunted,
I felt, not just by his father and their troubled relationship, but also by
the ghost of Richard II, whom he invokes at the end of the famous
'Upon the King' soliloquy. This seemed to me to reveal a massively
guilty man" (137). Guilty, perhaps, over his abandonment of his Irish
homeland, Branagh soon left the Royal Shakespeare Company in
search of Ireland's greener pastures, completing his fourth *Billy* production and writing a play, significantly, about a "schizophrenic" Ulster Protestant teenager (194). Branagh's relentless shuttling back and
forth between Will and Billy, England and Ireland, illustrates the
painful crux of Yeatsian self-conquest which, as Kiberd observes, invites haunting by alien selves, masks, and ghosts *without necessarily*

8. For an extensive treatment of this conflict between the Will and Billy principles see
my essay titled "Kenneth Branagh at the Quilting Point: Shakespearean Adaptation, Postmodern Auteurism, and the (Schizophrenic) Fabric of 'Everyday Life.'"

9. Branagh's autobiography, *Beginning*, is devoted to his reflections on the formation of
a "quintessentially English" identity through his first major foray into cultural and cinematic adaptation: the making of *Henry V*.

leading "to the discovery of an answering self within" (121). Uncannily acting out the relentless tensions endemic to his Shakespearean source of self-translation, Branagh altered his course, hoping to arrive at this promised end of self-possession by turning to the ultimate performance of surrogation: direction—and, more specifically, the cultural logic of late auteurism.

As suggested throughout this analysis, the postmodern auteur is both a haunting and a haunted figure, constructing a provisional, pastiche agency from the ever-mutating vehicle of mass culture. But for Branagh, the often-euphoric fragmentation of the postmodern is held in check by his status as a postcolonial subject; for it is one thing to capitalize on the leveling promise of postmodernity in order to overcome a devastating history of sectarian dynamics, but it is another thing altogether to remove oneself "from that condition into one in which all these lesions and occlusions are forgotten, in which the postmodernist simulacrum of pluralism supplants the search for a legitimating mode of nomination and origin" (Deane 19).[10] This search for a legitimating mode of nomination and origin defines the unfinished cultural business of the postmodern auteur, writ large in the project of "adaptation"—cultural and cinematic—that Kenneth Branagh undertakes in his Shakespeare films.

Branagh's search for a legitimating mode of nomination and origin led him to form his own production company, which he named—in keeping with the self-begetting ethos of the Irish—"Renaissance." Having left the RSC still in the debilitating throes of his double life, Branagh

10. This is the double-edge of postmodernism, which at once facilitates and threatens the formation of postcolonial identities, as Simon During notes:

the concept of postmodernity has been constructed in terms which more or less intentionally wipe out the possibility of post-colonial identity. Indeed, intention aside, the conceptual annihilation of the post-colonial condition is actually necessary to any argument which attempts to show that "we" now live in postmodernity. For me, perhaps eccentrically, post-colonialism is regarded as the need, in nations or groups which have been victims of imperialism, to achieve an identity uncontaminated by universalist or Eurocentric concepts and images. Here the argument becomes complex, since post-colonialism constitutes one of those Others which might derive hope and legitimation from the first aspect of postmodern thought, its refusal to turn the Other into the Same. As such it is threatened by the second moment in postmodern thought. (449)

resolved to exploit the split ends of his identity through pastiche, founding Renaissance in an effort to create the cinematic equivalent of what he calls "total theatre"—a "combination of high and low culture that [i]s visually exciting, fast and intellectually stimulating" (*Beginning* 182). All too aware of "the barriers that separate Shakespeare and the theatre in general from a truly popular audience" (63), Branagh turned to a filmmaking practice that would offer "something for everyone" (193), creating Shakespeare movies that combine legendary thespians with up-and-coming Hollywood heartthrobs, literary classics with Pop history, and a uniquely English sense of entitlement with a trendy multicultural mystique. This postmodern crossing of aesthetic boundaries between high and low culture also extends to national borders, reconciling the Will and Billy principles by positioning Shakespeare as the site of a national-popular sensibility. For while Branagh's choice of Shakespeare is an obvious reflection of his modernist quest for a "quintessentially English" identity, then his cinematic approach to Shakespeare— translating the Bard into the postmodern idiom of popular film—is an equally distinctive tribute to his Irish heritage.[11] Indeed, Branagh's desire to perform in the first place was born of his participation in the communal practices of Ulster everyday life. Fondly, he recalls vying for attention among his family and friends during their "collective yarn sessions," wherein "the past was strongly alive in everyday discourse and was relished by all generations" (13). Thus, while Branagh clearly

11. By associating "high" and "low" with England and Ireland, respectively, I am working within Branagh's own experience and description of these places. For Branagh, England signifies high culture through RADA, the RSC, and later, the patronage of Prince Charles, whereas Ireland signifies low culture in Branagh's own nostalgic recollections of his Ulster life—a hodge-podge of "drinking," "storytelling," and "the crack" (*Beginning* 81). The "crack" is an Irish combination of social drinking, storytelling, one-upmanship, and people "all jammed into somebody's tiny front room, squatting on the floor and perching on the ends of sofas" (*Beginning* 14–15). In an ethnographic study titled *Clashing Symbols*, Lucy Bryson and Clem McCartney analyze how "everyday" practices become an art form in the context of Northern Ireland's annual King Billy celebrations. Such commemorative practices include white-washing homes, hoisting flags, buying new clothes and shoes, and painting "kerb stones, bus shelters, lamp posts and pillars" (131), all of which signify Ulster's Unionist loyalty. See particularly the chapter on "Symbols in Everyday Community Life." Significantly, de Certeau explains that "everyday practices" are often "tactical in character," and suggest possibilities for aesthetic and cultural reclamation by enabling "victories of the 'weak' over the 'strong'" through "clever tricks, knowing how to get away with things, 'hunter's cunning,' maneuvers, polymorphic simulations," and so on (xix). This "everyday life" approach to Shakespeare provides the raw materials of Branagh's "quilting operation."

adopts Shakespeare—the historic signifier of all things "quintessentially English"—as his surrogate father, he simultaneously *adapts* Shakespeare for others, converting a debilitating sense of "belonging nowhere" into an "experimental 'mixing and meshing'" that people can enjoy everywhere. The success of this "still critical" postmodernism is evident in the reception of Renaissance's debut in—of all places—Belfast: "There was a funny sort of inverted snobbery and pride about my involvement with Shakespeare," Branagh relates. "They liked the idea of one of their lads showing the English how to do it...The recurring uneasiness that I felt about my Irishness was beginning to disappear" (213).

What an exploration of Branagh's work reveals, then, is that while the early modern auteur-function is associated with the unsettling and "Puckish" production of montage effects, the postmodern auteur-function derives from the flip-side of montage: "ideological quilting." Slavoj Žižek explains that "society is always traversed by an antagonistic split which cannot be integrated into the symbolic order," and the stake of ideological quilting "is to construct a vision of society which does exist, a society which is not split by an antagonistic division, a society in which the relation between its parts is organic, complementary" (*Sublime* 126). This illusion of organic society is achieved, in part, through the designation of a "quilting point," the "nodal point" that unites "the multitude of 'floating signifiers' in a given ideological field" and performs "the totalization by means of which this free floating of ideological elements is halted, fixed—that is to say, by means of which they become part of the structured network of meaning" (Žižek, *Sublime* 87). As suggested earlier, this is, ironically, the very role that Branagh ascribes to Shakespeare, the figure who quilts together the loose ends of his fractured identity even as he facilitates the broader company mission of "fulfill[ing] all the Renaissance creeds of life-enhancing populism" (*Beginning* 199).

Branagh's approach to casting arrangements within his films offers a specific demonstration of how his theory of ideological quilting works in practice. Aspiring "to create a level playing field" of actors through ensemble casts comprised of RSC veterans alongside inexperienced Shakespeareans and non-English actors, Branagh explains that

I...like the clash, if you like, of accents and sounds, so that we don't try to homogenize the sound of Shakespeare, which again, in its clichéd form, is equated with some kind of overblown theatrical delivery, usually English in accent....

In casting different groups of people, however, you...start to create a more
level playing field...from quite different cultural viewpoints. (Qtd. in
Crowdus 36)

As a "clash" becomes a "quilt," Branagh comes closer to fulfilling his
objective of "reach[ing] as many people as possible" by "present[ing]
popular art. Not poor art or thin art or even 'arty' art, but popular art
that would expand the mind and the senses and really entertain" (*Beginning* 193). Beneath this postmodern sales pitch, however, Branagh's
films play out a far more complex negotiation between his promise of
aesthetic populism and his modernist pursuit of a singular identity—
echoing, in unintended tribute, the historical tensions between individual and collaborative constructions of agency that divide the Shakespearean corpus against itself. And this is the point at which the line
between adapting Shakespeare and adopting him becomes provocatively fuzzy, for as Kiberd observes, it "is one thing to imitate your
Shakespearean father, but it is quite another to...turn him into a revised version of yourself" (274). Indeed, more significant than Branagh's
self-serving revisions of Shakespeare are the ways in which *Shakespeare*
revises *Branagh,* as the crisis of legitimacy that haunts the Shakespearean
corpus finds a body and a battleground through which to wage its ongoing battle for authorization.

Branagh's crisis of authorization is articulated in the tensions his
films generate between reception and production—tensions which, in
turn, stem from a conflict between the directorial body and the acting
body. (The geopolitical "bodies" at stake in this conflict will be explored
in Chapter Six.) In the context of the performative logic of late auteurism, the directorial body, generally speaking, is less easily colonized than the acting body, for the postmodern auteur preemptively divides and conquers the self by continually dispersing and reinventing
it along an "extratextual path." This radical relocation of authorial
agency from the sphere of production to reception leads to the *reductio
ad absurdum* that "auteur movies" are, paradoxically, "made before
they get made" (Corrigan 105). Conversely, the actor's body—while capable of having a similar affect on film reception in "star" discourse—
is a distinctly more vulnerable body. As W. B. Worthen argues, despite
the attempt of actor training to render this body pre-cultural and pre-
ideological, "the text of the social—behavior, language—is registered as
bodily nature" and, therefore, inescapably inscribed on the actor's
body (*Shakespeare and the Authority* 111). What happens, then, when the

director's body and the actor's body belong to the same person? It is not uncommon for directors—most notably, Hitchcock—to "pop up" in their films in ways that intentionally disrupt the diegesis and bemuse or baffle audiences; others, like Orson Welles, exploit the merger of directorial vision and performing vessel in ways that magnify the significance of both auteur and actor, often to such a powerful degree that we cannot tell where the diegesis ends and reality begins. By contrast, Branagh's "two bodies"—not unlike the medieval king's—are dramatically discontinuous, for they belong to the postmodern and the postcolonial, respectively. Indeed, if Branagh's "divine" directorial body supports a vision of Shakespearean community as the seamless product of ideological quilting, then his "natural" actor's body bears the scars of this process, emerging in his often extraordinary attempts to present his own body as a healthy alternative to the recurring specter of the body-in-pain.

Branagh's acting body generates a narrative quite different from the directorial body's proleptic, even apotropaic rhetoric of inclusion, for in the course of production, this body emerges rigidly poised against the very differences Branagh courts at the level of reception. In *Henry V*, for example, Branagh's body is armor-laden and literally steeled against attack. As I argue in the following chapter, however, this defensive strategy is aimed not at the French but at the geopolitical confusion embodied in the Irish Captain Macmorris, the figure who pushes the king's "two bodies" and Branagh's two identities as a Belfast native and an honorary Englishman to the breaking point. Serving as a provocative "sequel" to *Henry V*, *Dead Again* also revolves around the theme of identity confusion. This Hitchcockian thriller is the story of an amnesia victim (played by Emma Thompson) and a detective (played by Branagh) who is hired to find out the victim's true identity before false prophets and would-be murderers do. Projecting his own fears of colonized identity onto a surrogate psyche, Branagh-as-detective cleverly positions himself as the guarantor of "proper" identities which, as he knows all too well, *is* a matter of life or death. In *Peter's Friends* and *Much Ado About Nothing*, the process of "healthy" identity-formation is inscribed not on the *tabula rasa* of the mind, but rather, directly on the body. Though one might expect Branagh to play the titular character in *Peter's Friends*, Branagh casts himself as a relatively minor character—one of "Peter's friends"—all of whom gather at Peter's house for a holiday reunion. But as friendships devolve into fights and holiday spirits give way to depression, the difference between Branagh and Peter acquires major significance. Representing the spread of social dis-ease that threatens to disband the reunion, Peter ushers in the New Year by announcing his status as a diseased body par excellence: the AIDS victim. Consequently, *Much Ado About Nothing* works hard to distinguish this pale, enfeebled, deficient body from the impeccably healthy bodies of its cast members, who appear robust and tan from a shooting schedule that literally takes place under the Tuscan sun. What is particularly interesting about this film is the way in which Branagh's directorial promise of making *Much Ado* a Shakespeare film for "the world" (*Much Ado Screenplay* x) is belied by the caste system that the film unconsciously endorses in positioning the one naturally dark-skinned actor, Denzel Washington, at the margins of its Utopian community. Serving as a convenient synecdoche for all the non-white others that the film's putatively international scope fails to encompass, Washington functions more powerfully as a reminder of how "the Irish"—and, by extension, Branagh—"became white," that is, by subscribing to the same system of discrimination in America that the English subjected the Irish to in Britain.[12]

Branagh's later films, particularly *Mary Shelley's Frankenstein* and *Hamlet*, accentuate the tensions between his actorly attempt to naturalize his exclusive entitlement to a "proper" English identity and his directorial rhetoric of life-enhancing populism. What distinguishes *Mary Shelley's Frankenstein* and *Hamlet* from Branagh's earlier films, however, is the fact that the conflict between production and reception is not projected onto a marginalized other but, rather, is inscribed on the signifying surface of Branagh's own body. In his notes on the making of *Mary Shelley's Frankenstein*, Branagh the director announces his desire to make Victor into "less of an hysteric" and, he adds, "a little more physical, earthy…a powerful figure [who] has more to lose" ("Frankenstein Reimagined" 17, 19). Consequently, Branagh the actor responds by radically changing the appearance of his own body, converting it from a non-descript, amorphous softbody into a chiseled Hollywood hardbody. The hardbody, as Susan Jeffords defines it in her work on Hollywood masculinity, represents a fantasy of male self-fashioning.

12. I refer here to the title of Noel Ignatieff's fascinating exploration of the Irish in America, *How the Irish Became White*. In his notes on the production of *Much Ado about Nothing*, Branagh claims that he wanted to make the film "as international as possible" (*Much Ado Screenplay* x). For a thorough analysis of the racial politics of Branagh's *Much Ado about Nothing*, see my essay titled "*Much Ado about Nothing?* Shakespeare, Branagh, and the 'National-Popular' in the Age of Multinational Capital."

Smooth, consistent, and masterful in its refusal to be "'messy' or 'confusing,'" the hardbody is defined by "hard edges, determinate lines of action, and clear boundaries" (27), offering a self-affirming rebuttal to the hysterical "softbody's" haunting message of lack. Indeed, the hysterical body continually broadcasts its own deficiencies "by transforming anxieties and desires into somatic manifestations" written on the body (Bronfen xii). It is no wonder, then, that Branagh wishes to make Victor into "less of an hysteric" and, ideally, a little more "powerful." What we must ask, however, is what *Branagh* has "to lose"—should his directorial cure or actorly hardbody prove insufficiently powerful?

Branagh's directorial interest in reducing Victor's "hysteria" and his actorly conversion into a hardbody suggests a cause-and-effect relationship that generates yet another chapter in his ongoing attempt to revise his story of origins. Indeed, Branagh's interest in Victor's so-called hysteria is not casual, for Branagh's "self-begetting" style is dependent on keeping his own "ustera," the wandering Irish womb he has so successfully wandered *away from*—at bay. In this context, then, it is somewhat less surprising that this film (which is more aptly titled *Kenneth Branagh's Frankenstein*) begins by violently cutting the maternal womb from the picture. Completely revising Shelley's treatment of Victor's mother who, in the novel, dies of scarlet fever, Branagh reimagines her demise as a death by Caesarian section. While all matricidal impulses revolve around "[t]he desire to obliterate incoherences and flaws inflicted on us by genealogy" (Bronfen 14), matricide-by-Cesarean section takes this desire to the extreme, for it implies a rejection not only of genealogy but also of the entire process of *natural* birth. Thus, Branagh's decision to stage the death of the mother from a Cesarean section is particularly ingenious, for it enables him to stage a fantasy resolution to the crisis of his own birth. And what better way to deliver what Branagh claims to be the most faithful filmic version of Mary Shelley's *Frankenstein* ever made than by actually participating in the fantasy of male parthenogenesis staged by the novel, giving birth to himself anew from the gaping womb of Victor's dead mother?[13]

The problem occurs, however, when the parthenogenic meets the pathogenic, for what Branagh's filmmaking enterprise gives birth to is

13. Of course, the irony of Branagh's attempt to reinvent himself at the expense of Mary Shelley's own noted anxieties about childbirth is that this directorial move invokes, quite unoriginally, British director Ken Russell's film *Gothic* (1987), which pictures Mary Shelley having repeated nightmares about childbirth.

an *hysterical* hardbody. Though the idea of a hysterical hardbody sounds like a contradiction in terms, the hysterical softbody and the Hollywood hardbody share a common ontology; both resonate as compensatory strategies for obscuring trauma—for smoothing over an embarrassing weakness or lack through "improper recourse to the language of the body" (Bronfen 117). Furthermore, both phenomena arise from a perceived weakness in the status of paternal authority and, subsequently, a crisis of identification. It is particularly significant, then, that in contrast to Shelley's novel, wherein the symbolic authority or Law of the Father is never called into question, in Branagh's film, the father is quickly proven impotent—and worse, he is the husband-Doctor who performs the deadly C-section on Victor's mother—ironically, only hours after she has publicly exhorted Victor to become "an even greater doctor than [his] father."[14] The result is a crisis of identification for Branagh's Victor; for what is the son to do when the father, heralded as the finest doctor in Geneva, turns a C-section into a vivisection on his own wife? How now is the Law of the Father to be respected, let alone emulated? Prompted by the specter of paternal impotence, Victor devolves from mad scientist to mad Max, progressively stripping away layers of clothing to reveal *Branagh's* hysterical hardbody. Thus what is encoded in this scene is "the impossibility of the hysteric's appeal to paternal authority" (Bronfen 167), as Branagh's unprecedented revisions of Shelley's text relentlessly reveal *his own* failure to identify with and acquire acceptance into the Law of the Fatherland. And lest we forget, Branagh's lack of entitlement to a quintessentially English identity was due to his mother tongue: the accent that betrayed his Irish origins.

Thus in *Mary Shelley's Frankenstein,* Branagh goes one step further in his project of Yeatsian self-conquest, revising his personal history in the spirit of a Freudian "family romance." As Freud explains, the "family romance" is a common fantasy in which children imagine replacing their biological parents with new and improved ones.[15] Branagh's lifelong romance with English literary classics is a variation on this theme, for in adapting Mary Shelley's novel to the screen, Branagh hopes to adopt this quintessentially English mother alongside his Shakespearean father. But this audacious mission is fraught with irreconcil-

14. Taking symptomatic liberties with Shelley's text, Branagh converts Victor's father from a Judge to a Doctor, raising the stakes of Victor's identification with him by conspicuously creating a "like father, like son" career trajectory between them.

15. See Freud's essay on "Family Romances."

able tensions between director and actor, reception and production, culminating in Branagh's hysterical conversion into a hardbody. Similar to the strategies of distinction employed in his earlier films, Branagh's rigid physique suggests a psychosomatic attempt to resist comparison with the "messy and confusing" body of the Creature, whose grotesque hybridity recalls Branagh's traumatic experience of cultural monstrosity and symbolic orphanhood. And while Branagh succeeds in temporarily glossing over these inconsistencies in his life by recolonizing his body in his art, the real victim of the monstrous analogy generated by this film is Branagh the director. For if we read between the lines of the poorly sutured surfaces of Victor's monster, we may discern in these scars a gruesome parody of Branagh's directorial project of ideological quilting: the geopolitical borders that comprise and compromise the postcolonial body-in-pain.

Though *Mary Shelley's Frankenstein* did not receive the popular recognition that Branagh had hoped for in making his biggest-budget film to date (it was, in fact, a box-office disaster), he did get one step closer to his dream of achieving a naturalized English identity. For in the course of production, Branagh scratched Emma Thompson off his dance card to continue his nightmarish waltz with Helena Bonham Carter, who played Elizabeth to his Victor in the film. Adding a final twist to Shelley's tale of incest and intrigue, Branagh—unlike Victor—gets the girl and, for a time, the Hollywood ending, as he becomes an honorary member of the Bonham Carter clan—one of the last remaining aristocratic, and, indeed, quintessentially English families.

Bardy by Brawn-agh

The bookend film to *Mary Shelley's Frankenstein, Hamlet* marks the apotheosis of Branagh's family romance. If, in his *Hamlet* prequel, *A Midwinter's Tale*, Branagh's actorly body is conspicuously absent, then in *Hamlet*, Branagh's emphasis on size and scale returns with a vengeance as he sets out—like Hamlet himself—to prove himself a "good" son to his Shakespearean father once and for all.[16] But what stands out in this

---

16. Branagh describes *A Midwinter's Tale* as a "little *Hamlet* film" (qtd. in Arnold 41).

Figure 5. Branagh's buffed Victor embraces Elizabeth (Helena Bonham Carter) and a "quintessentially English" identity in *Mary Shelley's Frankenstein*. TriStar Pictures, 1994. Photo: David Appleby. Courtesy of Photofest.

film even more than Branagh's chiseled physique is *Shakespeare's* body. Shot in eighty millimeter film and hyped as the only "full-text" film version of *Hamlet* ever made, this four-hour epic self-consciously subscribes to the view that size matters, as Branagh's comments on the film suggest: "We want this *Hamlet* to be a big, big treat. We're trying for more epic sweep than is usually contemplated...there will be thousands of extras for some sequences. The Ghost is going to be a lot scarier than some faintly benign old sot walking on stage in a white shirt. It ain't gonna be three-and-a-half hours of talking heads'" (qtd. in Arnold 36–37). Branagh's somewhat strained appropriation of American slang, replete with the bravura promise of a "big and bad" *Hamlet*, smacks of overcompensation, suggesting his deep-seated insecurities about taking on this quintessentially English role. More provocatively, his remarks betray a certain degree of anxiety about the fortitude of the Shakespearean "corpus" in an all-action, no-talking-heads culture. Like Hamlet's own struggle with the exposure of his father's weaknesses, Branagh's rhetoric encodes his own fears about the vulnerabilities of his Shakespearean source which, as we have seen throughout this analysis, suggests the ultimate body-in-pain. But Branagh deftly deflects this anxiety onto surrogate fathers, claiming that the main challenge he faces in adapting *Hamlet* is contending with "the ghosts of other performances" (qtd. in Crowl 6). Serving as a sequel to the matricidal fantasy staged in *Mary Shelley's Frankenstein*, *Hamlet* invites Branagh both to worship and to kill the paternalistic "ghosts" of other *Hamlet* performances in a film that is, ultimately, less about a pouting prince's aspirations to the Danish throne than it is about this displaced Irishman's aspirations to the mantle of English theatrical royalty.[17]

Much has been made of the fact that it was Derek Jacobi's impersonation of Hamlet that jump-started Branagh's love-affair with Shakespeare back when he was merely a wide-eyed fifteen-year-old from Belfast. At a time when Branagh claimed to be interested only in soccer and girls, he was surprised to find his attention riveted on a television serialization of Robert Graves's *I, Claudius*. As he recalls: "I was particularly impressed by the actor playing the title role. His name was Derek Jacobi" (Introduction, *Hamlet* xi–xii). Inspired by Jacobi's acting, Branagh purchased his first ticket to a Shakespeare play—*Hamlet*—in which the fabled actor was playing the lead. And the rest is history. After seeing Jacobi's performance, Branagh "resolved to become an actor," exclaiming: "I believe that much of what has followed in my life was affected by that experience" (xii). Indeed, just over a decade later, in 1988, Jacobi directed Branagh as Hamlet in Renaissance's theatrical production of the play. Yet Branagh's memories of this dream-come-true were not fond: "I felt much more crushingly the weight of the ghosts of other performances," he claims, recalling his intimidation by "the weight of expectation that comes with any young actor playing the role.... It was not a relaxed experience" (qtd. in Crowl 6). But in 1996, Branagh was able to get his revenge by playing Hamlet to Jacobi's Claudius, as well as by directing the film himself, consolidating his creative energies in an effort

---

17. For an elaborate discussion of Branagh's extra-cinematic intentions and identifications, see Courtney Lehmann and Lisa S. Starks, "Making Mother Matter: Repression, Revision, and the Stakes of 'Reading Psychoanalysis Into' Kenneth Branagh's *Hamlet*."

to replace the memory of his theatrical father in the popular imagination. The problem is, however, that while Shakespeare's Hamlet ultimately proves himself a good son by following the Ghost and killing Claudius, Branagh's celluloid prince appears more intent on following in Claudius's, that is, *Jacobi's* immortal footsteps.

Here again a conflict between Branagh's "two bodies" emerges, for while Branagh the actor hopes to exorcise the ghost of Jacobi's Hamlet, Branagh the director clearly emulates Jacobi. This extra-diegetic fascination is apparent in the uncanny family resemblance the film establishes between stepfather and son. In contrast to the other members of the court, Hamlet and Claudius are the only two figures who have bleach-blonde hair cut in a military flat-top style, which accentuates their difference from the distinctly non-cropped, darker hair of the rest of the cast. Likewise, their costumes distinguish them from the crowd: Claudius and Hamlet both wear black, plain, and form-fitting outfits which they occupy with the stiff posture of bowling pins, quite unlike the relaxed poses, softer hues, and more lavish designs bedecking the other members of the vaguely nineteenth-century court. These pale, svelte, and decidedly phallic images of Claudius and Hamlet could not be further removed from the image of Old Hamlet, whose peppery hair, incandescent eyes, gargantuan physique, and sulfurous breath make a grotesque spectacle of Shakespeare's more sympathetic Ghost. Consciously or unconsciously, then, the film posits a mirroring relationship between Jacobi's Claudius and Branagh's Hamlet that clearly articulates Branagh's desire to be like Jacobi—to be, in effect, his natural son.

At one level, this extraordinary physical resemblance suggests that Branagh identifies with Jacobi in imaginary terms as his "ideal ego." Imaginary identification, as Žižek explains, involves imitating the other "at the level of resemblance—we identify ourselves in the image of the other inasmuch as we are 'like him'" (Žižek, *Sublime* 109). But why, then, doesn't Branagh simply cast Jacobi as Old Hamlet, making it easy for this would-be son to be like his otherwise inimitable Shakespearean precursor? The answer, I would argue, is because Branagh must come to identify with Jacobi in *symbolic*, rather than imaginary, terms; he must succeed from the realm of the "ideal ego" to that of the "ego ideal" by identifying himself with precisely the point at which Jacobi is "inimitable, at the point which [he] eludes resemblance" (Žižek 109). This transition from imaginary to symbolic identification entails a pivotal change of perspective in which the subject learns to align himself *not* with the position from which he appears likable to himself but with the position from which he appears

Figure 6. "Little more than kin?" Branagh's Hamlet bears a striking family resemblance to Derek Jacobi's Claudius. Julie Christie completes the love triangle as Gertrude. Castle Rock Entertainment, 1996. Photo courtesy of Photofest.

likable to *others*. In casting Jacobi as Claudius, Branagh cleverly streamlines both of these identificatory gazes by evoking the primal scene of his adolescent, imaginary desire to be like Jacobi in *I, Claudius* and by placing his Hamlet in a symbolic position to "kill" this father-figure according to the dictates of the play. Consequently, as Branagh's Hamlet thrusts the poison down the throat of Jacobi's Claudius, he is quite literally giving Jacobi a taste of his own medicine. Supplanting his lifelong experience of transferential desire for Jacobi, Branagh reconciles auteur and actor as he stage-directs and succeeds Jacobi as Hamlet. But it is not until Jacobi's final day on the set that Branagh's succession is complete, when Jacobi "springs a surprise" on him:

> He holds up red-bound copy of the play, that successive actors have passed on to each other with the condition that the recipient should give it in turn to the finest Hamlet of the next generation. It has come from Forbes Robertson, a great Hamlet at the turn of the century, to Derek, via Henry Ainley, Michael Redgrave, Peter O'Toole and others—now he gives it to Ken. (Jackson 206)

Like father, like son. No longer the Belfast-born step-son of the English theater, Branagh is hereby offered a new patrilineage by none other than Derek Jacobi, who christens him both natural son of and heir apparent to English theatrical royalty.

It seems particularly significant as well as strange that Branagh selected Belfast for *Hamlet's* United Kingdom debut, staging a return to the primal scene of his birth—and rebirth—with the Renaissance Theatre and Film Company. But for an audience eager to claim this prodigal son as their own, disappointment followed. Rather than acknowledging his familial and political debt to Belfast, Branagh opted to absent himself from a potentially infelicitous encounter with his own site of origin, preferring to remain, like Hamlet, at "school"—in Hollywood—where he was learning how to become an American in Robert Altman's *The Gingerbread Man*. In keeping with the haunting spirit of *Hamlet*, however, Branagh was present at the premiere as a ghost, that is, in the form of a videotaped message voicing his support for "First Run Belfast," the local charity sponsoring the study or staging of drama *outside* of Northern Ireland (Burnett 82). Thus Branagh completes his family romance by setting a ghostly precedent for subsequent generations, offering them tacit encouragement to follow his lead in "adapting" to greener, quintessentially English pastures—perhaps even to become, like Branagh himself, ghost sons of a willfully forgotten Ireland in favor of Shakespeare's sceptered isle.

After several intervening non-Shakespearean films, Branagh adds a coda to his repertoire of cinematic and personal adaptation with a musical version of *Love's Labour's Lost*. A far cry from Shakespeare's prominence and preeminence in *Hamlet*, in *Love's Labour's Lost*, the Bard plays second fiddle to twentieth-century troubadors like Irving Berlin, Cole Porter, and George Gershwin. In his reflections on this film in relation to his career as an actor, Branagh claims that as far as he is concerned, it "is dangerous to have a single hero" ("Salerno Transcript," http://www.branaghcompendium.com/artic-sal99.htm)—an admission that contextualizes his otherwise abrupt turn away from all things English in favor of distinctly American genres and icons. Anxious, perhaps, to avoid the kind of hero worship that threatened to sabo-tage his *Hamlet*, in *Love's Labour's Lost* Branagh trades Derek Jacobi for Fred Astaire, as his actorly body attempts to take on the ultimate illusion of transcendence: Americanization.

Our first indication that Branagh has crossed the Atlantic in hopes of reinventing himself on American shores is the film's carefully selected location in place and time. Skillfully avoiding the aura of repression that plagues Shakespeare's unconventional comedy, Branagh situates *Love's Labour's Lost* in the thick of the wildly expressive musical culture of the nineteen thirties, setting the film before America's involvement in World War Two but conspicuously after the repeal of prohibition. While this setting offers Branagh a wide range of musicals to emulate, it is clear from the film's opening scene that his point of reference for the mood of *Love's Labour's Lost* is the sauntering grace of Fred Astaire and, more specifically, *Top Hat* (Mark Sandrich 1935)—the Astaire/Rogers classic that Branagh screened for the cast and crew on the first day of rehearsal. Despite the fact that Branagh modestly assures the media that "I'm not Fred Astaire...I can tell you" (qtd. in "The Guardian Interview," http://branaghcompendium.com/articntfguard99.htm), his bodily transformation from a hardbody to a considerably more delicate slimbody clearly generates an illusion of height and grace befitting compari-son with Astaire. But Branagh's emaciated look in this film seems to work too hard for this analogy, for he much more clearly resembles another dance hero of the 1930s: James Cagney.

James Cagney might be called the working-class Fred Astaire. Known for his unusual combination of gangster and dancer roles and his bulldog energy, this Irish-American actor played parts in the thirties that correspond in stunning ways to Branagh's own postmodern penchant for merging high and low culture in the name of "life-enhancing populism." Preceding Astaire's *Top Hat* by two years was Cagney's role as the tap-dancing entrepreneur who puts the show on at all costs in *Footlight Parade* (Lloyd Bacon 1933)—a Busby Berkeley classic famous precisely for the goofy mix of "singing, dancing, and synchronized swimming" that *Love's Labour's Lost* sets out to emulate (qtd. in Thompson 31). Before this film, however, was Cagney's even more memorable performance as the gangster in *Public Enemy* (William Wellman 1931). This film left an indelible mark on Branagh's career, for his professional transition from the Royal Shakespeare Company to Renaissance hinged on the success of the Company's debut play, *Public Enemy*—the semi-autobiographical story of a working-class Belfast teenager who, in Branagh's own words, has "a Jimmy Cagney fixation" (*Beginning* 169). But it is Cagney's role as the aspiring actor-manager Bottom in Max Reinhardt and William Dierterle's 1935 version of *A Midsummer Night's Dream* that seals these unmistakably proto-Branagh identities with a Shakespearean imprimatur. Like "bully Bottom," Branagh has always wanted to "play all the parts" in an effort to overcome his suspicious Shakespearean credentials as the Belfast-born grandson of "rude mechanical" dockworkers. Unlike Bottom and, for that matter, Cagney,

Figure 7. Tap dancing or tapped out? An elegant but emaciated Branagh in *Love's Labour's Lost.* From left to right: Alessandro Nivola, Alicia Silverstone, Matthew Lillard, Carmen Ejogo (partially visible), Adrian Lester, Emily Mortimer, Kenneth Branagh, and Natascha McElhone. Miramax Films, 2000. Photo: Laurie Sparham. Courtesy of Photofest.

Branagh has succeeded in this enterprise only by repressing his working-class Irish origins.

Perhaps this explains Branagh's conspicuous erasure of Cagney from his musical tribute to the 1930s, as well as the reason that, when asked about Cagney's influence on the film, Branagh's associates rigorously deny any association with this screen legend of the 1930s who, like Branagh, is patently "no Fred Astaire." But if Branagh really believes that it is "dangerous to have a single hero," then why not embrace both Astaire *and* Cagney—the ideal coordinates of his personal and professional enterprise of bringing together high and low, national and popular in the name of Shakespeare? Quite simply, Cagney represents the wrong national-popular culture, for he threatens the film's glamorous, *Top Hat*-like diegetic reality with *the* reality of class and social antagonisms stemming from his irrepressible identity as a working-class Irish-American—an identity immortalized in his musical tribute to the 1930s: *Yankee Doodle Dandy* (Michael Curtiz 1942). There is little doubt that *Love's Labour's Lost* owes as much to Cagney and *Yankee Doodle Dandy* as it does to Astaire and *Top Hat.* However, in order for Branagh's audience to believe in the escapist fiction of the "high life" his film works so hard to construct, any hint of the "low life"—the labor, sweat, alienation, and bodily expenditure associated with both dance and industrialization so prominent in Cagney's films—must be repressed. Ultimately, then, Branagh's actorly pursuit of Americanization in *Love's Labour's Lost* reveals what his directorial body constantly attempts to hide: that a melting pot, in which post-colonial identities are subject to often violent erasure, is preferable to the hard labor of ideological quilting.

∽✕∾

Despite Branagh's directorial attempts to engineer the reception of his films as an inclusive experience of "life-enhancing populism," his actorly body consistently sacrifices the "popular" to the "national"— the quintessentially English or even American identity that promises to erase the scars of his postcolonial experience and make the project of ideological quilting unnecessary in the first place. Yet in positioning Shakespeare as a "quilting point," Branagh's adaptations bring this analysis of the contested makings of the auteur full circle. For as Žižek explains, "perceived as a point of extreme saturation of Meaning," the quilting point merely "holds the place of a certain lack" (*Sublime* 99). What better metaphor for the Shakespearean corpus— its historical function as a host for infinite, idiosyncratic investments and its material status as a prolific marker of absence? Indeed, in its perilous migrations between possession and dispossession, this corpus suggests a model of the more willful, but no less precarious, metamorphoses of the postmodern auteur. In bringing this complex legacy to bear on his own status as a postcolonial subject and an aspiring auteur, Kenneth Branagh challenges contemporary consumers of Shakespeare to detect and to connect with the pulse beneath the glossy surface of his films, wherein the constitutive tensions, contradictions, and remainders *remind us* of the importance of keeping both Shakespeare and the figure of the Author, auteur, or what you Will, from becoming "dead again." For it is not just authors who have been "crying out for life," as Hillel Schwartz concludes in *The Culture of the Copy:* "Our self-portraits now neither anchor nor extend us because we are no longer sure of ourselves as originals, no longer sure of what it means to be inspirited" (140). Through haunted by multiple selves, Branagh's cinematic portraits extend our understanding of authorship and originality in our contemporary culture of the copy, exceeding their filmic frame and brimming over to become signs of a time which, perhaps despite itself, is deeply inspirited by Shakespeare.

6

"There Ain't No 'Mac' in the Union Jack"

Adaptation and (O)mission in *Henry V*

[The "author-function"] is situated in the breach, among the discontinuities, which gives rise to new groups of discourse and their singular mode of existence.

—Foucault, "What Is an Author?"

Once more unto the breach, dear friends, once more.

In his exploration of the challenges facing contemporary film culture, Leo Braudy positions the postmodern auteur at a crossroads:

It is a time of dissatisfaction with the single story and yet a growing uneasiness with heartless and endless referentiality. It is also a time of hyperconsciousness of film history, fed by the availability of old films on cable channels and in video stores. How then does a filmmaker accomplish something personal that will attract an audience and assert the continuity of his or her own career? The two main ways seem to be the much-less-traveled road of originality and the crowded highway of remaking, where the filmmaker's individual and moral aesthetic sensibility is defined by its meditation on the works of the past. (332)

Braudy's reflections on the unfinished business of the postmodern auteur oddly resurrect the classic conception of the film-artist as a figure who, in Andre Bazin's words, "choos[es] in the artistic creation the *personal factor* as a criterion of reference, and then posits its permanence and even its progress from one work to the next" (qtd. in Stam et al. 190, emphasis added). But as Braudy acknowledges, the increasingly centrifugal forces of film reception undermine the prospect of developing an oeuvre over time, tempering the history-making aspirations of the auteur with the following choice: to make or to re-make? According to Fredric Jameson, this is a false choice, for in a world in which "stylistic innovation is no longer possible," the crowded highway of remaking is the *only* road, yet it, too, leads to a dead-end wherein we find ourselves "condemned to seek the historical past through our own pop images and stereotypes about that past, which itself remains forever out of reach" ("Postmodernism and Consumer Society" 194). What both Jameson and Braudy point to is a crisis of temporality within postmodern culture, a crisis that is both perceived and experienced as a "schizophrenic" onslaught of "pure and unrelated presents in time" (Jameson, *Postmodernism* 27).[1] The formal consequence of this temporal compression is legible in its debilitating identity-effects, as Jameson explains: the subject of postmodernity "has lost its capacity actively to...organize its past and future into coherent experience" and, therefore, "it becomes difficult enough to see how the cultural productions of such a subject could result in anything but 'heaps of fragments'" (25). For Kenneth Branagh, the heaps of fragments of postmodern cultural production are inextricable from his postcolonial experience of sectarianism. It is no wonder, then, that he situates his filmmaking enterprise firmly within the crowded highway of remaking, which provides him with an opportunity to meditate on and revise *his own* past. And in this respect, Branagh's Shakespearean adaptations do more than retrace already familiar territory, for they offer a glimpse of the much-less-traveled road of originality *within* the crowded highway of remaking: the detour forged by "homeopathic techniques."

In an infrequently cited interview about the future of the subject within the chaotic space-time of postmodernism, Jameson makes passing reference to the idea of "homeopathic techniques" which, he explains, use the very logic of postmodernism to "go through and be-

---

1. Jameson uses schizophrenia as a diagnostic model for characterizing the affective pathologies of postmodernity. According to Jameson, the postmodern condition has led to a breakdown not only of historical memory but also of personal identity, wherein one is "condemned to live a perpetual present," a present wherein the experience of "temporality, human time, past, present, memory" have little connection with each other. "In other words," Jameson concludes, this "schizophrenic experience is an experience of isolated, disconnected, discontinuous, material signifiers that fail to link up into a coherent sequence" ("Postmodernism and Consumer Society" 195).

yond" it ("Regarding Postmodernism" 60). The cultural logic of late auteurism offers a compelling example of how this theory might be employed in practice, mobilizing the schizophrenic temporality of contemporary consumer culture to create a provocative compression of the "high"
modernist notion of artistic production within a "low" postmodern mode
of commercial reception. Branagh's marketing campaign for his 1989 film
of *Henry V* demonstrates a masterful deployment of homeopathic techniques, as he attempts to convince moviegoers that Shakespeare's
Henry and pop culture's Batman are of "the same world" (Branagh, qtd.
in Light 19). On one level, Branagh's interest in targeting Batman fans
for *Henry V* is a transparent attempt to convert a high culture icon into
the idiom of mass culture and, more specifically, into the bottom-line
language of box-office returns. But on another level, there is a more than
casual link between Henry and Batman, for while these reluctant heroes
may not be *in* the same world, they are, in fact, *of* the same world. Indeed, both Henry and Batman lead double lives and, despite their ongoing attempts to reinvent themselves, they are haunted by a disturbing
relationship to the past which, ultimately, proves inescapable. Thus,
while Branagh's glib juxtaposition of the futuristic world of "Batman"
and the distant past of "Shakespeare" initially smacks of blank parody,
upon closer examination, these "pure and unrelated presents in time"
suggest a self-reflexive invocation of the schizophrenic poles of
Branagh's own identity, as a figure whose life-long efforts to create a
continuum between past and future, high and low, national and popular come to fruition only in art. For Branagh, then, as for Luhrmann, the
pastiche ethos of the postmodern auteur reso-nates not only as a homeopathic alternative to blank parody but also as the mark that separates the
makers from the mere re-makers: "Not that I'm against nicking things,"
Branagh explains. "I do it all the time—from life, or from other actors.
It's just that a really good actor will put such borrowings into his own
soil and make them his own" (*Beginning* 57).

But *which* soil will Branagh choose for the cultivation of his auteurist
enterprise? That is the question in *Henry V*, wherein Branagh's aesthetic
preoccupation with positing an enabling relationship to time—writ
large not only in his choice of a history play and the temporal compression of his marketing rhetoric but also in his portrayal of a "schizophrenic" hero—is a veil for his distinctly more personal preoccupation
with space.[2] And, simply put, there are some spaces that time *cannot*

2. Both literary and film critics have dubbed Henry V a "schizophrenic" character. As
William Shaw remarks: "The character of Henry is frequently described in terms of his

heal; for as Jameson explains, the colonial experience is what is always "located elsewhere, beyond the metropolis, outside of the daily life and existential experience of the home country, in colonies over the water whose own life experience and life world—very different from that of the imperial power—remain unknown and unimaginable" ("Modernism and Imperialism" 50–51). Quite unlike Shakespeare and Batman, England and Ireland are patently *not* "of the same world." Although Branagh seeks to bridge this space through ideological quilting, we are reminded that the quilting operation hinges on a manipulation of time that creates an illusion in space; it is born of an impulse to *suspend* social antagonisms, to create a fixed or "eternal present" in which society functions—magically—without acknowledging the real sociopolitical differences that make it tick.[3] Quite ingeniously, then, in adapting a play fraught with geopolitical antagonisms of class, country, and creed, Branagh generates an illusion of a harmonious society through "soil" itself—his preferred medium for quilting across markers of distinction in a film he envisions as a "filthy, vicious scrum" (*Henry V Screenplay* 83). Testifying to the success of this "smear" campaign, Peter S. Donaldson contends that in the film, "the manners of the aristocracy are sometimes nearly as crude as those of the 'base' characters; and the grime of the battle alludes, I think, to that of the tavern" (64). Indeed, in the battle scenes in particular, the distinction-eclipsing effects of Branagh's mud-strewn mise-en-scène were so powerful that, as Branagh notes, the production crew had problems "keep[ing] control of the narrative.... The mud was getting deeper and each day was merging with the next. We needed a computer to work out who fought who" (*Beginning* 235).

---

split or dual 'presence'—not in the quasi-mystical sense of 'The King's Two Bodies,' but as two, separate, unrelated beings, one public, one private; one present, one absent; one speaking, one silent; one good, one evil" (117).

3. Jameson explains that the "eternal present" is an illusion arising from the tensions between two distinct temporal modalities within postmodern culture: consumerism and nostalgia. On the one hand, the eternal present is created by the dizzying rate of consumption and recycling of products under late capitalism, wherein a preoccupation with surfaces precipitates a loss of historical depth-perception and an illusory absence of historicity. On the other hand, the eternal present is marked by the decelerating, counterclockwise impulse of nostalgia, an attempt to renegotiate the discriminating, division-inflected phenomenon of commodity logic by fostering an illusion of a "collective 'objective' spirit" (*Postmodernism* 25) through which "social divisions are suspended or overcome...by an appeal to some higher (and imaginary) principle of collective and social unity" (*Political Unconscious* 292).

While mud may be Branagh's medium of choice for creating a caste-less society temporarily suspended in the time-warp of war, it is not long before we realize that Branagh's Henry is the real mortar keeping this social fantasy in tact. As Linda Charnes might argue, what is at stake in the Agincourt sequence in particular is nothing less than "how both consumers and producers of cultural texts re-member histories, their own and those of others" ("What's love" 11). For Branagh, this process of re-making history begins with Henry's famous rebuke to the French emissary Montjoy: "We are but warriors for the working day" (*Henry V Screenplay* 81). Despite Henry's self-effacing efforts to convert the office of kingship into just another nine-to-five, this line never fails to sound disingenuous. However, when we as consumers remember Branagh as the working-class product of Belfast, the line acquires sudden sincerity. Once again eliding past and future through clever cinematic allusion, Branagh proceeds to insert himself in the breach of the workaday world only to rise above it all, by becoming—"in an explosion of outrage"—dirty Harry (*Henry V Screenplay* 81).[4] Covered in mud and seething with anger, Branagh's Henry replies to Montjoy's persistent requests for the king's ransom with the force of "make my day": "Come thou no more for ransom...They [the French] shall have none I swear, but these my joints" (82). Eclipsing the warring "we" in the glory-seeking "me," Branagh hereby articulates the social fantasy around which his conception of the postmodern auteur-function is structured. For if, as countless critics have suggested, France is merely a decoy for the persistence of internal antagonisms between England and its regional territories, then as "dirty Harry," Branagh imagines his very joints stretching across the divide of cultural difference to re-attach these severed bodies. Attesting to the appeal of this fantasy of leadership in our own disjointed culture, one critic observes that "Branagh can show us leadership as a hard-won personal achievement, rather than, as with Olivier, the divine right of kings and movie stars.... and his education of a king says a good deal to all of us who have to assume responsibility by learning it the hard way, on the job, in the dirt" (Simon 58). But the lesson learned in Branagh's education of a king will be a hard one. For under the auspices of this brooding, bloody, post-Fauklands critique of war, Branagh's dirty Harry emerges as Mr. Clean,

---

4. For an extensive analysis of the function of mud in *Henry V*, see Don Hedrick's essay on Branagh's film, "War Is Mud: Branagh's Dirty Harry V and the Types of Political Ambiguity."

positing himself as the site of a narrative of transcendence that hinges on keeping the rest of us on the job, in the dirt, and, ultimately, in our place.

In an essay called "What's Love Got to Do with It? Reading the Liberal Humanist Romance in Shakespeare's *Antony and Cleopatra*," Charnes explores how narratives of transcendence, and particularly love, become the source of a "sacralizing epistemology" in Shakespeare's plays. Defined as that which is *"Other than* the political" (4), love is aligned with timeless values that are situated above the sphere of war and politics even as it serves as a seductive smokescreen for oppressive relations of power. Yet Charnes's argument is less concerned with "what's love got to do with it" than with determining what's *Shakespeare* got to do with it: how is Shakespeare being appropriated to legitimize contemporary political agendas with his "timeless" imprimatur? Charnes's explanation for the sudden and ubiquitous presence of the Bard in mass culture is his "position as iconic guarantor of liberal humanism, at a time when as a society we desperately need to find ways to justify our moral authority as we throw our weight around" ("What's Love" 12). Linking the self-legitimating narratives of transcendence generated by liberal humanist critics to those produced by the world of realpolitik, Charnes claims that "what gets prosecuted in the New World Theatre in the name of Freedom and Democracy" is not that far removed from "what gets prosecuted in literary and cultural production in the name of Love" and literary Canon formation (12). And Shakespeare is, of course, at the center of this liberal humanist tradition, awarding transcendence not to the proud but to the few, for Shakespeare is ultimately "used to reinforce our sense of 'distinction'" (Charnes 12). So what's Branagh got to do with it? In *Henry V*, Branagh's "education of a king" takes the tradition of liberal humanist criticism one step further, as Branagh sets himself up as a *critic* of Shakespeare only to rise from the mud—Golem-like—as a liberal humanist hero. In a brilliant authorial gambit, Branagh creates a sacralizing epistemology of the auteur as king, as he becomes a modern day guarantor and granter of the divine right of transcendence which, as we shall see, he reserves exclusively for himself.

ᴖᴗᴖ

In the workaday world beyond the diegesis, Branagh's portrait of King Henry as "dirty Harry" suggests a provocative allusion to the "dirty work" that Timothy Corrigan identifies as "the business of being an auteur" (104). For the link between Branagh's working-class background and his portrait of a king who "shows us leadership...the hard way, on the job, in the dirt" is no mere coincidence but rather a savvy promotional scheme designed to situate his filmmaking persona within the perceptual schemes of mass culture. Indeed, Branagh's remarkable success in promoting, funding, and creating *Henry V* has everything to do with his ability to sell *himself* as Henry. Throughout the making of *Henry V*, Branagh demonstrates his "commercial conditioning" as a postmodern auteur by repeatedly merging the rhetoric of self-expenditure with a self-consciousness about accounting for the film's financial costs, focusing less on the artistic nature of his achievements than on "his achievements in staying within his budget and adhering to a strict production schedule" (Bristol 100). Not surprisingly, Branagh also creates a tie-in for the film's release that merges the commercial with the personal: an autobiography titled *Beginning*. Modeled on Sir John Gielgud's *Early Stages*, *Beginning* was written at the precocious age of twenty-eight and pictures Branagh as the newly crowned king on the cover. Anticipating resistance to this audacious marketing move, Branagh explains on the first page: "So why write this? Money" (*Beginning* ix). But while the dirty work of money and marketing may be the big picture, it is not the whole story, for as early as 1984 when he starred in Adrian Noble's production of *Henry V* with the RSC, Branagh was caught up in a drama of identification with Shakespeare's Henry: "Henry was a young man, and so was I. He was faced with an enormous responsibility. I didn't have to run the country and invade France, but I did have to control Brian Blessed and open the Stratford season" (*Beginning* 141). Five years later on the set of his film version of *Henry V*, Branagh updated this series of parallels, insisting on the relationship between Henry the "boy king" and himself as "baby director" (*Beginning* 226). In comparing Branagh's film with Olivier's, then, most critics have observed that while Olivier's adaptation involves a king whose "personality is complete at the start," Branagh's adaptation is "a trial by combat of the young King's personality" (Donaldson 61), "deeply developmental" and "a bildungsroman" (68). In other words, Branagh's adaptation is *about* the young king's adaptation to a position of authority, providing a perfect analogy for Branagh's own experience as a first-time director and aspiring auteur. This merging of film and autobiography, character and actor, fiction and reality, is all but announced in Branagh's stage directions for Henry's initial entry: "At last we see the young monarch's face. He is twenty-

seven years old and the leader of the most powerful country in the medieval world. This solitary, pensive boy in 'the very May morn of his
youth' is King Henry V of England" (*Henry V Screenplay* 7). The gratuitous reference to Henry's exact age, a detail that is not relayed to the
film audience, suggests the force of Branagh's fantasy of identification,
for he, too, is twenty-seven years old when this scene is shot, as well as
more than a little apprehensive about directing the power-house players
assembled for his cast.

Modeling the commercial savvy of the postmodern auteur, Branagh's
rhetoric of identification travels along an "extratextual path" to connect
the drama staged by the film with the drama surrounding the making
of the film, as the military exigencies of Henry's campaign are revisited
in the marketing exigencies of Branagh's filmmaking campaign. In his
own words, Branagh's objective in selling himself as Henry is to generate "a realistic collaboration between the worlds of commerce and art"
(*Beginning* 197)—a collaboration which, as Michael Bristol argues, "has
never been more artfully negotiated than in Kenneth Branagh's recent
film version of *Henry V* and in the media event surrounding it" (97). In
planning this media event, Branagh imagines himself as a "warrior for
the working day" on the front lines of consumer culture: "If I believed
in the potential of this work I wanted it to be seen by a lot of people. For
this kind of work to be truly popular the public would need to know
who I was. I would have no qualms about extensive press coverage,
and I had to build as far as I could on my commercial possibilities" (*Beginning* 178). Articulating a virtual manifesto for the postmodern auteur, Branagh goes "unto the breach" that separates the worlds of commerce and art and emerges with an identity born of his "commercial
possibilities." And though Branagh links this identity with the popular,
his interest in courting the public is swiftly eclipsed by his investment
in the national, as he proceeds with renewed audacity to link Henry's
military campaign to his own media campaign to "save the British film
industry" (qtd. in Howell 124). Consequently, one reporter astutely observes that the "real chemistry" here is "not between actor and part,"
but between "the idea of the star as entrepreneur and the idea of the
King as a self-made man" (Mars-Jones, qtd. in Holderness 231). But I
would go one step further to suggest that the "real chemistry" is between Branagh's postmodern auteur-function and Henry's early modern "authority-function."

In contrast to theatrical productions of *Henry V*, wherein alienation
effects can serve as a distancing mechanism between actor and role, "in

the relatively naturalistic medium of the film, and of course under Branagh's own direction, there is no such system of checks and balances to subvert the invitation to empathetic identification with the psychology of power" (Holderness, "What 'ish' my nation?" 229). As I have suggested throughout this analysis, the psychology of power that the postmodern auteur exploits lies in an ability to engineer and control the way an audience receives a film, regardless of the message the film product actually delivers. In this context, then, we might view Shakespeare's King Henry as the "once and future" embodiment of the auteur-function; for not only does Henry go "unto the breach" between high and low culture, mainland and frontier, but also between the realms of production and reception through his masterful discursive attempts at Harfleur and Agincourt to script the outcome of his military campaigns. The classic example of this authority-function occurs in Henry's "St. Crispin's day" speech as he rallies his troops against all odds at Agincourt. This passage bears quoting at length:

> This day is call'd the feast of Crispian:
> He that outlives this day, and comes safe home
> Will stand a' tiptoe when this day is named,
> And rouse him at the name of Crispian.
> He that shall see this day, and live old age,
> Will yearly on the vigil feast his neighbors,
> And say, "To-morrow is Saint Crispian."
> Then will he strip his sleeve and show his scars.
> [And say, "These wounds I had on Crispin's day."]
> Old men forget; yet all shall be forgot,
> But he'll remember with advantages
> What feats he did that day. Then shall our names,
> Familiar in his mouth as household words,
> Harry the King, Bedford and Exeter,
> Warwick and Talbot, Salisbury and Gloucester,
> Be in their flowing cups freshly rememb'red.
> This story shall the good man teach his son;
> And Crispin Crispian shall ne'er go by,
> From this day to the ending of the world,
> But we in it shall be remembered—
> We few, we happy few, we band of brothers;
> For he to-day that sheds his blood with me
> Shall be my brother; be he ne'er so vile,
> This day shall gentle his condition;

And gentlemen in England, now a-bed,
Shall think themselves accurs'd they were not here,
And hold their manhoods cheap whiles any speaks
That fought with us upon Saint Crispin's day.

(4.3.40–67)

After this speech, the actual battle is irrelevant: the script is in place for audiences at home, abroad, under siege, and unborn. Such is the "psychology of power" Branagh taps into in attempting to draw financiers and potential Shakespearean proselytes into his drama of identification with King Henry, for his desire to establish the conditions of reception for a film that he describes as "quintessentially English" in spirit *and* "something for everyone" in scope is only slightly less ambitious. As a film featuring "an exciting linear plot, short scenes, great structural variety and several different strains of narrative providing a rich mixture of low-life sleaze, foreign sophistication, romance, action, philosophy and humour," Branagh's *Henry V* does indeed purport to offer something for everyone (*Henry V Screenplay* xiv). But in contrast to Shakespeare's play, wherein Henry's rhetoric accords with the outcome he promises, in Branagh's film, there is an insurmountable "breach" separating reception and production, national and popular. For while it is one thing to direct *Henry V* by establishing a profitable series of parallels between the "dirty work" of Henry's military campaign and the marketing campaigns of the postmodern auteur, it is another thing altogether to *play* Henry V. In this debut film, then, we see the split between auteur and actor at its inception. What distinguishes this conflict from its manifestation in Branagh's later films, however, is the fact that because Branagh is playing a king who not only has two bodies, but whose psychology of power is dependent on his schizophrenic relationship to them, Branagh's actorly body must also divide in order to conquer this role. But will his transcendent vision of the monarch split at the seams of this half-English, half-Welsh hero?

Indeed, *Henry V* is a very carefully chosen first foray into filmic adaptation for Branagh, who locates in this play not only his own history-making designs as a director but also the challenge of a lifetime as an actor; for Henry is not merely a schizophrenic character—he is also a figure who identifies with a frontier country known for its madness: Wales. However, our first indication that Branagh is attempting to streamline these geopolitical complexities into a "quintessentially English" vision of royalty resides in the fact that his research for the part

Figure 8. Branagh's Henry V at the breach of Harfleur: where there's a Will, there's a Billy. Samuel Goldwyn, 1989. Photo courtesy of Photofest.

came largely from an interview with Prince Charles.[5] Again attempting to control both the reception and production of his creative energies, Branagh quickly becomes both interviewer and interviewee at his private conference with the heir apparent, informing Charles that "I'm not intending my Henry V to be an impersonation of you, but I simply wanted to explain some of my feelings about the character, particularly his role as king" (*Beginning* 142). Branagh's principal thesis is that royalty "involve[s] the suppression of many facets of one's character" (142) and, significantly, this theory recapitulates his philosophy of acting, which revolves around "submerg[ing] your identity fully into someone else's" (42). Appropriately, this is precisely how Shakespeare's young king ultimately approaches his own schizophrenic identity: by submerging useless "Hal" and ruthless "Henry" into "Harry"—generating, in the process, a transcendent vision of the Nation that achieves at least temporary consonance with the popular. Branagh, however, struggles to put this theory into practice, for at a pivotal point in the film—at the breach of Harfleur—we find that one of his king's two bodies belongs to King Billy, Northern Ireland's folkloric hero. Appearing atop a rearing white horse, flailing a sword, and donning a red and blue uniform with gold detail, Branagh's Henry suddenly transforms into a tableau of King Billy at the breach of the river Boyne, an image that appears in wall murals all over Ulster. And to match this iconic resurgence of his cultural schizophrenia, Branagh's Henry momentarily lapses into the lyricism of the Irish brogue, trilling the last few words of inspiration to his tired troops as follows: "For there is none of you so mean and base / That hath not *noble lustre in your eyes*" (*Henry V Screenplay* 39, emphasis added). Fortunately, by the end of the Harfleur speech, Branagh regains control over Henry with an appeal to the timeless Shakespearean identity markers "God for Harry, England, and Saint George!" (39) which, at least for now, "halt the sliding" of his split personality and enable him to pass this test of his quilting operation quite literally with flying colors.

But Branagh's enthusiastic description of this scene of transcendence is, perhaps, wishful thinking, for the process of *dis*membering history—

5. In diplomatic fashion, Branagh suggests that Prince Charles "strike[s] a balance between responsibility and compassion," a more benign version of "the ruthless killer and the Christian king" embodied in Shakespeare's Henry (*Beginning* 143). Significantly, through the course of the film's production, Charles became the official patron of Renaissance.

his own and others'—can not be accomplished with a quick edit. As Charnes observes, "the degree of misrecognition needed to subsidize our investment in any notion of transcendent anything is matched only by the degree of violence that erupts when our real conditions of existence intrude on the fantasy" ("What's Love" 12). In his comments on the character of Henry V, Branagh clearly recognizes the fact that Henry's pursuit of a transcendent vision of the Nation is achieved only at the expense of his violent rejection of his "former tavern life," that is, his literal rejection of the "low" life for a "higher" calling (*Henry V Screenplay* 12). Consistent with his gritty critique of war, then, Branagh also exaggerates the violence of this process of rejection, show-casing off-stage events such as the hanging of Pistol and the death of Falstaff to underscore Henry's break with these "low lifes." But what Branagh misrecognizes is the degree of violence with which he wages his more personal campaign against his own Irishness, writ large in his consistent mistreatment of the Irish Captain Macmorris.[6] Having come dangerously close to representing, rather than repressing, the splits in his complex psychological portrait of King Henry that define his own experience as a postcolonial subject, Branagh must extend the disciplining of his actorly body to his directorial body which, paradoxically, must prevent his own film from becoming "altogether directed by an Irishman" (*Henry V*, 3.2.66).

Macmorris's ability to undermine Branagh's mission of dissolving social antagonisms into a transcendent vision of nationhood is apparent even before his first on-screen appearance. Why, for example, when Captain Gower informs Fluellen that "The Duke of Gloucester, to whom the order of the siege is given, is altogether directed by an Irishman" (*Henry V Screenplay* 41) does Branagh make this line read as a complaint, omitting the compliment that finishes Gower's line in Shakespeare's text: "a very valiant gentleman, i' faith" (3.2.67)? This omission is particularly curious given that it playfully invokes Branagh's direction of *Henry V* and his campaign to save the British film industry. Clearly, Branagh wishes to circumvent the centrifugal effect his own Irishness could have on an adaptation of a play already littered with Irish, Scottish, Welsh, and English antagonisms. In Shakespeare's *Henry V*, these

---

6. Commensurate with Henry's own past, Branagh refers to his "former life" in light of the tavern culture he associates with "a love of drinking, of storytelling, of the crack" (*Beginning* 81).

antagonisms are respectively embodied in the four Captains: Macmorris, Jamy, Fluellen, and Gower. But unlike the other Captains, Macmorris is a figure whose language distinguishes him as the incurable subject of colonial confusion; his tortured syntax and incoherent regional inflection disclose a crisis of self and national identity. The classic example of Macmorris's "schizophrenia" occurs in his response to a provocation from the Welsh Captain Fluellen, who accuses the Irish nation of military inferiority:

> FLUELLEN: Captain Macmorris, I think, look you, under your
>   correction, there is not many of your nation—
> MACMORRIS: Of my nation? What ish my nation? Ish a villain, and a
>   basterd, and a knave, and a rascal. What ish my nation?
>   Who talks of my nation? (3.2.120–24)

By contrast, in Branagh's film, Macmorris's all-too-familiar "Anglo-Irish sense of belonging nowhere"—of belonging to no "nation"—is stripped away and replaced with a reactionary, gratuitous anger, typical of the stereotype of the "wild Irish": "What ish my nation? Who talks of my nation is a villain and a bastard and a knave and a rascal" (*Henry V Screenplay* 58). This reductive treatment of the Irish is perfectly in keeping with the political ideology of Shakespeare's day, for as Jonathan Dollimore and Alan Sinfield explain, "[t]he assumption that the Irish were a barbarous and inferior people was so ingrained in Elizabethan England that it seemed only a natural duty to subdue them and destroy their culture" (224–25). Branagh's cuts to Macmorris's character work with a similar violence to render him a barbarian exception to the United Kingdom rule.

Macmorris is a character who embodies what I wish to call the "frontier perspective," for as a regional figure whose difference cannot be assimilated, Macmorris surfaces as a reminder of the space that separates everyday life on the frontier from that on the mainland.[7] Rather than

---

7. A strange on-location scene sets the tone for this frontier perspective. At the beginning of Shakespeare's act two, Branagh adds a personal flourish by positioning the Chorus "standing on a grassy cliff edge, looking out to sea" (*Henry V Screenplay* 20), presumably looking from the White Cliffs of Dover to France. But this view out to sea could be toward another land off the coast of England and another kind of "enemy": Ireland. This twist would dovetail rather neatly the with Chorus's simultaneous complaint: "Oh England!...Were all thy children kind and *natural*!" (20, emphasis added). Though the Chorus is describing the pending traitors' scene with Scroop, Cambridge, and Grey, this com-

extending his quilting operation across the Irish frontier, Branagh reinforces the cultural and geopolitical distance separating the Irish Captain from his Scottish, Welsh, and English counterparts by indulging in
a series of stereotypes. As suggested above, Macmorris's character, while
somewhat of a stock character in Shakespeare's play, becomes in
Branagh's film an exaggerated stereotype of the "wild Irishman"—
drunk, belligerent, and distinctly Catholic. And even though Branagh
reduces Macmorris's part to mere lip service, cutting his lines by more
than half, Branagh chooses to retain the Captain's Catholic mantra "so
Chrish save me," accentuating the enduring distinction between the
largely Catholic nation of Ireland and the "purified" Protestant nations
of Scotland, Wales, and England. Still more striking is the way in which
Branagh uses Macmorris to revise his own autobiographical "beginnings," for the actor who is playing the Irish Captain is none other
than John Sessions, Branagh's close friend and classmate at the Royal
Academy of Dramatic Art. Indeed, Sessions's Macmorris returns
Branagh to the primal scene of his quest for a quintessentially English
identity at a time when he was desperately seeking to distance himself
from the tradition of stage Irish. Having developed his own form of elo-
cutionary training designed to out-English the English, Branagh put his
new accent to the royal test when he outbid John Sessions for the opportunity to perform before the Queen and Prince Philip during their
visit to RADA. Sessions requested a three-minute solo improvisation
and Branagh countered with an offer to play Hamlet, as he relates:

> Hugh [the director] laughed. "Oh no. Oh no, no. no." (More laughter) "It's
> simply not possible, John. Your language is quite unacceptable...there could be
> a national incident....I simply can't take the risk."
> There was room, however, for the extremely boring and conventional stu-
> dent who came up with the least original idea.
> "Could I do a bit of Hamlet?" (*Beginning* 66)

Nearly ten years later, Branagh's *Henry V* provides the ideal coda to this
scene of amateur egos in-the-making, for in casting Sessions as the "wild

---

bination of frontier perspective, "natural children," and betrayal has rich implications.
Perhaps Branagh, also facing out to sea as he directs this scene, at once resents his status
as a non-native of England even as he laments the betrayal he commits against his homeland in the name of a naturalized or "quintessentially English" identity. It is this split perspective—this simultaneous glance in opposing directions—that comprises Branagh's
schizophrenic characterization of Henry V.

and apparently deranged" Irishman (*Henry V Screenplay* 41) while allocating the part of the quintessentially English king to himself, Branagh all but seals his victory in this quest to become more English than the English.

> "My Master is a great tyrant," said a Negro, according to a popular quip of the day.
> "He treats me as badly as if I was a common Irishman."[8]

The most stunning example of Branagh's use (and abuse) of Macmorris as proof of his own Englishness is revealed in the Irish captain's physical appearance. As in Shakespeare's play, Jamy and Macmorris emerge from the mines at Harfleur weary from battle; but in Branagh's version, Macmorris is the only character who emerges almost completely "blackened" (*Henry V Screenplay* 40). This image of Macmorris evokes yet another stage tradition associated with the Irish: the minstrel tradition. Given the historical slander of the Irish as "white niggers," it "is surely no coincidence," as Noel Ignatieff explains, "that so many of the pioneers of blackface minstrelsy were of Irish descent" (42). It is particularly interesting to note the effect this tradition had on Branagh who, as a teenager, became fascinated by his brother's "blacked up" impersonation of a "York Street shoe-shine"—a performance which, Branagh claims, sparked his interest in the theatrical arts (*Beginning* 16). But in the context of *Henry V,* the "blacked up" appearance of Macmorris does not evoke Branagh's nostalgia; rather, it demonstrates his continued rejection of Irish stock figures and, in broader terms, the prospect of solidarity with his homeland. The Irish, as Ignatieff points out in his fascinating study of *How the Irish Became White,* were often considered to be "an intermediate race located socially between black and white" (76). As we have seen, Branagh experienced this disabling liminal status in the form of his Anglo-Irish sense of "double isolation." Thus, in conjuring this specter of the "black Irish" only to parody it, Branagh demonstrates how *he* "became white," that is, by rejecting all

8. According to Noel Ignatieff's analysis of *How the Irish Became White,* this quote typifies and derives from the complex relationships between Irish- and African-Americans on the minstrel stage.

things not quintessentially English.[9] And if we dig further into this image of the Irish captain emerging from the mines, we might also see the burned-out shadow of a coal miner—a figure who clearly evokes the coalfield strikes of the mid-eighties which Branagh's *Henry V* followed hard upon. As Paul Gilroy explains in *There Ain't No Black in the Union Jack*, during this historic labor crisis, the figure of the miner was lumped together with the Irish and the blacks, who collectively came to represent "the enemy within" the United Kingdom, threatening the smooth workings of Thatcherite conservatism with the lived reality of alienated labor, wage exploitation, and racism (34).[10] In this context, the caricature of the Irish Captain Macmorris as a "blacked up" miner uncannily condenses all existing threats—past and present—to Branagh's vision of a national-popular Shakespeare, a vision that is viable only insofar as certain representatives of "the people" are kept on the job, in the dirt, and *in their place*. For all these reasons, then, there ain't no "Mac" in Branagh's Union Jack.

The success of ideological quilting lies in its ability to efface its own traces, for as Žižek reminds us, its totalizing effects do not "abolish the endless floating of signifiers without residue" (*Sublime* 100). Despite Branagh's directorial acts of damage control and his actorly embodiment of a king whose two bodies rise triumphant from the battlefield to create a shining synecdoche for a "united" kingdom, the residue of his attempts to abolish the threat of his Irishness emerges in the form of a Welsh decoy: Fluellen. Though it is not uncommon for stage productions of *Henry V* to accentuate Fluellen's role, I will argue that for Branagh, Fluellen's character has geopolitical implications that far exceed the Welsh Captain's standard treatment as an amusing representative of ethnic pride. Indeed, in Branagh's film, Fluellen, as one reviewer notes, is "*intemperately* inflamed by ethnic pride" (Lane 34, emphasis added). It is particularly odd, then, that instead of provoking

9. Ignatieff explains that in the blend-in-or-bust context of nineteenth- and twentieth-century America, the Irish had "to learn to subordinate county, religion, or national animosities...to a new solidarity based on color—" (96).

10. There was also solidarity among these common enemies to the state, as one propaganda poster suggests: "The Experience of Irish people, Black people and the Miners are Same" (qtd. in Gilroy 41).

Branagh's resistance, Fluellen (played by Ian Holm) exercises a certain fascination over him. Indeed, Branagh's admiration for Fluellen's "ethnic pride" is encoded not only in his stage directions describing the Welsh warrior as a "[m]ost loyal...fierce, eccentric disciplinarian, Welsh to his very bones" (*Henry V Screenplay* 39), but also in his attempts to create a series of structural homologies between Fluellen and Henry. For example, following Henry's magnificent Harfleur speech, Branagh cuts Pistol's parodic version of "to the breach" and jumps directly to Fluellen's "Up to the breach, you dogs! Avaunt you cullions!" (39), reinforcing Henry's battle cry in Fluellen's more colloquial register. Later, on the eve of Agincourt, Branagh has both Henry *and* Fluellen go on "rounds" throughout the camp, eventually crossing paths to provide Henry with another opportunity to translate his own crisis of cultural ambivalence into a display of admiration for "the unswerving loyalty of the Welshman" (87).[11] Finally, in a series of battle scenes at Agincourt, Branagh positions Fluellen—who does not fight in Shakespeare's text— in military poses similar to Henry's, producing an effect that goes so far as to "equat[e] Henry with Fluellen" (Breight 104).

The relationship that Branagh establishes between Henry and Fluellen is essentially one of "mimicry." According to Homi K. Bhabha, in the dialectic between colonizer and colonized, mimicry "represents an ironic compromise," articulating the desire for *"a subject of difference that is almost the same but not quite"* (86). Accordingly, if Ireland "was, and remains...[England's] bad conscience" (Dollimore and Sinfield 226), then of the three frontier countries represented in *Henry V*, Wales is, as Dollimore and Sinfield conclude, "the most tractable" from geographic, linguistic, and religious perspectives (224).[12] In other words, Wales and Fluellen invoke a frontier that is almost the same as the mainland, maintaining the modicum of resemblance through which mimicry insinuates itself as an "authorized versio[n] of otherness" (Bhabha 88). But according to Bhabha, the dynamics of mimicry revolve

---

11. Keeping a watchful eye over the soldiers and other Captains, Fluellen "stands behind this peaceful scene for a moment, before moving on around the camp"; then, as if following *Fluellen's* lead, Henry proceeds to "mak[e] his way through the camp, meeting with some of his soldiers" (*Henry V Screenplay* 61).

12. Dollimore and Sinfield explain that in Shakespeare's day, "Ireland was the great problem....The population was overwhelmingly Catholic and liable to support a continental invader, and resistance to English rule proved irrepressible, despite or more probably because of the many atrocities committed against the people..." (224).

around *menace* as well as resemblance (86) and, in this respect, Wales is almost the same as the mainland but *not quite different enough* from Ireland. Indeed, Wales, too, is a frontier country associated with a kind of cultural madness; for confirmation of this suggestion, we need only look back to *1 Henry IV* to find Fluellen's Shakespearean predecessor, Captain Glendower, passionately raving about his ability to "call spirits from the vasty deep" as well as to "command the devil" (3.1.52, 55–56). And like Branagh's relationship to Ireland, Wales exerts a powerful, if often unstated, pull on Shakespeare's Henry, whose heritage is similarly split between the English mainland and the Welsh frontier. Thus, while it seems as though this mimicking relationship between Henry and Fluellen will generate a seamless displacement of Branagh's repressed identification with Ireland, the consummate irony of this compromise is that it merely takes Branagh on a Welsh detour back to his Irish homeland.

Serving as a form of "camouflage," mimicry, as Bhabha explains, works through metonymy, generating "a form of resemblance " that is displayed only "in part[s]" (90). This dynamic of partial resemblance is the source of the most fascinating performance decision Branagh makes for the crucial "disguised king" sequence on the eve of Agincourt: playing Henry with a Welsh accent. This is our first indication that Henry's mimicking relationship with Fluellen is converting to menace, for a "stable, essential, unified national identity absorbs, refines, and neutralizes difference, but remains itself unchanged by those differences" (Brinker-Gabler and Smith 9). Though Branagh explains away his adoption of a regional inflection as an attempt "to underline the king's disguise" (*Beginning* 154), we might recall the Lacanian dictum that the truth has the structure of a fiction.[13] In other words, the more Branagh's Henry learns to enjoy this fiction of Welshness, the closer Branagh gets to the truth of his Irishness and, consequently, his irrepressible "schizophrenia." Accordingly, following the decisive victory at Agincourt, Branagh's filmic fantasy of transcendence splits at the seams of his Welsh disguise. As Fluellen describes England's historical victory over

13. Citing Lacan's observation about the relationship between truth and fiction, Žižek explains that " 'Truth' is definitely not a kind of surplus *eluding* us again and again; it appears, on the contrary, in the form of traumatic *encounters*—that is, we chance upon it where we presumed the presence of 'mere appearance'" (*Sublime* 190). In other words, the " 'shock of the truth' consists in its sudden emergence in the midst of the realm of reassuring phenomena" (190).

the French led by Henry's great-uncle Edward III, the Black Prince of Wales, Branagh's Henry appears to struggle against this assertion of family resemblance with his Welsh ancestor and even "breaks into an involuntary laugh" (*Henry V Screenplay* 92). It is not long, however, before laughter converts to tears, as Fluellen exposes the cultural breach separating Henry and, by extension, Branagh, from a quintessentially English identity: "and I do believe your Majesty takes no scorn to wear the leek upon Saint Davy's day" (92). In keeping with the metonymic effects of mimicry, here, Fluellen's insistence upon Henry's Welshness tacitly exposes Branagh's Irishness, as the leek becomes a metonymic substitute for the "W" brandished by William of Orange and the Welsh celebration of Saint Davy's day slides easily into the Ulster Protestants' observation of King Billy's day.[14] The telltale sign that this metonymy effect is taking place is revealed in the moment of "textual excess" that follows Fluellen's statement, a moment that "discloses an ideological 'stress point' by evoking an emotional affect which remains unexplained by the contingent dramatic circumstances" (Holderness, "'What ish my nation?'" 233). This moment of excess occurs when, in response to Fluellen's inquiry about the leek, Henry offers the following confession "through tears which he cannot prevent" (*Henry V Screenplay* 92): "I wear it for a memorable honour; For I am Welsh, you know, good countryman" (92).

As Branagh's Irishness leaks through Henry's Welsh facade, this revelation of his frontier identity creates a breach in his king's two bodies, exposing the residue or leftover of his quilting operation. Žižek's reading of the leftover and its relationship to the social structure is instructive here. In Shakespeare's *Henry V*, the social structure is constituted around a prevailing "lack." In other words, subjects interact with each other on the basis of a shared "breach" in the fabric of class, ethnicity, or creed, while the social fantasy of the play radiates from the figure of the monarch, who exists to fill in or conceal these breaches through the rhetoric of mud and blood. But as Dollimore and Sinfield contend, the fatal flaw in the ideology of rule featured in Shakespeare's play resides precisely in its "fantasy of establishing ideological unity in the sole figure of the monarch" (225), for not even this celebrated "warrior for the working day" can stretch without splitting upon certain ideological pressure

14. The "W" is worn on King Billy's Day, celebrated annually on July 12 in Ulster, to commemorate the 1690 Battle of Boyne. The "W" is a central part of King Billy's iconography, signifying William.

Figure 9. Branagh's Irishness "leeks" through his Welsh façade as Fluellen (Ian Holm) informs him that "All the water in wye cannot wash the Welsh blood out of your body." Samuel Goldwyn, 1989. Photo courtesy of Photofest.

points, setting the stage for the emergence of the leftover. According to Žižek, the leftover materializes in the following paradox: "this structural network of relations, can establish itself only in so far as it is embodied in a totally contingent material element, a little-bit-of-Real which, by its sudden irruption, disrupts the homeostatic indifference of relations between subjects" (183). This is exactly how the leek/leak functions in *Henry V:* to disclose the Real of social antagonisms that Shakespeare's play and Branagh's film conspire to occlude. What is so stunning about this scene in Branagh's film is the way his own lack is brought to bear on this enduring leak in the symbolic order. For the leek materializes what Henry's Welsh accent merely suggests—that there is a difference, as Bhabha puts it, between "being English and being Anglicized" (90). This is the cold wisdom that Fluellen proceeds to share with Branagh's Henry, who continues to sob uncontrollably as he listens to the Welsh Captain exclaim: "All the water in Wye cannot wash your Majesty's Welsh blood out of your body, I can tell you that" (*Henry V Screenplay* 92). Indeed, there is no end to the current of social antagonisms and no beginning to a hoped-for catharsis in a film that begins by making big promises "for everyone" but ends with the whimper of identities in ruins. For beneath the begrimed image of an English king and a Welsh soldier "plangently embracing in a symbolic ritual of national unity," we recognize the more haunting vision of "an Irishman and a Scot weeping over the historical devastations of British imperialism" (Holderness, "'What ish my nation?'" 234).

It is for this reason that Branagh makes one final attempt to dissolve the geopolitical devastations of space into time—and, more specifically, into the time it takes for him to emerge as a liberal humanist hero. Envisioning his climactic exit from Agincourt as "the greatest tracking shot in the world" (*Beginning* 235), Branagh focuses on an image of Henry carrying a dead boy over his shoulder, as he wades through the carnage to the crescendo of the *Non Nobis* hymn. Though Branagh describes this scene as the film's climactic critique of war, it more obviously suggests the cinematic apotheosis of Branagh. For in this tableau of boy and king, Branagh encapsulates—across five-hundred feet of tracking platforms—his journey from baby director to Academy Award nominee in a shot that creates a sacralizing epistemology of his own career, following his footsteps from the hard way to the high way of the auteur-king.

Appropriately, Branagh's auteurist mission in *Henry V* rests upon one final omission: the Chorus's allusion to Essex returning from Ireland "[b]ringing rebellion broached upon his sword" (5.1.32). But what I would call the "Essex function" of broaching or eradicating difference is considerably far removed from Henry's early modern authority-function and Branagh's postmodern auteur-function of quilting across the breach between dissident constituencies. The elimination of this line from the film thus reveals a lesson learned, albeit "the hard way," about the pathology of authorship in both early modern and postmodern culture. For despite Branagh's failed attempt to bridge the gap between a "quintessentially English project" and a Shakespeare film "for everyone," what he learns is that he must go unto this breach between high and low, national and popular, not once more, but *ever* more. Perhaps, then, in a cultural moment wherein aspiring authors are destined to repeat the styles of the past, the only hope of variation lies, paradoxically, in repetition—in an ethos not of broaching but of poaching. Such is the method embedded in the madness of early modern authorship, wherein the repetition and recontextualization of preexisting texts generates "leaks" or "breaches" in the authority of the original even as this authority becomes the shaky ground of new authorial missions. And isn't this, after all, what defines the unfinished cultural business of adaptation? Offering a variation on this theme, Branagh's remake attempts not to create but to conceal the social breaches in Shakespeare's play in hopes of generating a retake on his own skewed personal and cultural experience. But by the conclusion of the film, it is clear that this dirty work remains unfinished. It is little wonder, then, that after shooting the triumphant but traumatic leek scene, Branagh went home feeling "exhausted and somehow defeated, and for no good reason, burst into tears. I felt as if I had come back form the war" (*Beginning* 236). Once more unto the breach, dear Ken, once more.

7

Shakespeare in Love

Sex, Capitalism, and the Authorial Body-in-Pleasure

While Baz Luhrmann conjures the life-infusing spirit of Shakespeare in his quest against the dead letter of the legend, Kenneth Branagh attempts to embody this spirit in his personal and political pursuit of a national-popular cinema. Neither, however, succeeds in his respective mission to the extent that *Shakespeare in Love* does in bringing to life its vision of Shakespeare the Author as an Ur-Auteur. Resuming the search begun by Washington Irving, *Shakespeare in Love* returns from Stratford-upon-Avon having broached rebellion against the much-maligned body of the Bard on its celluloid sword. Indeed, what makes *Shakespeare in Love* such a provocative end-point for this analysis is its focus on the authorial body as the privileged site of the adaptation process. In this sexy film about the spirit-made-flesh, authorship is anchored in and made accountable to the body—in all its vulnerability and virility. Quite unlike the other adaptations we have explored in this analysis, in *Shakespeare in Love* the role of the actual film director, John Madden, is rendered almost invisible, subordinated to this diegetic dream of quite literally raising Shakespeare from the ranks of death and its perpetual paramour: impotence. This bedroom farce thus reimagines the "death of the Author" as a "little death" by playfully linking poetic labor to sexual expenditure. In so doing, however, *Shakespeare in Love* poses a theory of authorial production that is grounded in the conspicuous consumption of the *female* flesh, redefining the "dirty work" of the postmodern auteur not in the spirit of Shakespeare's early modern legacy, but in the flesh of late capitalism's dirty deals to commodify the body itself, all the while disguising this mission as a labor of love.

As I have argued throughout this analysis, in the wake of poststructuralist critiques of the Author, the Shakespearean "corpus" has been the locus of a particular kind of violence, born of the impetus to mutilate, maim, and un-name the authorial body in an effort to valorize the

Text. While this exorcism of the Author in academic culture presents us with a striking image of the body-in-pain, popular culture—and Hollywood film in particular—has often stemmed this deconstructive tide by resurrecting Shakespeare in the form of a body-in-pleasure. Significantly, from its inception, cinema has claimed the ontological priority of bodies over texts; and films such as *Shakespeare in Love*, which approach the Shakespearean text by fetishizing the overtly sexualized authorial body, seem to realize this cinematic dream with a vengeance. What, then, might this sexualized body have to tell us about Shakespeare's *textual* remains? Focusing on Shakespeare's latest incarnation as a cinematic romance hero in *Shakespeare in Love*, I will explore the way in which this corpus, in all its incarnations—bodily, textual, commercial, and critical—returns from the dead to implore us not to love but, rather, to enjoy.

In *Shakespeare in Love* "enjoyment" revolves deliriously around the act of consumption. Thus, instead of aligning Shakespearean authorship with the production-driven energies associated with early capitalism and the Elizabethan theatrical marketplace, this film ultimately positions Shakespeare the Author as an invention and, in fact, endorsement of *late* capitalism. The experience of enjoyment-as-consumption is a prerogative of late capitalistic society, deriving from a crucial mutation in the status of cultural authority, specifically, the authority of the "Master." If, as Žižek explains, precapitalistic society is structured by a belief in the regulatory function of a singular authority or Master, a figure who reflects a stable paternal signifier and exists as a model of the "ethics of self-mastery and 'just measure,'" then within capitalism, this regulatory function of the Master "becomes suspended, and the vicious circle of the superego spins freely" (*Tarrying* 210). In other words, the nature of the Master's function as a collective superego changes; rather than serving as an agent of prohibition, the Master's imperative is reconstituted as an *invitation* to consume and, therefore, to enjoy "freely"— without restraint. In this context, then, "to obey" *is* "to enjoy."[1] Poised on the brink of transition from feudalism to capitalism, the Elizabethan

---

1. In *Tarrying with the Negative*, Žižek explains the imperative to enjoy within late capitalism through the following example drawn from the commercialization of everyday

England of *Shakespeare in Love* is a society in the throes of economic and social chaos, seeking a Master who can articulate a new conception of value—monetary and human—appropriate to the fiscal and ethical changes demanded by the rise of capitalism. As we shall see, "Master Will" fits this bill, but only in the guise of the late capitalistic Master of enjoyment, for rather than emerging as a producing text, he materializes as a consuming and, indeed, consummating body.

In its portrait of a theatrical marketplace beset by the plague of early capitalism, *Shakespeare in Love* localizes the culture-wide growing pains of Elizabethan England in its opening images of the body-in-pain. The first such body we encounter belongs not to Shakespeare but to Philip Henslowe (Geoffrey Rush) who, the film informs us, is "a businessman with a cash flow problem," a phrase which smacks anachronistically of late-capitalistic slang. But the subsequent title card sends us swiftly back to the Elizabethan marketplace with an advertisement for a play called THE LAMENTABLE TRAGEDIE OF THE MONEYLENDER REVENG'D. Engaged in a real-life drama, Henslowe is strapped to a chair on stage, where he is being tortured with hot coals for his failure to pay his debts to the vengeful moneylender, Hugh Fennyman (Tom Wilkinson). Tabulating Henslowe's debt, Fennyman's thug claims that they have been "bitten" for "Twelve pounds, one shilling and four pence...including interest" (Norman and Stoppard 1–2). Curiously inflected with an image of orality, this line suggests the ravenous mouth of a marketplace fully committed to usury, burning its bottom-line mentality into the bottom of Henslowe's boots.[2] Prone, enfeebled, feminized, and filthy, Henslowe's body is more than just a body-in-

---

life: "consider the labels on food cans full of pseudoscientific data—this soup contains so much cholesterol, so many calories, so much fat...(Lacan, of course, would discern behind this replacement of direct injunction by the allegedly neutral information the superego imperative '*Enjoy!*')" (218). Two provisos must be articulated at this point in order to contextualize my reading of *Shakespeare in Love*. First, it is important to note that Lacan distinguishes between "enjoyment" (as *jouissance*, or pleasure-in-pain) and "pleasure." I use these terms interchangeably in my argument, which relies more heavily on cultural materialism than psychoanalysis for its theoretical foundations. Second, it must also be acknowledged that for the sake of clarity, I am oversimplifying "precapitalism" by setting it up as a kind of "straw man," rather than exploring the various nuances in and abuses of its system of "self-mastery and just measure."

2. Thomas Moison observes that usury, while exploited not only by "capital-hungry merchants" but also by "Parliament and the Queen herself," was still considered to be a morally suspect practice in Elizabethan England (192). See Moison's essay " 'Which is the merchant here? and which the Jew?': Subversion and Recuperation in *The Merchant of*

pain, for in this scene it acquires the more specific contours of what Susan Jeffords calls a "softbody." In her book titled *Hardbodies: Hollywood Masculinity in the Reagan Era,* Jeffords explains that the "softbody" typically emerges during a time of national crisis, when patriarchal authority—embodied in the symbolic figure of the Master—is in a state of atrophy, weakened by some emasculating economic, social, or political threat (12). As suggested by the opening scene of *Shakespeare in Love,* Elizabethan England is a culture in need of a Master to regulate its strumpet-like embrace of exchange values within the emergent theatrical marketplace, as well as to restore enabling models of distinctly male power during the emasculating reign of Elizabeth I. Henslowe's last-ditch offer to Fennyman of a partnership in a new comedy by "Will Shakespeare," a name conspicuously foreshortened to connote desire itself, seems to initiate precisely this quest.

But the next body we encounter in *Shakespeare in Love* does little to placate the sense of dis-ease that permeates this opening image of Elizabethan culture, for this body is, as Henslowe memorably puts it, "Nobody": it's "[t]he author" (Norman and Stoppard 50). And so we are introduced to Will Shakespeare (Joseph Fiennes), a playwright whose humble surroundings, composed of crumpled paper balls and broken quills, playfully suggest the dismembered status of the Shakespearean corpus. Will's "corpus," meanwhile, is in even worse shape. Ignoring Henslowe's desperate entreaties for the completion of his new play, Will heads to his analyst, bitterly complaining about his writer's block: "It's as if my quill is broken," he exclaims. "As if the organ of the imagination has dried up. As if the proud tower of my genius has collapsed" (10). If Henslowe's body is threatened with indigence, Will's body is threatened by impotence: not only is he unable to produce poetry, but, more importantly, he is unable to consume women. "Broken," "dried up," and "collapsed," Will's body, by his own admission, is also a "softbody." But this softbody is more complicated than Henslowe's, because at this point it expresses alienation from rather than complicity with the succubus-like forces of the burgeoning Elizabethan marketplace. "Once," Will laments, "I had the gift...I could make love out of words as a potter makes cups out of clay...for sixpence a line I could cause a

---

Venice." Significantly, the name alone of the principal capital-hungry entrepreneur in *Shakespeare in Love,* Fennyman, reflects his entrenchment in the emergent Elizabethan marketplace, for "Fennyman" is an Anglicization of the word "Pfennigmann" or "pennyman."

riot in a nunnery" (Norman and Stoppard 9). Will's complaint plainly indicates that his poetic inspiration came freely to him so long as it was, in fact, a "gift." The problem is that now the work of his hands cannot be separated from its market value. Indeed, Will's equation of poetry first with "pottery" and then with "pence" alludes to the much larger cultural shift from use value to exchange value beginning to take place in early modern culture. For like pottery, Will's poetry once had a "riotous" and distinctly human quality; now, however, both poetry and pottery fall victim to the leveling, quantity-intensive logic of the commodity form which, as Herbert Marcuse argues, reduces not only all forms of art but also all realms of culture to commercials, so that "[t]he music of the soul is also the music of salesmanship" (72). Echoing this tune, Will laments his futile search for a "soulmate" in a world in which love is for sale from Black Sue, Fat Phoebe, Rosaline, and Aphrodite, and where, consequently, there is no place for true love poetry—only the relentless demand for comedy and "a bit with a dog" (Norman and Stoppard 18).

At this point in the film, then, Will's professional and personal failures may be read as a form of resistance to the alienating forces of the marketplace that seek to co-opt and corrupt his art and life for "sixpence a line." Will's loss of poetic and sexual prowess, in other words, may signal at least an unconscious refusal to buy into the crass consumer logic that prostitutes his genius and his person. As Jeffords might conclude, Will's inability to generate poetic lines defies not only the all-important bottom line but also the idea of social definition more generally—the hard edges, lines, and boundaries that distinguish the socially legible hardbody from the anomalous, "messy" and "confusing" softbody (27). In this state, Will resembles the disruptive figure of the "rebel-poet" who, Marcuse explains, flouts the established order by refusing to "earn a living, at least not in an orderly and normal way" (59). It is at the beginning, therefore, rather than the end of the film that Will represents the "poet of true love" because only here does he maintain a properly "romantic" existence—one that exudes "aesthetic incompatibility with the developing society" (60). Although the dilemma between art and commerce that the film dramatizes is a cliché of late as opposed to early capitalism, it is not long before the Shakespearean corpus itself becomes the source of this burgeoning dilemma, when Heminge and Condell urge the "great Variety of Readers" to "Judge your sixe-pen'orth, your shillings worth, your five shillings worth at a time, or higher, so you rise to the just rates, and welcome. *But what ever you do, Buy"* (*Riverside Shakespeare* 95, emphasis added). Poised at the inception of this imperative to "buy," Will soon learns that his aesthetic incompatibility with the world around him stems from his failure to engage in proper *consumption* and, consequently, from his failure to adopt the late capitalist solution: "enjoy!"

✎

Thus what begins as a critique of the dehumanizing drive to produce within early capitalism quickly becomes an endorsement of the desire to consume associated with late capitalism. Will's visit to his "shrink"—itself a conspicuous allusion to the film's preoccupation with late capitalism and the cult of self-help—prompts him to buy into this latter choice when Dr. Moth (played by Anthony Sher) supplies him with a prescription for pleasure. Simply put, Dr. Moth persuades Will to desublimate his repressed passions which, rather than being channeled into art, can be enjoyed in life—a form of therapy that foregrounds consumption as a cure-all for the incommensurate ailments of the soul. Offering Will an asp-shaped bangle for a modest fee, Dr. Moth instructs him to write his name on a piece of paper, feed it through the mouth of the snake and, finally, place the snake charm on his lady's wrist. Presumably, his lady will proceed to dream of him and his poetic "gift" will be restored. The fact that this gift is no longer free, however, indicates that Will has begun to buy into the logic of the marketplace; he has been charmed by the snake and is now falling from pseudo-alienation into willing complicity with the forces of capitalism. Indeed, in its role as a mystical go-between for Will and his lady, as well as for Will and his poetry, the magic snake bracelet alludes to the ways in which the fetishization of commodities within capitalism reduces social relations between people to "the fantastic form of a relation between things" (Marx 321). Not surprisingly, this axiom also describes the brief course of Will and Rosaline's relationship. With the help of the snake charm, Will doesn't even really need Rosaline for inspiration or, for that matter, sexual gratification. He is able to produce the first scene of *Romeo and Rosaline* (formerly *Romeo and Ethyl, the Pirate's Daughter*) with little more than a passing kiss from his lady-muse; and his far more passionate act of kissing his new-wrought pages—followed by the climactic exclamation "God, I'm good!"—renders his satisfaction with "things" virtually complete. But Will is being groomed for a late-capitalistic variation on this theme, which stipulates that gratification can be obtained immediately through "relations" with people that produce "things"—we need only recognize the exchange value that "Juliet" commands over "Rosaline" in *Romeo and Juliet*. Quite provocatively, then, the image of the snake with the mouth that *consumes before it can produce* presents us with a virtual tableau of the libidinal economy destined to restore Will's gift—but only at the expense of the lady of *his* dreams.

If, as Marcuse explains, proper desublimation involves "replacing mediated with immediate gratification" (72), then in *Shakespeare in Love*, it is not until Will's conversional encounter with the Master of the Revels that he learns how to enjoy without limits. From a historical perspective, the Master of the Revels is a figure easily aligned with the "Master" of pre-capitalist society, for both are authority figures who exist to censor and restrict the excess traditionally associated with the human libido. More specifically, the Master's function "is to dominate the excess by locating its cause in a clearly delimited social agency" (Žižek, *Tarrying* 210). In Elizabethan England, one such potentially dangerous social agency was the institution of the public theater, and the Master of the Revels was the figure who, representing the Crown's interests, maintained regulatory power over it. But in *Shakespeare in Love*, the Master of the Revels (Simon Callow) is more accurately described as a "master of reveling," for he re-opens the theaters not because they have been purged of the social threat of plague and moral corruption but because of his own naked self-interest in enjoying Burbage's (and Will's) mistress, Rosaline:

> WILL: You have opened the playhouses?
> TILNEY: I have Master Will.
> WILL: But the plague...
> TILNEY: (Sighs) Yes, I know. But he [Burbage] was always
>   hanging around the house.
>
> (Norman and Stoppard 26)

Clearly, when the censor himself has re-opened the playhouses solely for the purposes of getting the men out of their houses, the new ethos of self-indulgence has overtaken the old ethics of self-mastery and restraint.[3] As this scene suggests, then, within capitalism, there is no "clearly delimited social agency" to guard against, for everyone—even

3. This image of the Master of the Revels as a Master of Enjoyment is strikingly similar to the Freudian figure of the pre-Oedipal or totemic father who monopolizes enjoyment by hoarding all the women and, therefore, must be killed. From the standpoint of cinematic intertextuality, the fact that Simon Callow plays this figure, after having played the celibate priest Mr. Beebe in *A Room with a View* (1987) and the gay Scotsman in *Four Weddings and a Funeral* (1994), is particularly interesting.

the Master charged with protecting society—is a potential threat. But rather than increasing the prohibitions already in place in this every-man-for-himself environment, capitalism "solves" the problem of so-cial antagonisms inherent to it by taking the path of least resistance, that is, by encouraging everyone to busy themselves with consumption and, in so doing, increase the cycle of production.

Cued by the Master of the Revels, Will becomes a kind of "no holds Bard," allowing his repressed desires to roam free. In this incarnation, Will most resembles the subject of late capitalism, a figure who is not so much a person as a "place" traversed by free-ranging and often conflicting desires associated with the confusing affective cues of con-sumer culture. The subject of late capitalism is a subject in search of im-ages that will regulate his or her passions, or, as Žižek puts it, images that will *"organize our enjoyment"* (*Tarrying* 206)—a figure on a billboard or a face on TV capable of mastering and making sense of the myriad desires that the subject seems to experience all at once. Before emerging as a figure capable of mastering his own and others' desires as a Holly-wood Hardbardy, Will becomes a site of multiple, even subversive pas-sions, for the first image that momentarily regulates his desire is that of a handsome young man, Thomas Kent. Of course, the off-screen audi-ence is privy to the fact that this handsome young man with whom Will becomes infatuated is really a lovely young lady, Viola de Lesseps (Gwyneth Paltrow), and so the subversive potential of Will's desire is quickly "straightened out."[4] But even Will's patently heterosexual de-sire for Viola is potentially subversive in its rejection of existing hierar-chies of class and gender. For example, when Will learns that Viola is betrothed against her will to the aristocrat Wessex, "Thomas" asks him if "a lady born to wealth and noble marriage can love happily with a Bank-side poet and player?" Without thinking, Will responds: "Yes, by God! Love knows nothing of rank or riverbank!" (Norman and Stoppard 66). At this point, Will and "Thomas" kiss, as if to seal their pledge of so-cially disruptive desire. But the revolutionary romantic energy of *Shakespeare in Love* stops here—where the buck begins—as the bottling up of Will's impromptu speech in convenient couplets such as "rank" and "bank" implies. Indeed, Will *will* take his desire straight to the bank,

---

4. This scene of homoerotic affection alludes to an earlier but quickly dismissed plot-line for *Shakespeare in Love* imagined by Stephen Greenblatt, who suggested to the film-makers that they make the affair not between Will and Viola but between Will and Christopher Marlowe. Most likely, *Shakespeare in Love* would have been more interesting but less of a box-office smash under Greenblatt's "direction."

once he realizes that in consuming Viola, he can (re)produce her—as a play—and so work becomes play, and play becomes the masterwork of *Romeo and Juliet*.

This mystifying merger of work and play is precisely the logic that *Shakespeare in Love* applies to its representation of authorship which, I shall argue, also represents the interests of what Theodor Adorno and Max Horkheimer call "the culture industry." The culture industry is a catch-all phrase for sites of mass entertainment within late capitalism: television, record companies, Harlequin romance novels, and, above all, Hollywood. The culture industry refers to the commercialization of culture and the process whereby "art," masquerading as culture, becomes an industrial product. According to this logic, "art" is created not by some solitary genius but by market trends, mass production, tailorization, reproduction, and, of course, consumption. The way that the culture industry disguises this industrial process and seduces consumers into believing that mass entertainment is "high" art or culture is by disguising work in play, business in pleasure, labor in leisure. For the culture industry and its products are, according to Adorno and Horkheimer, "sought after as an escape from the mechanized work process" in order to "recruit strength in order to be able to cope with it again" (137). But the catch is that enjoyment also becomes mechanized—courtesy of two-hour movies, three-day mini-series, sixty-minute records—to the point where it "is entirely extinguished in fixed entertainments" (106). Simply put, what drives the culture industry is the idea that the more efficiently we spend our leisure time, the better workers we become; therefore, the culture industry and its products convince us to work more so we can play more.

Shakespeare in Love adopts a similar approach to authorship, by representing the work of playwriting as something that is enhanced by indulging in play itself. Materializing Shakespeare's dismembered or even non-existent "corpus" as a smooth, sexually viable hardbody is part and parcel of this late capitalistic fantasy. But before this body can become a playmaking and lovemaking machine, it must be established that it exists in the first place—a feat which the film accomplishes in the following exchange between Will and Viola:

> VIOLA: Answer me only this: are you the author of the plays of
> William Shakespeare?
> WILL: I am.

> (Norman and Stoppard 68)

Figure 10. Foreplay to the play: Will (Joseph Fiennes) and Viola (Gwyneth Paltrow) redefine collaboration in John Madden's *Shakespeare in Love*. Miramax Films, 1998. Photo courtesy of Photofest.

In an instant, the four-hundred-year-old memory of Shakespeare's missing body and Will's messy softbody is erased, for the success of this multiple-Oscar-winning film hinges on our willingness to believe not only that this is Shakespeare but that this is Shakespeare "in love." What follows is a vision of the Author-as-Master, a figure whose ability to produce "riotous" passions in others is ideally suited both to meet and to manufacture the needs of late capitalist culture. This is a Master who *enjoys*—and who, by extension, can teach *us* how to enjoy. Indeed, *Shakespeare in Love* banks on the fact that as subjects of late capitalism, we, too, are in need of images to "regulate our passions"; and what better image to lend meaning to our own potentially wayward desires than the specter of Shakespeare raised from the dead through the special effects and sublime affect of love?

Born of the unmistakable style of the culture industry, Will and Viola's love generates an extraordinarily efficient merger of work and play. This merger is inscribed, appropriately, in the film's magnificent montage effects, as dress rehearsals from "The Rose Theatre" are inter-cut with undressed rehearsals in "Viola's bedroom." In both locations, lines of the play we recognize as *Romeo and Juliet* are uttered and lived, blurring the boundaries between business and pleasure, work and play, even further. The result is something akin to method acting meets "the rhythm method":

WILL and VIOLA are both out of bed, halfway through dressing. Still rehearsing.

> WILL: Good night, Good night. As sweet repose and rest
> Come to thy heart as that within my breast.
> O wilt thou leave me so unsatisfied?
> VIOLA: That's my line!
> WILL: Oh, but it is mine too!

INT. THE ROSE THEATRE. STAGE. NIGHT.

> VIOLA AS ROMEO: O wilt thou leave me so unsatisfied?
> SAM AS JULIET: What satisfaction can'st thou have tonight?
> VIOLA AS ROMEO: The exchange of thy love's faithful vow for mine.

INT. [THE] DE LESSEPS HOUSE. VIOLA'S BEDROOM. NIGHT.
WILL and VIOLA are back on the bed, kissing and making love.

> WILL: My bounty is as boundless as the sea,
> My love as deep:....
> VIOLA AND WILL: (*continuing the speech with him*)...the more I give to thee
> The more I have, for both are infinite....
> WILL: Stay but a little, I will come again.

(Norman and Stoppard 82–83)

As dramatic collaboration is reduced to copulation, rhymed couplets emerge from the rhythms of orgasm, and the seminal work of *Romeo and Juliet* is born. "I would not have thought it," Viola exclaims after making love with Will: "There is something better than a play" (70). What Viola doesn't realize at this point is that lovemaking is the same thing as playmaking; she is Master Will's masterpiece-in-the-making, and the more they play, the more *of* the play, *Romeo and Juliet,* they pro-duce. And there is no chicken-and-egg confusion as to who or what "comes" first here, for the film makes it very clear that Will's authorship of *Romeo and Juliet* is based on his sexual enjoyment of Viola as foreplay to his creation of *the* play.

Brilliantly reversing the Marxist dictum that within capitalism, relations between people take the form of relations between things, *Shakespeare in Love* convinces us that people can have relations to produce things—and as we all know, the play's the thing. Will and Viola's effortless creation of *Romeo and Juliet* thus represents a fantasy of what I will call "good capitalism," which naturally appears to privilege human values over exchange values. The central value of "good capitalism" is, therefore, love. But not just any love will do, for this must be a love, as Viola dreamily puts it, "that overthrows life. Unbiddable, ungovernable, like a riot in the heart, and nothing to be done, come ruin or rapture. Love like there has never been in a play" (Norman and Stoppard 21). The two models of "love" represented in *Shakespeare in Love*, namely, the dreary Wessex-Viola union and the dreamy Will-Viola union correspond to what Lawrence Stone describes in *The Family, Sex and Marriage in England* as the "clear dichotomy between marriage for interest, meaning money, status or power, and marriage for affect, meaning love, friendship or sexual attraction" (86). Like Shakespeare's Romeo and Juliet, whose union implicitly critiques the socioeconomic institution of arranged marriage, Viola and Will are clearly ahead of their time, for their love has at least the potential to transgress the institutional boundaries of class, gender, sexuality, and the theater itself. Consequently, Will and Viola's relationship anticipates the "riot" of the bourgeoisie revolution, following which, sexual and economic success were widely considered to be the fruits of individual initiative and industry, rather than property and pedigree. Functioning under the veil of "good lovin'," then, this is "good capitalism."

What is really at stake in the film's vision of "good capitalism," however, is its privileging of an all-consuming desire that leads to the consummate production of a most profitable play. And plays cannot ultimately be isolated from things—that is, from the vicious cycle of commodity production—just as bodies engaged in the spectacle of lovemaking cannot ultimately be insulated from the specter of (alienated) labor. Accordingly, the more that art imitates life and work mirrors play in *Shakespeare in Love*, the more the film suggests the naturalization of the industrial cycle of commodity production in the healthy, buffed surfaces of Will's laboring body. Similar to the framing of Branagh's Victor in *Mary Shelley's Frankenstein*, Will is shot in ways that progressively expose more and more of his flesh, as the camera develops a fetishistic fascination with his tricep muscle—an icon of "the hard edges, determinate lines of action, and clear boundaries" (Jeffords 27) that distinguish his new and improved hardbody from its impotent precursor. Supporting him as he hovers intimately over Viola, Will's tricep—captured in profile—leads down in a hard, straight line to the hand that writes *Romeo and Juliet,* suggesting the teleology of Shakespearean authorship as a labor that begins and ends in the mystery of love. What gets truly mystified in this film, however, is not love, but labor; for Will's apotheosis as the Hollywood Hardbardy assumes the form of a chiseled physique that churns away in the business of pleasure without sweating or showing any other symptoms of exertion. This is because the only labor at stake in the film's vision of authorial production is, in fact, consumption; and, as suggested in Will and Viola's erotic dialogue, the more Viola gives to Will, the more he has, for both her supply and his demand are "infinite." Thus, consumption begets production which, in turn, leads to more consumption—an ideology decidedly connected to the deterritorializing logic of late capi-talism, which seeks to convince us that by enjoying without limits, we actually become more creative, more productive and, ultimately, more satisfied individuals. But by the same token, *Shakespeare in Love*'s vision of sexual desublimation as the key to authorial creativity exposes the film's complicity with the industrial cycle—that is, with the exploitation of alienated labor that the film takes pains to naturalize through the *chic* of sex. For sex is not associated with production so much as it is associated with *re*production—and reproduction, as Adorno and Horkheimer conclude, serves to confirm only "the immutability of circumstances" (149). Far from producing infinite pleasure, then, *Shakespeare in Love*'s vision of desublimation is not only repressive but, more importantly, oppressive.

The logic of repressive desublimation is, according to Herbert Marcuse, paradoxical, for it invokes a situation whereby the "range of socially permissible and desirable satisfaction is greatly enlarged" but "through this satisfaction, the Pleasure Principle is reduced" (75). This paradox hinges on the way enjoyment masquerades as freedom within the cultural logic of late capitalism. Žižek explains that capital exercises "the ultimate power of 'deterritorialization,'" liberating us from the constraints of "every fixed social identity" (*Tarrying* 216). This freedom from socially prescribed roles is extended even further within late capitalism, wherein "the traditional fixity of ideological positions (patriarchal authority, sexual roles, etc.) becomes an obstacle to the unbridled commodification of everyday life" (216). If we read between the lines, we find that this freedom from ideological fixity is actually a ruse of late capitalism, for the only true freedom it grants is the unbridled freedom *to consume* and, by extension, to enjoy. Knowing that all people do not have equal access to enjoyment, it is also clear that late capitalism deterritorializes desire only to reterritorialize society according to its own economic interests. Indeed, what *Shakespeare in Love* cannot ultimately conceal beneath the spectacle of sex, the drug of romance, and the rocking and rolling of heavenly bodies is the fact that there are consequences to consumption, for as Will becomes the manly poet of true love, Viola must become the feminized object of exchange, a cycle that reveals the extent to which one man's enjoyment is another (wo)man's exploitation.

In *Shakespeare in Love,* the specter of repressive desublimation emerges most emphatically in the *other* transactions that take place behind closed doors in the de Lesseps household: the property dealings over and for Viola's body. The film cleverly convinces us to buy into Will and Viola's comparatively liberated working relationship by situating it in relation to the practice of "bad capitalism" exercised by figures such as Viola's father, Lord Wessex and, to a lesser extent, Fennyman. Indeed, while Will and Viola are engaging in the pleasures of the flesh, Lord Wessex (Colin Firth) and Sir Robert de Lesseps (Nicholas Le Prevost) are trafficking in it—"bargaining for a bride," as Viola's mother (Jill Baker) coldly describes the dowry negotiations (Norman and Stoppard 37). Inquiring about the quality of the goods, Wessex asks: "Is she fertile?" The vulgarity of this question is topped only by Robert de Lesseps's reply: "She will breed. If she do not, send her back." The horrors of this bad capitalism culminate in the following phallocratic exchange between father and future son-in-law:

> WESSEX: Is she obedient?
> SIR ROBERT: As any mule in Christendom. But if you are the man
>   to ride her, there are rubies in the saddlebag.
> WESSEX: I like her. (Norman and Stoppard 42)

With the deal thus made, Wessex, the film's sardonic version of *Romeo and Juliet*'s Paris, lays claim to his purchase by informing Viola that he has purchased her from her father and that he is her new "six-day lord and master." This, of course, is Master Will's cue to rescue Viola from the exploitative clutches of bad capitalism and to introduce her to the ways of good capitalism, writ large in the mystery of playmaking through lovemaking, or, production through consumption.

Quite deftly, then, by generating a decoy for its own heartless business maneuvers in the figures of Wessex and Robert de Lesseps, the film encourages us to enjoy Will and Viola's happy, hardy, liberating breed of capitalism without seeing its soft, slimy underbelly. Representing a caricature of "bad capitalism," Wessex and de Lesseps enable the film to mask economic issues in ethical ones, a diversionary tactic which, as Jameson concludes, "is a very different proposition from that diagnosis...whose prescription would be social revolution" (*Signatures of the Visible* 32). Thus it is not long before we realize that the riotous, revolutionary freedoms that *Shakespeare in Love* grants in the name of desublimated desire are not free at all; rather, the frenzied emotions of liberated love and unmitigated enjoyment merely mimic the capriciousness of the commodity form itself. And not even Will and Viola's love is immune to the shattering effects of the glass ceiling, for Viola will soon be called upon to perform the role of the commodity she always already was. In the meantime, however, by deflecting its own exploitative economic practices onto the exaggerated evil of characters such as Wessex and de Lesseps, the film slyly substitutes the fiction of bad capitalism for the reality that *all* capitalism is bad from the standpoint of those denied the "freedom" to consume and enjoy.

Shakespeare in Love goes even further in its attempt to promote its "feel good" vision of capitalism by reterritorializing the desire of the vicious financier, Fennyman. As the only internal spectator witnessing the piecemeal evolution of *Romeo and Juliet*, Fennyman's increasingly enrapt gaze is implicitly aligned with our gaze. His conversion from bad capitalism to good capitalism, therefore, is designed to mitigate potential skepticism on the part of the off-screen audience. Through the combined magic of love and theater, Fennyman grows convinced that his latest investment is shaping up as something more than a profit-or-perish phenomenon—so much so that he eventually assumes a part in the play himself and even becomes a "born again theatre groupie" (Norman and Stoppard 87). A similar smoke-and-mirror trick of "good capitalism" occurs when, shortly after the Master of the Revels closes The Rose, Burbage offers The Curtain to his chief competitors, Henslowe's players—another gesture designed to conceal the brutal realities of market competition in the gentlemen's agreements associated with the film's fiction of good capitalism. Perhaps inspired by Burbage's example, Fennyman proceeds to cross over the river that divides the base, repressive business practices of the Wessex-de Lesseps merger from the elevated, desublimated bliss of Will and Viola's transactions and, in so doing, he becomes more than a patron of the arts: he becomes the leading patron of the culture industry. But "the deception" central to the culture industry, as Adorno and Horkheimer explain, lies not in the fact that it "supplies amusement but that it ruins the fun by allowing business considerations to involve it in the ideological clichés of a culture in the process of self-liquidation" (143).

The closer we get to the end of *Shakespeare in Love*, at which point all the liberal claims about men and women being free to follow their desires uninhibited by gender, class, or custom come tumbling tragically down, the more the film relies on its clichéd quest to show us "the truth of love." With Fennyman now among those converted by the shared truths of love, theater, and "good capitalism," the only remaining obstacle to the film's complete reterritorialization of the collective libido is Queen Elizabeth herself—the figure who, historically, "just said no" to enjoyment—and whose distinctly non-femmebody in this film (as compared with Shekhar Kapur's *Elizabeth* [1998], for example), appears rigidly and castratingly poised against it. When the subject of love is raised at a royal function, the Queen (Dame Judi Dench) complains that "playwrights teach nothing about love, they make it pretty, they make it comical, or they make it lust. They cannot make it true." Viola, lost in her rapturous love for Will, naturally forgets her place and objects: "Oh, but they can!" The result is a wager that Will, disguised as Viola's country cousin, sets at the amount of fifty pounds, to which the Queen responds: "Fifty pounds! A very worthy sum on a very worthy question. Can a play show us the very truth and nature of love? I bear witness to the wager, and will be the judge of it as occasion arises" (Norman and Stoppard 94–5). Working together like a well-oiled machine, Will and Viola hereby establish the terms of their own "self-liquidation," for this is the bet that will liberate Will from the life of a hired player at the price of selling Viola into domestic slavery.

Perhaps the single most disturbing deception enacted by *Shakespeare in Love* is its representation of a love which, in the beginning, creates riot in the heart, but in the end, prefers ruin to rapture. In the final third of the film, troubling questions are raised about Will and Viola's relationship—questions, for instance, about Will's present wife and Viola's future husband that threaten to destroy the pleasing homeostasis achieved by their lovemaking. When pressed about her betrothal to Wessex, Viola says to Will: "What will you have me do? Marry you instead?"

> WILL: (*brought up short*) To be the wife of a poor player—
> can I wish that for Lady Viola, except in my dreams?
> And yet I would, if I were free to follow my desire in the
> harsh light of day.

VIOLA: *(tartly)* You follow your desire freely enough in
the night. (89)

These mutual snipes, which point to irreconcilable tensions between
Will and Viola, are abandoned in favor of a sexual resolution. Similarly,
when Viola temporarily leaves Will, having learned of his Stratford wife,
Will claims in his defense: "My love is no lie. I have a wife, yes, and I
cannot marry the daughter of Sir Robert de Lesseps. It needed no wife
come from Stratford to tell you that. And yet you let me come to your
bed" (112). And he will "come again," as Will once promised Viola, for
here, too, conflict is displaced and replaced with sexual pleasure. "Pleasure," as Adorno and Horkheimer explain, "always means not to think
about anything, to forget suffering even where it is sham. Basically it is
helplessness. It is flight; not, as is asserted, flight from a wretched reality,
but from the last remaining thought of resistance" (144). Indeed, toward
the end of the film, we must wonder what has happened to Will and
Viola's revolutionary desire to wreak havoc with social conventions and
to love each other without limits. Will's uninspired response to the devastating force of circumstances that divides him from Viola is to convert
his play to tragedy, while Viola ultimately consents to marry Wessex,
albeit with a wry twist: "I see you are open for business," she says to
him as she witnesses the dowry changing hands, "so let's to church"
(Norman and Stoppard 128). Will and Viola's increasing complicity with
the oppressive social order that surrounds them suggests the insidious
influence of capital which, having deterritorialized their desire and
freed them from "all fixed social identities" in order to facilitate their enjoyment of each other, now reterritorializes their desire in its own image:
Viola generates a socially conservative merger of money and land, while
Will wins the £50 wager and with it, entry into the lucrative, upwardly
mobile "company" of the Lord Chamberlain's Men.

In love enjoyment was coupled with a deification of man, who vouchsafed it;
it was the human emotion proper. Finally it was revoked as a sexually conditioned value judgment. In the pietistic adoration of the lover, as in the bound-
less admiration he commanded from his sweetheart, the actual slavery of
woman was glorified anew.

—Theodor W. Adorno and Max Horkheimer,
Dialectic of Enlightenment

What, then, is the truth of love in *Shakespeare in Love?* The truth of love in *Shakespeare in Love* is more accurately described as the irony of romance. "It is perhaps the most extravagant irony in the history of women," observes Jan Cohn, "that romantic love, with its source in the celebration of woman in chivalric romance, should have become a means for exacerbating the powerlessness of women" (129). At the conclusion of *Shakespeare in Love,* Will becomes the poet of true, or rather, "romantic" love, and Viola, now powerless in petticoats, is sold into a life of domestic slavery on a Virginia tobacco plantation. The film's choice of the feminized landscape of Virginia furnishes subtle clues into the stark reality of Viola's pending violation as Wessex's wife, for we know that both flesh and land are fertile sites destined to be pillaged for profit. Even before Viola is shipped off to Virginia, the film suggests that the empowerment she once shared with Will was, in fact, illusory; for in her emergency appearance in the debut of *Romeo and Juliet,* Viola no longer plays the young wayfarer, Romeo, but rather the Capulet commodity Juliet—a reminder that she "wears the pants" only in fiction—not in the real performance where money is on the line and the "truth of love" is at stake. And, as Adorno and Horkheimer observe, "Language based entirely on truth simply arouses impatience to get on with the business deal it is probably advancing" (147). There is no doubt about the business transaction taking place at the end of *Shakespeare in Love,* wherein the trafficking in female flesh proceeds by royal decree. Were "the very truth and nature of love" really at stake here, the Queen would keep the business deal for Viola from advancing. Instead she demands that Wessex pay Will for losing the wager, though it is obvious that it is Viola who is being purchased at this price, confirming the fact that in this culture of consumption, "exchange value, not truth value counts" (Marcuse 57).

It seems only appropriate that the Master of the Revels should return for an encore performance at this time, emerging somewhat curiously as the Old Master of prohibition, inveighing against public lewdness. But it is too late for the now defunct order of "self-restraint" and "just measure" to be reestablished. Signaling how completely this culture has been retrained to enjoy, the Queen herself overrules the Master of the Revels in favor of the new Master, Master Will, whose play of *Romeo and Juliet*—if the truth be told—comments on the defeat of true love and "the triumph of invested capital, whose title as *absolute master* is the meaningful content of every film, whatever plot the production team may have selected" (Adorno and Horkheimer 147, emphasis added). The final apotheosis of the figure of the Master in *Shakespeare in Love* thus represents a compromise between the Old Master of precapitalism and the New Master of enjoyment, combining archaic prohibitions with reckless hedonism. For above all, Master Will encourages us to *cultivate the will:* to work not for hire, but for a higher purpose, that is, to "play." The merger that occurs at the end of the film to sanctify this new understanding of work and play is the implied merger of Will and Fennyman, playwright and financier. Becoming joint patrons of the culture industry, Will and Fennyman will work together to convert what Adorno and Horkheimer call the liberating "festival" of enjoyment into the repressive "farce" of socially controlled satisfaction: "The[se] masters introduc[e] the notion of enjoyment as something rational, a tribute paid to a not yet wholly contaminated nature; at the same time they try to decontaminate it for their own use, to retain it in their higher form of culture.... until, ultimately, it is entirely extinguished in fixed entertainments" (105–6).

These fixed entertainments serve a crucial purpose in *Shakespeare in Love*, by reminding us to *master our wills* when the more painful affects and effects of love threaten to spoil the fun at the film's conclusion. Indeed, to mitigate the pain we might feel for Viola, *Shakespeare in Love* convinces its off-screen audience that her tragic fate also has a higher purpose: she will be recycled. Thus, as Viola undertakes her future "with tears and a journey" (150), we are encouraged to enjoy the journey—assured, like the wildly applauding on-screen audience—that Will will "write her well" for *Twelfth Night*. And as the film closes with Will's handwriting superimposed on an image of Viola trekking across a sandy coastline, *Shakespeare in Love* brilliantly relocates Shakespeare the Author from early modern England to our own postmodern consumer society, recycling the Bard not as the Marlboro Man of Southern Virginia but as the daydream believer of Southern California: Hollywood.

For all the academics who have "just said no" to the popular pleasure promised by the cinematic celebration of the Author in *Shakespeare in Love*, the film makes good on its attempt to offer something for everyone by staging the death of the Author. In the closing moments of *Romeo and Juliet*'s debut, Will, the author, counterfeits Romeo's death so convincingly that Viola's Nurse (Imelda Staunton) believes that Will himself is dead, a realization that causes her to cry out in agony from the audience. Momentarily rupturing the diegesis of the play within the film, the Nurse's exclamation—"Dead!"—serves as a reminder to the off-screen audience that this author will, in fact, not "come again." But the film's more obvious privileging of the name "Will," which functions as a synonym for desire as well as for the last will and testament that survives the death of the physical body, frustrates the potential for a proper poststructuralist burial of the Author, implying that this corpus will, happily, *never* rest in peace. Indeed, the battle over the screenplay of *Shakespeare in Love* alone suggests the ways in which that strange surplus called "Shakespeare" continues to come back—from the future or, for that matter, from the dead—to challenge our understanding of what constitutes an author. For example, although Marc Norman and Tom Stoppard won the Oscar for "best original screenplay," these authors were accused of borrowing heavily from another collaboratively composed book, *No Bed for Bacon*, by Caryl Brahms and S. J. Simons. And it is perhaps even more ironic that a screenplay about the singular genius of Shakespeare not only portrays this "author" randomly cannibalizing the ideas of others but also revolves around Shakespeare's writing of *Romeo and Juliet*, a play which, as we have seen, undermines the very prospect of originality as a product of legendary transmission. For better or for worse, then, the Shakespearean corpus is the site of what can only be described as an enduring *surplus* value—and, as such, suggests the ultimate commodity fetish.

Significantly, Marx thought it apt to liken commodity fetishism to the experience of "mystery," "magic," and "necromancy," the very terms used to describe authorship in *Shakespeare in Love*. For many years, these terms also described the equally romantic fetishization of the Author in academic culture. But even though we can now clear ourselves, at least in *theory*, of the charge of romancing the dead, we might consider the possibility that the status of the Author's body in academic discourse has always been less about theoretical revelations than it is about the revolutions of our own desires. For it is clear that while academic and popular culture strongly disagree about Shakespeare's status as an author, both share an undeniable fascination, whether expressed through violence or veneration, with the authorial body. By way of concluding, then, I would argue that one reason we take so much pleasure in dismembering the Author—and Shakespeare in particular—is that the Author is guilty of what Žižek calls the "theft of enjoyment." According to Žižek, enjoyment is precisely what is ascribed to the Other because we cannot come to terms with it in ourselves. The

theft of enjoyment, therefore, is what is "imputed to the Other, and...
conversely, the hatred of the Other's enjoyment is always the hatred of
one's own enjoyment" (*Tarrying* 206). Might we substitute "Author"
for "Other" here? After all, isn't the figure of the Author charged with
robbing all the other agents involved in literary production—silent col-
laborators, invisible prompters, compositors, printers, audiences, and,
chiefly, critics—of their fair share of the pleasure pie? What is so instructive about recent films that romance Shakespeare is that they expose what always already exists in this corpus: the specter of enjoyment
and the bodies that perpetuate it—whether they belong to authors, actors or, for that matter, academics. Unwittingly, then, the ultimate act of
mystification undertaken by *Shakespeare in Love* lies in its preservation
of the "mystery" housed in the *critical* enterprise, for by boldly imput-
ing enjoyment to a figure for whom we cannot even locate a body—let
alone a single, authoritative textual corpus—it provides the perfect
alibi for the desire we refuse to locate in ourselves: the enjoyment of our
own authority.

Postmortem

"By William Shakespeare"

Throughout this inquiry into early modern and postmodern conditions of authorial (im)possibility, I have consistently emended the term author to auteur. But what is to be gained by this emendation for studies of Shakespeare's dramatic legacy? We might begin to answer this question by reexamining the phrasing of this legacy in the 1623 Folio. In their appeal to "the great Variety of Readers," John Heminge and Henry Condell offered neither Shakespeare's "body" nor "Shakespeare's" book but rather his "remaines" (94), a word befitting their desire "to shew their gratitude both to the living, and the dead" (94).[1] Like the ruins of Sycamore Grove, "remains" imply a peculiar inheritance, one that is both permanent and unfinished. In addressing the postmodern consumer, then, Heminge and Condell might have packaged Shakespeare's remains with the added label: "assembly required." Indeed, this injunction to assemble is precisely what it means "to inherit," for, as Derrida reminds us, inheritance is not about the passive reception of a gift; rather, it is about the active construction of a legacy:

> An inheritance is never gathered together, it is never at one with itself. . . . *one must* filter, sift, criticize, one must sort out several possibles that inhabit the same injunction. . . . if the readability of a legacy were given, transparent, univocal, if it did not call forward and at the same time defy interpretation, we would never have anything to inherit from it. (16)

This is why the death of the Author and more recent critical efforts to render the authorial aura "dead again" acquire a peculiar redundancy in their encounters with Shakespeare, whose remains initiated the task

---

1. The entire quotation appears as follows: "*In that name therefore, we most humbly consecrate to your H.H. these remaines of your servant Shakespeare; that what delight is in them, maybe ever your L.L. the reputation his, & the faults ours, if any be committed, by a payre so carefull to shew their gratitude both to the living, and the dead, as is*" (*The Riverside Shakespeare* 94).

of deconstruction long ago, producing an inheritance that requires assembly. How these remains will be handled in the future remains to be seen—and screened.

Indeed, given the historic reciprocity that has existed between cinema and Shakespeare since the dawn of the motion picture industry, it seems likely that the destinies of both are intertwined. Whereas cinema once relied on Shakespeare for cultural legitimation, Shakespeare now needs cinema for cultural longevity in a world that increasingly privileges images over words as well as visual literacy over more traditional reading practices. How this provocative collaboration will end is, as *Shakespeare in Love* reminds us, "a mystery." Offering one prognosis, Timothy Corrigan projects into the landscape of the future the image of a "cinema without walls"—a place wherein social, economic, and aesthetic barriers come crumbling down, supporting, in their absence, "a cross-cultural dreaming in a variety of directions" (5). Though Corrigan does not explicitly invoke Shakespeare as an agent of "cross-cultural dreaming," Shakespearean drama, as we have seen, is both a harbinger of and a home to these cultural montage effects. Balancing this optimistic prediction is the more nihilistic image of Sycamore Grove from *William Shakespeare's Romeo + Juliet*, which presents us with a cinema with walls but no center. This tableau of a frame struggling to support *what is not there* is a provocative metaphor for the ongoing collision of Shakespeare, authorship, and cinema with which this project has been concerned. For if we read the writing on these proto-and post-cinematic walls, we might find the "insignia trait" of Shakespeare. After all, isn't the practice of Shakespearean authorship a site of our projections—the cultural, psychological, critical, and aesthetic rituals through which we traverse this specter of ruins wrapped around a void? And aren't these tenacious remains, like the ruins of Sycamore Grove, at once degenerate and regenerate? Nevertheless, the answer to the question of how to keep *this* auteur from becoming "dead again" will always require assembly, for it will depend on the possible legacies that Shakespeare's dramatic remains configure in a given cultural moment.

I have explored the variety of auspices that these remains take on, all of them inscribing a story of authorship within a culture that demands its erasure. In *Romeo and Juliet* and *Hamlet*, the remainder crystallizes in the authorial legacy that is inscribed on the bodies of the protagonists themselves. In Branagh's corpus, the remainder surfaces in the stain of an alienated homeland that emerges in the figure of the "enemy within," a reminder of the Irish "source" that haunts Branagh's filmic fantasies of Englishness. In *William Shakespeare's Romeo + Juliet*, Baz Luhrmann goes right to the source of the legend that condemns aspiring auteurs to repeat the dead styles and language of the past only to create an apocalyptic vision of the death of cinema itself in Sycamore Grove. Signaling a departure from these more high-minded and heavy-handed approaches to Shakespeare's authorial legacy, *A Midsummer Night's Dream* and John Madden's *Shakespeare in Love* convert the negative "patterns of energy cathexis" that traverse the Shakespearean corpus into comic remainders that remind us of the special *affects* that keep this corpus alive and kicking—come ruin or rapture. But like the more serious cultural tensions that *Dream* anticipates in its production of montage effects, *Shakespeare in Love* leaves us with the disturbing realization that when sexual labor is mystified as "love" there is dangerously little to laugh about. Ultimately, then, what both Shakespeare's plays and recent film adaptations of them foreground is the contestatory nature of inheritance, leaving us with a struggle over remains, as we work to "filter, sift, criticize" and, ultimately, to control the ghosts that we are in a position both to exorcise and inherit.

It seems oddly fitting, then, that Hollywood is currently under siege by a revenge plot that we might call "the return of the Author." What is at stake in this battle is "possessory credit," as screenwriters challenge the directorial monopoly on the phrase "a film by," hoping to possess—in fact—the fictions they are consigned merely to haunt as unacknowledged authors. Consequently, the industry is taking the looming threat of a writers' strike scheduled to occur any time after May 1, 2001, very seriously, preparing dozens of hastily produced films in order to stave off anticipated losses during the summer, the high season for film consumption. Observes one industry employee: "I was at Warner Brothers yesterday and the lot's already dead."[2] Like Romeo, the auteur, too, may be "already dead" if the writers succeed in their quest to obtain "possessory credit." For according to theorists such as Timothy Corrigan and Dudley Andrew, the paratextual agency embodied in the phrase "a film by" is perhaps the only hope of keeping the auteur from becoming "dead again" in a culture that is more concerned with the commerce of the paratext than the content of the film-text. Yet surely this is to underestimate the power of that which is "in the film-text

2. This quotation is from Jean Hodges, a prop food creator, cited in an Associated Press article by Gary Gentile (http://news.excite.ca/printstory/news/ap/010427/15/hollywood-strike-impact).

more than the film-text," for the third term that emerges from this fortuitous collision between writers and directors is, in fact, auteur, a term
which, like "montage," has no precise English corollary. Conceptually
encompassing both writing and direction to embody " 'filmic writing'
in its social relations" (Browne 1), the term "auteur" signals a process of
contestation that both precedes and exceeds the film-text, all the while
leaving room, somewhere between the lines—and walls—for the projection of meaning. Thus, the strike that is threatening to shut down the
film industry is very much a "matter of vocabulary" or, more appropriately, a *vocabulary that matters*. And isn't this, after all, what "the desire
called cinema" is all about—the para-doxical yearning for presence
which, ultimately, can only be realized through absence? Though no
adaptation of Shakespeare has a credit sequence reading "screenplay
by William Shakespeare," this is, as I have tried to demonstrate, what
Shakespeare's plays were—screens—with holes in the middle that
prompt us to go where "authors" fear to tread, forcing us to engage
with the absence that leaves in its wake the makings of the auteur.

In search of what I will describe, by way of conclusion, as "the desire
called Shakespeare," Washington Irving cathected his own "film" into
the vacancy born of the Bard's missing remains, recalling, as he "trod
the sounding pavement," that "there was something intense and
thrilling in the idea, that, in very truth, the remains of Shakespeare were
mouldering beneath my feet" (229). The desire called Shakespeare is indeed a thrill-ride that takes shape as a form of "cross-cultural dreaming" and a transhistorical nightmare, connecting us to the aspirations
and the anxieties that prevail through and in spite of the practice of authorship in early modern and postmodern culture. Whether expressed
in terms exultant or execrable, the desire called Shakespeare—from the
Bazmark inspired by "William Shakespeare" to the anonymous "marks
on the page" urging us to forgo the search for Shakespeare—is, quite
simply, what *authorizes* our desires. But is the thrill gone? And if so,
will it come back? As I have argued throughout this analysis, the desire called Shakespeare comes back from the future—in effect, from
cinema—whose own monstrous ontology functions "to show" and "to
warn" us about the futility of the clash between critical voice-overs that
seek "revenge" against what they cannot see and cinematic images that
attempt to "remember" what was never there.[3] As the ongoing threat in

---

3. I am referring here to the Latin etymology of the word "monster," from *monere* (to
warn) and *monstrare* (to show).

Hollywood of a screenwriters' strike suggests, authorship is poised on the precarious brink "in-between-two-deaths"—between, that is, the manifest death of the Author in theory and the more devastating, symbolic death of authorial attribution in practice.[4] It is time, then, to initiate a process of *theoretical* adaptation that maintains poststructuralism's vital, counter-hegemonic approach to cultural production, while reinvesting authorship as a site both of the contestation over, and the construction of, legacies: historical, aesthetic, political and, yes, personal. There can be no doubt that the Author is dead, but why not retort: "long live the auteur"? To the imaginary label embossed on Shakespeare's remains, "some assembly required," I would thus add: "handle with care." For if what we *really* want is a Shakespeare without walls—a pluralistic space for the performance of an enabling relationship to authority—then we should take care to distinguish this desire from a world without Shakespeare.

Perhaps, as Orson Welles suggests, the trick is not to speculate about what brave new worlds lie behind the Bard's words but rather to enjoy the great Variety of *Shakespeares* created in their wake. "Shakespeare said everything," Welles once exclaimed. "Brain to belly; every mood and minute of a man's season. His language is starlight and fireflies and the sun and moon. He wrote it with tears and blood and beer, and his words march like heart-beats" (qtd. in Hill and Welles 22). This inextinguishable potency—and prospect—of life that is "in Shakespeare more than Shakespeare" has much to tell us about the history, as well as the future, of authorship in early modern and postmodern culture, if we are willing to follow this "perturb'd spirit" where it leads. In pursuing this challenging and, at times, monstrous collaboration between Romanticism and poststructuralism, theater and cinema, early modern and postmodern, we certainly forgo the opportunity to send this corpus fit and seasoned for its passage to Heaven, but we also resist towing the hard line of the Text that condemns Shakespeare to lead Authors into Hell. I propose a third possibility that meets somewhere in the middle, wherein—among the collisions of forward and backward projections that converge in the desire called "Shakespeare"—we may enjoy the journey.

4. The concept of being "in-between-two-deaths" (Lacan's *l'entre-deux-morts*) is the liminal position designated between the actual death of the physical body and the symbolic death of the deceased's living memory—the latter involving total eradication from the collective memory, symbolic community, or narrative history. See Žižek's *Enjoy Your Symptom!* (151–52).

Bibliography

Adorno, Theodor W., and Max Horkheimer. *Dialectic of Enlightenment*. 1944. Translated by John Cuming. New York: Continuum, 1999.

Agnew, Jean-Christoph. *Worlds Apart: The Market and the Theater in Anglo-American Thought, 1550–1750*. Cambridge: Cambridge University Press, 1986.

Anderegg, Michael. *Orson Welles, Shakespeare, and Popular Culture*. New York: Columbia University Press, 1999.

Andrew, Dudley. "The Unauthorized Auteur Today." In *Film Theory Goes to the Movies*, edited by Jim Collins, Hilary Radner, and Ava Preacher Collins, 77–85. New York: Routledge, 1993.

Armes, Roy. *Action and Image: Dramatic Structure in Cinema*. Manchester: Manchester University Press, 1994.

Arnold, Gary. "Branagh Breathes New Life into Classics." *Insight on the News*, 15 Jan. 1996, 37–38.

———. "To Film or Not to Film, That's the Quest." *Insight on the News*, 17 Feb. 1997, 40–41.

Aston, Elaine, and George Savona. *Theatre as Sign-System: A Semiotics of Text and Performance*. London: Routledge, 1991.

Ayers, P. K. "Reading, Writing, and *Hamlet*." *Shakespeare Quarterly* 44, no. 4 (1993): 423–39.

Barthes, Roland. "The Death of the Author." In *The Rustle of Language*, translated by Richard Howard, 49–55. Berkeley: University of California Press, 1989.

———. "Diderot, Brecht, Eisenstein." In *The Responsibility of Forms: Critical Essays on Music, Art, and Representation*, translated by Richard Howard, 89–97. Berkeley: University of California Press, 1985.

———. *The Pleasure of the Text*. Translated by Richard Miller. New York: Noonday Books, 1975.

———*S/Z*. Translated by Richard Miller. New York: Hill and Wang, 1974.

———. "The Third Meaning." In *The Responsibility of Forms: Critical Essays on Music, Art, and Representation*, translated by Richard Howard, 41–62. Berkeley: University of California Press, 1985.

Batman. Directed by Tim Burton. Warner Brothers, 1989.

Baudry, Jean-Louis. "Ideological Effects of the Basic Cinematographic Apparatus." In *Film Theory and Criticism*, 4th ed., edited by Gerald Mast, Marshall Cohen, and Leo Braudy, 302–12. Oxford: Oxford University Press, 1992.

Bazin, Andre, Jacques Doniol-Valcroze, Pierre Kast, Roger Leenhardt, Jacques Rivette, and Eric Rohmer. "Six Characters in Search of Auteurs: A Discussion about the French Cinema." In *Cahiers du Cinema: The 1950s*, edited by Jim Hillier, 31–46. Cambridge: Harvard University Press, 1985.

Bednarz, James P. "Marston's Subversion of Shakespeare and Jonson: Histriomastix and the War of the Theaters." *Medieval and Renaissance Drama in England: An Annual Gathering of Research, Criticism and Reviews* 6 (1993): 103–28.

Belsey, Catherine. *The Subject of Tragedy: Identity and Difference in Renaissance Drama*. New York: Routledge, 1985.

Benjamin, Walter. "The Work of Art in the Age of Mechanical Reproduction." In *Film Theory and Criticism*, 4th ed., edited by Gerald Mast, Marshall Cohen, and Leo Braudy, 665–81. Oxford: Oxford University Press, 1992.

Benson, Pamela Joseph. *The Invention of the Renaissance Woman: The Challenge of Female Independence in the Literature and Thought of Italy and England*. University Park, Penn.: Pennsylvania State University Press, 1992.

Bentley, G. E. *The Profession of Dramatist in Shakespeare's Time, 1590–1642*. Princeton: Princeton University Press, 1971.

Bhabha, Homi K. "Of Mimicry and Man: The Ambivalence of Colonial Discourse." In *The Location of Culture*, 85–92. New York: Routledge, 1994.

Blau, Herbert. "Rhetorics of the Body: Do You Smell a Fault?" In *Cultural Artifacts and the Production of Meaning: The Page, the Image, and the Body*, edited by Margaret J. M. Ezell and Katherine O'Brien O'Heeffe, 223–39. Ann Arbor: University of Michigan Press, 1997.

Blayney, Peter. "The Publication of Playbooks." In *a New History of Early English Drama*, edited by John D. Cox and David Scott Kastan, 383–422. New York: Columbia University Press, 1997.

Brahms, Carol, and S. J. Simon. *No Bed for Bacon*. 1941. Pleasantville, New York: Akadine Press, 2001.

Branagh, Kenneth. *Beginning*. New York: St. Martin's Press, 1989.

——. "Frankenstein Reimagined." In *Mary Shelley's Frankenstein: The Classic Tale of Terror Reborn on Film*, 19–29. New York: Newmarket Press, 1994.

——. "The Guardian Interview at the National Film Theatre." Interview by Michael Billington. *The Kenneth Branagh Retrospective*, 23 May 1999.http://branaghcompendium.com/articntfguard99.htm.

——. *Henry V, By William Shakespeare: A Screen Adaptation by Kenneth Branagh*. London: Chatto and Windus, 1989.

——. Introduction to *Hamlet, By William Shakespeare: Screenplay, Introduction, and Film Diary*, xi–xv. New York: W. W. Norton, 1996.

——. *Mary Shelley's Frankenstein: The Classic Tale of Horror Reborn on Film*. New York: Newmarket Press, 1994.

———. *Much Ado About Nothing by William Shakespeare: Screenplay, Introduction, and Notes on the Making of the Movie by Kenneth Branagh*. New York: W. W. Norton, 1993.

———"Salerno Transcript." Interview with Kenneth Branagh, 22 April 1999. Linea d'Ombra Film Festival. http://www.branaghcompendium.com/artic-sal99.htm.

Braudy, Leo. "Afterword: Rethinking Remakes." In *Play it Again, Sam. Retakes on Remakes,* edited by Andrew Horton and Stuart Y. McDougal, 327–34. Berkeley: University of California Press, 1998.

Breight, Curtis. "Branagh and the Prince, or a 'royal fellowship of death.'" *Critical Quarterly* 33, no. 4 (1991): 95–111.

Brinker-Gabler, Gisela, and Sidonie Smith, eds. "Introduction: Gender, Nation, and Immigration in the New Europe." In *Writing New Identities: Gender, Nation, and Immigration in Contemporary Europe,* 1–27. Minnesota: University of Minnesota Press, 1997.

Bristol, Michael. *Big-time Shakespeare.* London: Routledge, 1996.

Bronfen, Elizabeth. *The Knotted Subject: Hysteria and Its Discontents.* Princeton: Princeton University Press, 1998.

Brooke, Arthur. *The Tragicall Historye of Romeus and Iuliet.* 1562. *Brooke's 'Romeus and Juliet' Being the Original of Shakespeare's 'Romeo and Juliet.'* Edited by J. J. Munro. London: Chatto and Windus, 1908.

Brooks, Peter. *Reading for the Plot: Design and Intention in Narrative.* Cambridge: Harvard University Press, 1984.

Browne, Nick, ed. "Introduction: The Politics of Representation: Cahiers du Cinema 1969–1972." In *Cahiers du Cinema: 1969–1972: The Politics of Representation,* 1–20. Cambridge: Harvard University Press, 1990.

Bryson, Lucy, and Clem McCartney. "Symbols in Everyday Community Life." In *Clashing Symbols: a Report on the Use of Flags, Anthems, and Other National Symbols in Northern Ireland,* 125–43. Belfast: Queen's University of Belfast, 1994.

Bullough, Geoffrey. *Narrative and Dramatic Sources of Shakespeare.* 8 Vols. New York: Columbia University Press, 1957.

Burch, Noel. *Theory of Film Practice.* Princeton: Princeton University Press, 1981.

Burnett, Mark Thornton. "The 'Very Cunning of the Scene': Kenneth Branagh's *Hamlet.*" *Literature-Film Quarterly* 25, no. 2 (1997): 78–82.

Burt, Richard. *Unspeakable ShaXXXspeares: Queer Theory and American Kiddie Culture.* New York: St. Martin's Press, 1998.

Butler, Judith. *Bodies that Matter: On the Discursive Limits of "Sex."* New York: Routledge, 1993.

Calderwood, James. *Shakespearean Metadrama: The Argument of the Play in Titus Andronicus, Love's Labour's Lost, Romeo and Juliet, A Midsummer Night's Dream, and Richard II.* Minneapolis: University of Minnesota Press, 1971.

Carruthers, Mary. *The Book of Memory: A Study of Memory in Medieval Culture.* Cambridge: Cambridge University Press, 1990.

Caso, Adolph, ed. *Romeo and Juliet: Original Text of Masuccio, Da Porto, Bandello, Shakespeare.* Boston: Dante University of America Press, 1992.

Certeau, Michel de. *The Practice of Everyday Life.* Translated by Steven Rendall. Berkeley: University of California Press, 1984.

Charnes, Linda. "Near misses of the non-transcendent kind: reply to Richard Levin." *Textual Practice* 7, no. 1 (1993): 56–59.

——. *Notorious Identity: Materializing the Subject in Shakespeare.* Cambridge: Harvard University Press, 1993.

——. "What's Love Got to Do with It? Reading the Liberal Humanist Romance in Shakespeare's *Antony and Cleopatra.*" *Textual Practice* 6, no. 1 (1992): 1–16.

Chartier, Roger. *The Order of Books.* Translated by Lydia G. Cochrane. Stanford: Stanford University Press, 1994.

Chimes at Midnight. Directed by Orson Welles. Peppercorn Wormser (English language version), 1967.

City of Angels. Directed by Brad Silberling. Warner Brothers, 1998.

Cohen, Walter. *Drama of a Nation: Public Theater in Renaissance England and Spain.* Ithaca: Cornell University Press, 1985.

Cohn, Jan. *Romance and the Erotics of Property: Mass-Market Fiction for Women.* Durham: Duke University Press, 1988.

Colie, Rosalie L. *Shakespeare's Living Art.* Princeton: Princeton University Press, 1974.

Comolli, Jean-Louis, and Jean Narboni. "Cinema/Ideology/Criticism." In *Cahiers du Cinema 1969–1972: The Politics of Representation,* edited by Nick Browne, 58–67. Cambridge: Harvard University Press, 1990.

Copjec, Joan, ed. "The Phenomenal Nonphenomenal: Private Space in *Film Noir.*" In *Shades of Noir,* 167–97. London: Verso, 1993.

Corrigan, Timothy. *A Cinema Without Walls: Movies and Culture After Vietnam.* New Brunswick: Rutgers University Press, 1991.

The Crow. Directed by Alex Proyas. Dimension Films/Edward R. Pressman Film Corp., 1994.

The Crow II: City of Angels. Directed by Tim Pope. Dimensions Films/Jeff Most Productions, 1996.

Crowl, Samuel. "Hamlet 'Most Royal': An Interview with Kenneth Branagh." *Shakespeare Bulletin* 12, no. 4 (1994): 5–8.

Daney, Serge, and Jean-Pierre Oudart. "The Name of the Author (on the 'place' of *Death in Venice*)." In *Cahiers du Cinema 1969–1972: The Politics of Representation,* edited by Nick Browne, 306–24. Cambridge: Harvard University Press, 1990.

Dead Again. Directed by Kenneth Branagh. Paramount Pictures, 1992.

Deane, Seamus. Introduction to *Nationalism, Colonialism, and Literature,* by Terry Eagleton, Fredric Jameson, and Edward W. Said, 3–19. Minneapolis: University of Minnesota Press, 1990.

Deibert, Ronald J. *Parchment, Printing, and Hypermedia: Communication in World Order Transformation.* New York: Columbia University Press, 1997.

De Grazia, Margreta. "Sanctioning Voice: Quotation Marks, the Abolition of Torture, and the Fifth Amendment." In *The Construction of Authorship: Textual Appropriation in Law and Literature,* edited by Peter Jaszi and Martha Woodmansee, 281–302. Durham: Duke University Press, 1994.

——. "Shakespeare in Quotation Marks." In *The Appropriation of Shakespeare: Post-Renaissance Reconstructions of the Works and the Myth,* edited by Jean Marsden, 57–71. New York: St. Martin's Press, 1991.

——. *Shakespeare Verbatim: The Reproduction of Authenticity and the 1790 Apparatus.* Oxford: Oxford University Press, 1991.

De Grazia, Margreta, and Peter Stallybrass. "The Materiality of the Shakespearean Text." *Shakespeare Quarterly* 44, no. 3 (1993): 255–83.

Dekker, Thomas. *Satiromastix.* 1601. Edited by Josiah H. Penniman. Boston: D.C. Heath, 1913.

De Laurot, Yves. "From Logos to Lens." In *Movies and Methods,* edited by Bill Nichols. Vol. 1. Berkeley: University of California Press, 1976.

Derrida, Jacques. *Specters of Marx: The State of the Debt, the Work of Mourning, and the New International.* Translated by Peggy Kamuf. New York: Routledge, 1994.

Dillon, Janette. "Is There a Performance in this Text?" *Shakespeare Quarterly* 45, no 1 (1994): 74–86.

Dobson, Michael. *The Making of the National Poet: Shakespeare, Adaptation, and Authorship, 1660–1769.* New York: Oxford University Press, 1992.

Dollimore, Jonathan, and Alan Sinfield. "History and Ideology: The Instance of *Henry V.*" In *Alternative Shakespeares,* edited by John Drakakis, 206–27. London: Routledge, 1985.

——, eds. *Political Shakespeare: Essays in Cultural Materialism.* Ithaca: Cornell University Press, 1985. Reprint, 1994.

Donaldson, Peter S. "Baz Luhrmann's *Romeo + Juliet:* Media, Spectacle, Performance." Paper Presented at the Shakespeare Association of America. San Francisco, April 1–3, 1999.

——. "Taking on Shakespeare: Kenneth Branagh's *Henry V.*" *Shakespeare Quarterly* 42, no. 1 (1991): 60–71.

Donawerth, Jane. *Shakespeare and the Sixteenth-Century Study of Language.* Urbana: University of Illinois Press, 1984.

Drakakis, John, ed. *Alternative Shakespeares.* London: Routledge, 1985.

During, Simon. "Postmodernism or Post-colonialism Today." In *Postmodernism: A Reader,* edited by Thomas Docherty, 448–62. New York: Columbia University Press, 1993.

Dutton, Richard. "The Birth of the Author." In *Texts and Cultural Change in Early Modern England,* edited by Cedric C. Brown and Arthur F. Marotti, 153–78. London: Macmillan, 1997.

Eagleton, Terry. "Nationalism: Irony and Commitment." In *Nationalism, Colonialism, and Literature,* by Terry Eagleton, Fredric Jameson, and Edward W. Said, 23–39. Minneapolis: University of Minnesota Press, 1990.

Eisenstein, Sergei. *Film Form.* New York: Harcourt Brace, 1949.

Elizabeth. Directed by Shekhar Kapur. Polygram/Channel Four/Working Title Films, 1998.

Farrell, Kirby. *Shakespeare's Creation: The Language of Magic and Play.* Amherst: University of Massachusetts Press, 1975.

Feeney, F. X. "Vaulting Ambition." *American Film* 16, no. 9 (1991): 22–29.

Ferguson, Margaret. "*Hamlet:* Letters and Spirits." In *Shakespeare and the Question of Theory,* edited by Geoffrey Hartman and Patricia Parker, 292–309. New York: Routledge, 1985.

Footlight Parade. Directed by Lloyd Bacon. Warner Brothers, 1933.

Foucault, Michel. "What Is an Author?" In *Language, Counter-Memory, Practice: Selected Essays and Interviews by Michel Foucault,* edited by Donald F. Bouchard, 113–38. Ithaca: Cornell University Press, 1977.

Four Weddings and a Funeral. Directed by Mike Newell. Produced by Duncan Kenworthy, 1994.

Freud, Sigmund. "Family Romances." In *The Standard Edition of the Complete Psychological Works of Sigmund Freud,* translated and edited by James Strachey. Vol. 9. London: Hogarth Press, 1959.

———. *The Interpretation of Dreams.* Edited by James Strachey. New York: Avon Books, 1965.

———. "The Uncanny." 1919. *Studies in Parapsychology.* New York: Collier Books, 1963. 19–60.

Galloway, Andrew. "Authority." In *A Companion to Chaucer,* edited by Peter Brown, 23–39. Oxford: Blackwell Press, 2000.

Garber, Marjorie. *Shakespeare's Ghost Writers: Literature as Uncanny Causality.* New York: Routledge, 1987.

Gentile, Gary. "Hollywood Labor Strife Already Felt." http://news.excite.ca/printstory/news/ap/010427/15/hollywood-strike-impact.

Gielgud, Sir John. *Early Stages.* London: Macmillan, 1939.

Gilroy, Paul. *"There Ain't No Black in the Union Jack": The Cultural Politics of Race and Nation.* Chicago: University of Chicago Press, 1991.

Goffen, Rana. "Renaissance Dreams." *Renaissance Quarterly* 40, no. 4 (1987): 682–706.

Goldberg, Jonathan. "Hamlet's Hand." *Shakespeare Quarterly* 39, no. 3 (1988): 307–27.

———. *Writing Matter: From the Hands of the English Renaissance.* Stanford: Stanford University Press, 1990.

The Goo Goo Dolls. "Iris." *Dizzy Up the Girl.* Warner Brothers, 1998.

Gothic. Directed by Ken Russell. Pioneer Entertainment, 1987.

Gramsci, Antonio. *Selections from Cultural Writings* Edited by David Forgacs and Geoffrey Nowell-Smith. Cambridge: Harvard University Press, 1991.

Greenblatt, Stephen. "The Mousetrap." Paper presented at the Dartmouth School of Criticism and Theory, June 1996.

——. *Renaissance Self-Fashioning from More to Shakespeare*. Chicago: University of Chicago Press, 1980.

——. *Shakespearean Negotiations*. Berkeley: University of California Press, 1988.

Greene, Robert. *The Life and Complete Works of Robert Greene*, edited by Alexander B. Grosart. Vol. 12. New York: Russel, 1964.

Gurr, Andrew. *Playgoing in Shakespeare's London*. Cambridge: Cambridge University Press, 1987.

Hallet, Bryce. "British Love Romeo and Leave Titanic." *Sydney Morning Herald*, 21 April 1998, 7.

Hamlet. Directed by Kenneth Branagh. Castle Rock Productions, 1996.

Harris, Diana. "Violent Delights, Violent Ends: Baz Luhrmann's *Romeo + Juliet*." Paper presented at Shakespeare on Screen: The Centenary Conference. Malaga, Spain, Sept. 21–24, 1999.

Hartman, Geoffrey, and Patricia Parker, eds. *Shakespeare and the Question of Theory*. New York: Routledge, 1985.

Hawker, Philippa. "DiCaprio, DiCaprio, Wherefore Art Thou, DiCaprio?" *Meanjin*, March 1997, 6–15.

Heath, Stephen. "Comment on 'The idea of authorship.'" In *Theories of Authorship*, edited by John Caughie, 214–20. New York: Routledge, 1981.

Hedrick, Donald K. "War Is Mud: Branagh's Dirty Harry V and the Types of Political Ambiguity." In *Shakespeare, the Movie: Popularizing the Plays on Film, TV, and Video*, edited by Lynda Boose and Richard Burt, 45–66. London: Routledge, 1997.

Helgerson, Richard. *Forms of Nationhood: The Elizabethan Writing of England*. Chicago: University of Chicago Press, 1992.

Heminge, John, and Henry Condell. "To the great Variety of Readers." In *The Riverside Shakespeare*, 2d ed., edited by G. Blakemore Evans et al., 95. Boston: Houghton Mifflin,1997.

——. "To The Most Noble and Incomparable Paire of Brethren." In *The Riverside Shakespeare*, 2d ed., edited by G. Blakemore Evans et al., 93–94. Boston: Houghton Mifflin, 1997.

Henderson, Katherine Usher, and Barbara F. McManus, eds. *Half Humankind: Context and Texts of the Controversy about Women in England, 1540–1640*. Urbana: University of Illinois Press, 1985.

Henry V. Directed by Kenneth Branagh. Samuel Goldwyn/Renaissance Films, 1989.

Henry V. Directed by Sir Laurence Olivier. Paramount Pictures, 1944.

Heywood, Thomas. *An Apology for Actors*. 1611. New York: Johnson Reprint Corp., 1972.

Hill, Roger, and Orson Welles, eds. *Everybody's Shakespeare: Three Plays*. Woodstock, Ill.: Todd Press, 1934.

Hodgdon, Barbara. "*William Shakespeare's Romeo + Juliet:* Everything's Nice in America?" *Shakespeare Survey* 52 (1999): 88–98.

Holderness, Graham. " 'What ish my nation?' Shakespeare and National Identities." In *Materialist Shakespeare: A History*, edited by Ivo Camps, 218–38. New York: Verso 1995.

Holderness, Graham, and Bryan Loughrey, eds. *Shakespearean Originals: First Editions. The tragicall historie of Hamlet, Prince of Denmarke*. Hemel Hempstead: Harvester Wheatsheaf, 1992.

Hollows, Joanne, and Mark Jancovich, eds. "Introduction: Popular Film and Cultural Distinctions." *Approaches to Popular Film*, 1–14. Manchester: Manchester University Press, 1995.

Holmer, Joan Ozark. " 'Draw, if you be men': Saviolo's Significance for *Romeo and Juliet*." *Shakespeare Quarterly* 45, no. 2 (1994): 163–89.

Howell, Georgina. "Renaissance Man." *Vogue*, Sept. 1991, 534+.

Ignatieff, Noel. *How the Irish Became White*. New York: Routledge, 1995.

Irving, Katrina. "EU-phoria? Irish National Identity, European Union, and *The Crying Game*." In *Writing New Identities*, edited by Gisela Brinker-Gabler and Sidonie Smith, 295–314. Minneapolis: University of Minnesota Press, 1997.

Irving, Washington. "Stratford-on-Avon." In *The Sketch-Book*, edited by Susan Manning, 224–39. New York: Oxford University Press, 1996.

Jackson, Russell. "The Film Diary." In *Hamlet, By William Shakespeare: Screenplay, Introduction, and Film Diary*, 175–208. New York: W. W. Norton, 1996.

Jameson, Fredric. *The Geopolitical Aesthetic: Cinema and Space in the World System*. Bloomington: Indiana University Press, 1992.

——. "Modernism and Imperialism." In *Nationalism, Colonialism, and Literature*, by Terry Eagleton, Fredric Jameson, and Edward W. Said, 43–66. Minneapolis: University of Minnesota Press, 1990.

——. *The Political Unconscious: Narrative as a Socially Symbolic Act*. Ithaca: Cornell University Press, 1981.

——. "Postmodernism and Consumer Society." In *Movies and Mass Culture*, edited by John Belton, 185–202. New Brunswick: Rutgers University Press, 1996.

——. *Postmodernism, Or, The Cultural Logic of Late Capitalism*. Durham: Duke University Press, 1991.

——. "Postmodernism, Or, The Cultural Logic of Late Capitalism." In *Postmodernism: A Reader*, edited by Thomas Docherty, 62–92. New York: Columbia University Press, 1993.

——. *Signatures of the Visible*. New York: Routledge, 1992.

Jameson, Fredric, and Anders Stephanson. "Regarding Postmodernism—A Conversation with Fredric Jameson." In *Postmodernism/Jameson/Critique*, edited by Douglas Kellner, 43–74. Washington, D.C. : Maisonneuve Press, 1989.

Jardine, Lisa. *Still Harping on Daughters: Women and Drama in the Age of Shakespeare*. New York: Columbia University Press, 1989.

Jeffords, Susan. *Hardbodies: Hollywood Masculinity in the Reagan Era*. New Brunswick: Rutgers University Press, 1994.

Johnson, Brian D. "Souping up the Bard," *Macleans*, 11 Nov. 1996, 74–75.

Jones, Welton. "Triumph of Tragic Love Ensures Long Life of 'Romeo.'" *San Diego Tribune*, 12 April 1998, E1.

Jonson, Ben. *Every Man in His Humour*. 1598. Edited by Martin-Seymour-Smith. New York: W. W. Norton, 1966.

——. "To the memory of my beloued, the AVTHOR Mr. William Shakespeare: And what he hath left vs." In *The Riverside Shakespeare*, 2d ed., edited by G. Blakemore Evans et al., 97–98. Boston: Houghton Mifflin, 1997.

——. *Oberon*. 1611. *Ben Jonson*, edited by C.H. Herford, P. Simpson, and E. Simpson. 11 vols. Oxford: Clarendon Press, 1925–52.

——. *Poetaster*. 1601. Edited by Josiah H. Penniman. Boston: D. C. Heath and Corp., 1913.

——. *Timber; or, Discoveries made upon men and matter: as they have flow'd out of his daily readings; or had their refluxe to his peculiar notion of the times, by Ben Iohnson*. 1641. *Ben Jonson*, edited by C. H. Herford, P. Simpson, and E. Simpson. 11 vols. Oxford: Clarendon Press, 1925–52.

Kastan, David Scott. "Workshop and/as Playhouse: The Shoemaker's Holiday." In *Staging the Renaissance: Reinterpretations of Elizabethan and Jacobean Drama*, edited by David Scott Kastan and Peter Stallybrass, 151–63. New York: Routledge, 1991.

Kavanagh, James. "Shakespeare in Ideology." In *Alternative Shakespeares*, edited by John Drakakis, 144–65. London: Routledge, 1985.

Kernan, Alvin B. *The Playwright as Magician: Shakespeare's Image of the Poet in the English Public Theater*. New Haven: Yale University Press, 1979.

——. "Shakespearian Comedy and Its Courtly Audience." In *Comedy from Shakespeare to Sheridan: Change and Continuity in the English and European Dramatic Tradition*, edited by A. R. Braunmuller and J. C. Bulman, 91–101. Newark: University of Delaware Press, 1986.

Kiberd, Declan. *Inventing Ireland: The Literature of the Modern Nation*. Cambridge: Harvard University Press, 1995.

Kierkegaard, Søren. *The Sickness Unto Death: A Christian Psychological Exposition for Upbuilding and Awakening*. Edited and translated by Howard V. Hong and Edna H. Hong. Princeton: Princeton University Press, 1980.

Klein, Joan Larsen. *Daughters, Wives, and Widows: Writings by Men about Women and Marriage in England, 1500–1640*. Urbana: University of Illinois Press, 1992.

Knutson, Rosalyn. "Falconer to the Little Eyases: A New Date and Commercial Agenda for the 'Little Eyases' Passage in *Hamlet*." *Shakespeare Quarterly* 46, no. 1 (1995): 1–31.

Lacan, Jacques. "Desire and the Interpretation of Desire in *Hamlet*." In *Literature and Psychoanalysis, The Question of Reading: Otherwise,* edited by Shoshana Felman, 1–52. Baltimore: Johns Hopkins University Press, 1982.

——. "Seminar on 'The Purloined Letter.'" Translated by Jeffrey Mehlman. In *The Purloined Poe: Lacan, Derrida, and Psychoanalytic Reading,* edited by John P. Muller and William J. Richardson, 28–54. Baltimore: Johns Hopkins University Press, 1988.

Lane, Robert. "'When blood is their argument': Class, Character, and History-making in Shakespeare's and Branagh's *Henry V.*" *ELH* 61, no. 1 (1994): 27–52.

Lanier, Douglas. "Drowning the Book: *Prospero's Books* and the Textual Shakespeare." In *Shakespeare, Theory, and Performance,* edited by James C. Bulman, 187–209. London: Routledge, 1996.

Lehmann, Courtney. "Kenneth Branagh at the Quilting Point: Shakespearean Adaptation, Postmodern Auteurism, and the (Schizophrenic) Fabric of 'Everyday Life.'" *Post Script: Essays in Film and the Humanities* 17, no. 1 (1997): 6–27.

——. "Much Ado about Nothing? Shakespeare, Branagh, and the 'National-Popular' in the Age of Multinational Capital." *Textual Practice* 12, no. 1 (1998): 1–23.

Lehmann, Courtney, and Lisa S. Starks. "Making Mother Matter: Repression, Revision, and the Stakes of 'Reading Psychoanalysis Into' Kenneth Branagh's *Hamlet.*" *Early Modern Literary Studies* 6, no. 1 (May 2000):<URL:http://purl.oclc.org/emls/Q61/lehmham1.htm>

Leinwald, Theodore B. "'I believe we must leave the killing out': Deference and Accommodation in *A Midsummer Night's Dream.*" *Renaissance Papers* (1986): 11–30.

Levin, Richard. "On Defending Shakespeare, 'Liberal Humanism', Transcendent Love, and Other 'Sacred Cows' and Lost Causes." *Textual Practice* 7, no. 1 (1993): 50–55.

Light, Alison. "The Importance of Being Ordinary." *Sight and Sound* 3, no. 9 (1993): 16–19.

Loewenstein, Joseph. "*Idem:* Italics and the Genetic of Authorship." *Journal of Medieval and Renaissance Studies* 20, no. 2 (1990): 205–24.

——. "Printing and 'The Multitudinous Presse': The Contentious Texts of Jonson's Masques." In *Ben Jonson's 1616 Folio,* edited by Jennifer Brady and W. H. Herendeen, 168–91. Newark: University of Delaware Press, 1991.

——. "The Script in the Marketplace." In *Representing the English Renaissance,* edited by Stephen Greenblatt 265–78. Berkeley: University of California Press, 1988.

Love's Labour's Lost. Directed by Kenneth Branagh. Miramax, 2000.

Luhrmann, Baz. "A Note from Baz Luhrmann." In *William Shakespeare's Romeo + Juliet. The Contemporary Film, The Classic Play,* i–ii. New York: Bantam Doubleday Dell, 1996.

Lukacher, Ned. *Primal Scenes: Literature, Philosophy, Psychoanalysis.* Ithaca: Cornell University Press, 1986.

Lyotard, Jean-François. *Libidinal Economies.* Translated by Iain Hamilton Grant. Bloomington: Indiana University Press, 1993.

MacDonald, Russ. *Shakespeare and Jonson: Jonson and Shakespeare.* Lincoln: University of Nebraska Press, 1988.

Macherey, Pierre. "Creation and Production." In *Authorship from Plato to the Postmodern,* edited by Sean Burke, 230–32. Edinburgh: Edinburgh University Press, 1995.

Macrone, Michael. "The Theatrical Self in Renaissance England." *Qui Parle* 3, no. 1 (1989): 72–102.

Marcus, Leah. *Unediting the Renaissance: Shakespeare, Marlowe, Milton.* New York: Routledge, 1996.

Marcuse, Herbert. *One-Dimensional Man: Studies in the Ideology of Advanced Industrial Society.* Boston: Beacon Press, 1964.

Marston, John. *Histrio-mastix, or, The player whipt.* London: Thorp, 1610.

Marx, Karl. *Capital.* In *The Marx-Engels Reader,* 2d ed., edited by Robert C. Taylor, 294–438. New York: W. W. Norton, 1978.

Mary Shelley's Frankenstein. Directed by Kenneth Branagh. TriStar Pictures, 1994.

Masten, Jeffrey A. "Beaumont and/or Fletcher: Collaboration and the Interpretation of Renaissance Drama." In *The Construction of Authorship: Textual Appropriation in Law and Literature,* edited by Peter Jaszi and Martha Woodmansee, 361–81. Durham: Duke University Press, 1994.

Mathews, Peter. Review of *William Shakespeare's Romeo + Juliet. Sight and Sound* 7, no. 4 (1997): 63.

Matus, Irvin Leigh. *Shakespeare, In Fact.* New York: Continuum, 1994.

McLeod, Randall, ed. *Crisis in Editing: Texts of the English Renaissance.* New York: AMS Press, 1994.

McLuhan, Marshall. *The Gutenberg Galaxy: The Making of Typographic Man.* Toronto: University of Toronto Press, 1962.

Metz, Christian. "On the Notion of Cinematographic Language." In *Movies and Methods,* edited by Bill Nichols. Vol. 1. Berkeley: University of California Press, 1976.

A Midsummer Night's Dream. Directed by Max Reinhardt and William Dieterle. Warner Brothers, 1935.

A Midwinter's Tale. Directed by Kenneth Branagh. Castle Rock Productions, 1995.

Milton, John. *Areopagitica.* 1643. In *John Milton: Complete Poems and Major Prose,* edited by Merritt Y. Hughes, 716–49. New York: Macmillan, 1957.

Moison, Thomas. " 'Which is the merchant here? and which the Jew?': Subversion and Recuperation in *The Merchant of Venice.*" In *Shakespeare Reproduced: The Text in History and Ideology,* edited by Jean E. Howard and Marion F. O'Connor, 188–206. New York: Routledge, 1993.

Montaigne, Michel de. *The Essays of Montaigne.* 1580. Translated by J.M. Cohen. New York: Penguin, 1958.

Montrose, Louis Adrian. " 'Shaping Fantasies': Figurations of Gender and Power in Elizabethan Culture." *Representations* 1 (1983): 61–94.

Moore, Olin H. *The Legend of Romeo and Juliet.* Columbus: Ohio State University Press, 1950.

Moullet, Luc. " 'Sam Fuller: In Marlowe's Footsteps.' " In *Cahiers du Cinema. The 1950s: Neo-Realism, Hollywood, New Wave,* edited by Jim Hillier, 145–55. Cambridge: Harvard University Press, 1985.

Much Ado About Nothing. Directed by Kenneth Branagh. Renaissance Films, 1993.

Mullaney, Steven. *The Place of the Stage: License, Play, and Power in Renaissance England.* Chicago: University of Chicago Press, 1988.

Muller, John P., and William J. Richardson, eds. "Lacan's Seminar on the Purloined Letter: Overview." In *The Purloined Poe: Lacan, Derrida, and Psychoanalytic Reading,* 55–76. Baltimore: Johns Hopkins University Press, 1988.

Munsterberg, Hugo. "The Means of the Photoplay." In *Film Theory and Criticism,* 4th ed., edited by Gerald Mast, Marshall Cohen, and Leo Braudy, 355–61. Oxford: Oxford University Press, 1992.

Murray, Janet H. *Hamlet on the Holodeck: The Future of Narrative in Cyberspace.* New York: Free Press, 1997.

Murray, Timothy. *Like a Film: Ideological Fantasy on Screen, Camera and Canvas.* New York: Routledge, 1993.

Nairn, Tom. *The Break-up of Britain: Crisis and Neo-Nationalism.* London: NLB, 1977.

Naremore, James. "Authorship and the Cultural Politics of Film Criticism." *Film Quarterly* 44, no. 1 (1990): 14–23.

Norman, Marc, and Tom Stoppard. *Shakespeare in Love: A Screenplay.* New York: Hyperion, 1998.

Ong, Walter J. *Orality and Literacy: The Technologizing of the Word.* New York: Methuen, 1982.

Orgel, Stephen. "The Authentic Shakespeare." *Representations* 21 (1988): 5–25.

———. *The Illusion of Power.* Berkeley: University of California Press, 1991.

———. "What Is a Text?" In *Staging the Renaissance: Reinterpretations of Elizabethan and Jacobean Drama,* edited by David Scott Kastan and Peter Stallybrass, 83–87. New York: Routledge, 1991.

Osborne, Laurie E. "Staging the Female Playgoer: Gender in Shakespeare's Onstage Audiences." In *Enacting Gender on the English Renaissance Stage,* edited by Viviana Comensolu and Anne Russell, 201–17. Urbana: University of Illinois Press, 1999.

Parker, Patricia. *Shakespeare from the Margins: Language, Culture, Context.* Chicago: University of Chicago Press, 1996.

Pasolini, Pier Paolo. "The Cinema of Poetry." In *Movies and Methods,* edited by Bill Nichols. Vol. 1. Berkeley: University of California Press, 1976.

Pearce, Craig, and Baz Luhrmann. *William Shakespeare's Romeo + Juliet. The Contemporary Film, The Classic Play.* New York: Bantam Doubleday Dell, 1996.

Pearlman, E. "Staging *Romeo and Juliet:* Evidence from Brooke's *Romeus." Theatre Survey* 34 (May 1993): 22–32.

Pechter, Edward. *What Was Shakespeare? Renaissance Plays and Changing Critical Practice.* Ithaca: Cornell University Press, 1995.

Peucker, Brigitte. *Incorporating Images: Film and the Rival Arts.* Princeton: Princeton University Press, 1995.

The Piano. Directed by Jane Campion. CIBY 2000/Jan Chapman Productions, 1992.

Pittenger, Elizabeth. "Aliens in the Corpus: Shakespeare's Books in the Age of the Cyborg." In *Prosthetic Territories,* edited by Gabriel Brahm Jr. and Mark Driscoll, 204–18. San Francisco: Westview Press, 1995.

Propp, Vladimir. *The Morphology of the Folktale.* Translated by Laurence Scott. Austin: University of Texas Press, 1970.

Psycho. Directed by Gus Van Sant. Universal Pictures, 1998.

The Public Enemy. Directed by William Wellman. Warner Brothers, 1931.

Ray, Robert. *The Avant-Garde Finds Andy Hardy.* Cambridge: Harvard University Press, 1995.

Reid, Graham. *Billy: Three Plays for Television.* London: Faber, 1984.

A Room with a View. Directed by James Ivory. Produced by Ismail Merchant. Cinecom International Films, 1987.

Rose, Mark. "The Author in Court: *POPE v. CURLL* (1741)." In *The Construction of Authorship: Textual Appropriation in Law and Literature,* edited by Martha Woodmansee and Peter Jaszi, 211–29. Durham: Duke University Press, 1994.

Rupprecht, Carol Schreier, ed. "Divinity, Insanity, Creativity: A Renaissance Contribution to the History and Theory of Dream/Text(s). In *The Dream and the Text: Essays on Literature and Language,* 112–32. Albany: State University of New York Press, 1993.

Sarris, Andrew. "Notes on the Auteur Theory in 1962." In *Film Theory and Criticism,* 4th ed., edited by Gerald Mast, Marshall Cohen, and Leo Braudy, 585–88. Oxford: Oxford University Press, 1992.

———. "Towards a Theory of Film History." In *Movies and Methods,* edited by Bill Nichols. Vol. 1. Berkeley: University of California Press, 1976.

Scanlon, Larry. *Narrative, Authority, and Power: The Medieval Exemplum and the Chaucerian Tradition.* Cambridge: Cambridge University Press, 1994.

Schleiner, Winfried. "Imaginative Sources for Shakespeare's Puck." *Shakespeare Quarterly* 36, no. 1 (1985): 65–68.

Schmidgall, Gary. *Shakespeare and the Courtly Aesthetic.* Berkeley: University of California Press, 1981.

Schwartz, Hillel. *The Culture of the Copy: Striking Likenesses, Unreasonable Facsimiles.* New York: Zone Books, 1996.

Shakespeare, William. *Coriolanus*. In *The Riverside Shakespeare*, 2d ed., edited by
  G. Blakemore Evans et al., 1444–1485. Boston: Houghton Mifflin, 1997.
——. *Hamlet*. Edited by Susanne L. Wofford. New York: Bedford Books, 1994.
——. *1 Henry IV*. In *The Riverside Shakespeare*, 2d ed., edited by G. Blakemore
  Evans et al., 889–924. Boston: Houghton Mifflin, 1997.
——. *Henry V*. In *The Riverside Shakespeare*, 2d ed., edited by G. Blakemore
  Evans et al., 979–1015. Boston: Houghton Mifflin, 1997.
——. *1–3 Henry VI*. In *The Riverside Shakespeare*, 2d ed., edited by G. Blake-
  more Evans et al., 632–744. Boston: Houghton Mifflin, 1997.
——. *A Midsummer Night's Dream*. In *The Riverside Shakespeare*, 2d ed., edited
  by G. Blakemore Evans et al., 256–80. Boston: Houghton Mifflin, 1997.
——. *The Rape of Lucrece*. In *The Riverside Shakespeare*, 2d ed., edited by G.
  Blakemore Evans et al. 1816–36. Boston: Houghton Mifflin, 1997.
——. *Romeo and Juliet*. In *The Oxford Shakespeare: Tragedies*, edited by Stanley
  Wells and Gary Taylor, 1053–88. Oxford: Oxford University Press, 1987.
——. "Sonnet 111." In *The Riverside Shakespeare*, 2d ed., edited by G. Blakemore
  Evans et al., 1863. Boston: Houghton Mifflin, 1997.
——. *The Tempest*. In *The Riverside Shakespeare*, 2d ed., edited by G. Blakemore
  Evans et al., 1661–86. Boston: Houghton Mifflin, 1997.
——. *Venus and Adonis*. In *The Riverside Shakespeare*, 2d ed., edited by G. Blake-
  more Evans et al., 1799–1812. Boston: Houghton Mifflin, 1997.
Shakespeare, William, et al. *The Passionate Pilgrim*, 3d ed. Printed by W. Iag-
  gard, 1612.
Shakespeare in Love. Directed by John Madden. Miramax Films/Universal
  Pictures/The Bedford Falls Company, 1998.
Shapiro, James. "'Tragedies naturally performed': Kyd's Representation of
  Violence." In *Staging the Renaissance: Reinterpretations of Elizabethan and
  Jacobean Drama*, edited by David Scott Kastan and Peter Stallybrass,
  99–113. New York: Routledge, 1991.
Shaw, William P. "Textual Ambiguities and Textual Certainties in *Henry V*."
  Literature Film Quarterly 22, no. 2 (1994): 117-128.
Shelley, Mary. *Frankenstein or the Modern Prometheus*. 1818. New York: Penguin,
  1992.
Shurgot, Michael. "'Get you a place': Staging the Mousetrap at the Globe
  Theatre." *Shakespeare Bulletin* (Summer 1994): 6–9.
Simon, John. Review of *Henry V*. *National Review*, 19 March 1990, 57–58.
Sinfield, Alan. *Faultlines: Cultural Materialism and the Politics of Dissident Read-
  ing*. Berkeley: University of California Press, 1992.
——. "Heritage and the Market, Regulation and Desublimization." In *Political
  Shakespeare: Essays in Cultural Materialism*, 2d ed., edited by Jonathan Dol-
  limore and Alan Sinfield. Ithaca: Cornell University Press, 1985. Reprint, 1994.
Sir Thomas Moore. c. 1594.
Slater, Ann Pasternak. *Shakespeare the Director*. Sussex: Harvester Press, 1982.

Sleepy Hollow. Directed by Tim Burton. Paramount Pictures, 1999.

Smith, Dinitia. "Much Ado About Branagh." *New York,* 24 May 1993, 36–45.

Sontag, Susan. "Film and Theatre." In *Film Theory and Criticism,* 4th ed., edited by Gerald Mast, Marshall Cohen, and Leo Braudy, 362–74. Oxford: Oxford University Press, 1992.

Spillers, Hortense. "Mama's Baby, Papa's Maybe: An American Grammar Book." *Diacritics* (Summer 1987): 65–81.

Stallybrass, Peter. "Shakespeare, the Individual, and the Text." In *Cultural Studies,* edited by Lawrence Grossberg, Carey Nelson, and Paula Treichler, 593–612. New York: Routledge, 1992.

——. "Transvestism and the 'Body Beneath': Speculating on the Boy Actor." In *Erotic Politics: Desire on the Renaissance Stage,* edited by Susan Zimmerman, 64–83. New York: Routledge, 1992.

Stallybrass, Peter, and Allon White. *The Politics and Poetics of Transgression.* Ithaca: Cornell University Press, 1986.

Stewart, Garret. "Shakespearean Dreamplay." *ELR* 11, no. 1 (Winter 1981): 44–69.

Stone, Lawrence. *The Family, Sex and Marriage in England 1500–1800.* New York: Harper and Row, 1977.

Strictly Ballroom. Directed by Baz Luhrmann. Rank/M&A/Australian Film Finance Corp., 1992.

Taylor, Gary, and Michael Warren, eds. *The Division of the Kingdoms: Shakespeare's Two Versions of King Lear.* Oxford: Oxford University Press, 1983.

Thomas, Max W. "Reading and Writing the Renaissance Commonplace Book: A Question of Authorship?" In *The Construction of Authorship: Textual Appropriation in Law and Literature,* edited by Martha Woodmansee and Peter Jaszi, 361–81. Durham: Duke University Press, 1994.

Thompson, Bob. "Sing along with Shakespeare." *Toronto Sun,* 4 Aug. 1999, 31.

The Three Parnassus Plays. 1598–1601. Edited by J. B. Leishman. London: Iver Nicholson, 1949.

Tibbets, John C. *The American Theatrical Film: Stages in Development.* Bowling Green: Bowling Green State University Press, 1995

Titanic. Directed by James Cameron. Lightstorm Entertainment, 1997.

Top Hat. Directed by Mark Sandrich. RKO, 1935.

Travers, Peter. "Just Two Kids in Love." *Rolling Stone,* 14 Nov. 1996, 123–24.

U2. "The Fly." *Achtung Baby!* Island Records, 1991.

Warren, Michael. *The Complete King Lear, 1608–1623.* Berkeley: University of California Press, 1989.

Webster, John. *The White Devil.* 1612. New York: American Books, 1912.

Weimann, Robert. "'Appropriation' and Modern History in Renaissance Prose Narrative." *New Literary History* 14 (1983): 459–95.

——. *Author's Pen and Actor's Voice.* Cambridge: Cambridge University Press, 2000.

——. "Mimesis in *Hamlet*." In *Shakespeare and the Question of Theory*, edited by Geoffrey Hartman and Patricia Parker, 275–91. New York: Routledge, 1985.

——. *Shakespeare and the Popular Tradition in the Theater: Studies in the Social Dimension of Dramatic Form and Function*. Baltimore: Johns Hopkins University Press, 1978.

Welsh, Jim. "Postmodern Shakespeare: Strictly Romeo." *Literature-Film Quarterly* 25, no. 2 (1996): 152–3.

West Side Story. Directed by Robert Wise and Jerome Robbins. Mirisch/Seven Arts, 1961.

Whittier, Gayle. "The Sonnet's Body and the Body Sonnetized in Romeo and Juliet." *Shakespeare Quarterly* 40, no. 1 (1989): 27–41.

William Shakespeare's Romeo + Juliet. Directed by Baz Luhrmann. Twentieth Century Fox/Bazmark Productions, 1996.

Williams, Raymond. *Marxism and Literature*. Oxford: Oxford University Press, 1977.

Wilson, Richard. "The Kindly Ones: The Death of the Author in Shakespearean Athens." In *Literature and Censorship*, edited by Nigel Smith, 1–24. Cambridge: S. S. Brewer, 1993.

Wollen, Peter. *Signs and Meaning in the Cinema*. Bloomington: Indiana University Press, 1972.

Wood, Robin. "Ideology, Genre, Auteur." *Film Theory and Criticism*, 4th ed., edited by Gerald Mast, Marshall Cohen, and Leo Braudy, 475–85. Oxford: Oxford University Press, 1992.

——. "Introduction (1965)." In *Hitchcock's Films Revisited*. New York: Columbia University Press, 1989.

——. "Introduction (1988)." sIn *Hitchcock's Films Revisited*. New York: Columbia University Press, 1989.

Woodbridge, Linda. *Women and the English Renaissance: Literature and the Nature of Womankind, 1540–1620*. Urbana: University of Illinois Press, 1984.

Worthen, W. B. "Drama, Performance, Performativity." *PMLA* (October 1998): 1093–1107.

——. *Shakespeare and the Authority of Performance*. Cambridge: Cambridge University Press, 1997.

Wyrick, Deborah Baker. "The Ass Motif in *The Comedy of Errors* and *A Midsummer Night's Dream*." *Shakespeare Quarterly* 33, no. 4 (1982): 432–48.

Yankee Doodle Dandy. Directed by Michael Curtiz. Warner Brothers, 1942.

Žižek, Slavoj. *Enjoy Your Symptom! Jacques Lacan in Hollywood and Out*. New York: Routledge, 1992.

——. *For They Know Not What They Do: Enjoyment as a Political Factor*. London: Verso, 1991.

——. *Looking Awry: An Introduction to Jacques Lacan through Popular Culture.*
Cambridge: MIT Press, 1991.
——. *The Sublime Object of Ideology.* London: Verso, 1989.
——. *Tarrying with the Negative: Kant, Hegel, and the Critique of Ideology.*
Durham: Duke University Press, 1993.

Index

About the Author

Courtney Lehmann is Assistant Professor of English and Film Studies at the University of the Pacific. She is an award-winning teacher and co-editor, with Lisa S. Starks, of *Spectacular Shakespeare: Critical Theory and Popular Cinema.*